CW00689185

GLORIOUS GOODWOOD

HILL

GLORIOUS
GOODWOOD
CAMILLA CECIL,
GEORGE ENNOR & RICHARD ONSLOW

GLORIOUS GOODWOOD

Written by Camilla Cecil (*Summer At Goodwood, The Royal Connection, Characters Of The Course*),
George Ennor (*Stars Of The Future, The Sussex Stakes, Stepping Forward*)
and Richard Onslow (*The Goodwood Cup, The Stewards' Cup*).
Additional text by Philip Dodd.

Goodwood editorial consultants: Rosemary Baird and Peter Willett.

First published in 2002 by Kenneth Mason Publications Ltd.,
The Book Barn, White Chimney Row, Westbourne, Hampshire P010 8RS.

A catalogue record for this title is available from the British Library.

ISBN 0 85937 402 5

Art direction and design: Derek Slatter and Garold West.

Picture research: Derek Slatter with Ellen Westbrook at Goodwood.

Publishing consultant: Philip Dodd.

Printed and bound in Italy.

Above: *'Goodwood In Coronation Year', by William Cartledge, 1952.*
Below, left to right: *The Stewards' Cup (1933), The Chesterfield Cup (1902) and The Goodwood Gold Cup (1827).*

CONTENTS

FOREWORD

BY HIS GRACE THE DUKE OF RICHMOND AND GORDON

Horse racing at Goodwood has been part of my life for over 55 years. My earliest memory of going to the course is as a 16-year-old, when we set out from school on a gorgeous July morning in 1946 to see the opening day of the first Festival week after the end of the Second World War.

That night, my brother and I had a party for some of our friends from school and, for the first time in our lives, a few girls came! What I remember most from that meeting is the sheer excitement, heightened by the fact that there had been no racing on the course for seven years, and the mixture of sight, sound and smell, not forgetting the hats...

The greatest horse to win at Goodwood in my time was probably Brigadier Gerard. At Goodwood he won both the Sussex Stakes and the Celebration Mile in 1971, and in total 17 of his 18 races, including the 2,000 Guineas. Then in 1998 I was privileged to be present when Double Trigger, with Darryll Holland onboard that year, won the Goodwood Cup for the third time - a unique achievement.

Since those days, I have been lucky enough to be involved in the continuing development of the Racecourse, and have always been keenly aware of the history that stretches back over two centuries. Whenever I look at the marvellous George Stubbs painting of the 3rd Duke's racehorses that graces the jacket of this book, it makes me realise just how important it is to respect and value that tradition.

And also I realise how much racing at Goodwood means to other people, when we receive (not infrequent) requests from regular racegoers for their ashes to be scattered on the course!

Equally, though, to keep racing alive and progressing, Goodwood has tried to innovate and adapt wherever possible, whether by introducing the first racecourse PA system in the 1950s, enlarging the race programme from four to twenty days, or constructing new facilities like the March stand which HM The Queen opened in 1980 - a moment that made me especially proud - or the new paddock which first came into use in 2001. This effective blend of the old and new remains, I hope, one of Goodwood's most characteristic qualities.

Glorious Goodwood - this book - is an enduring reminder of everything that Goodwood has stood for: the history of the earliest days, when a bugler of the Sussex Militia signalled the start of races; the memorable finishes of great races to win the Goodwood Cup or the Sussex Stakes; and the jockeys and trainers whose personalities have enlivened each season.

Everyone here at Goodwood loves racing. This book is a chance for us all to share in celebrating the past 200 years - and, God willing, the next 200!

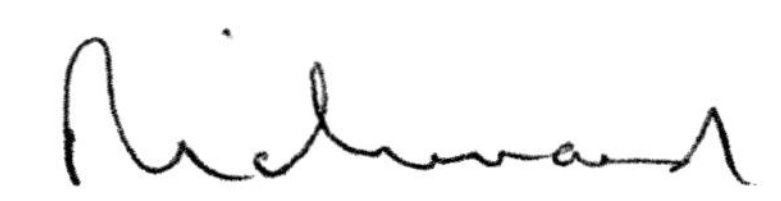

INTRODUCTION

BY SIR PETER O'SULLEVAN CBE

What brilliant timing for Goodwood's 200th anniversary to coincide with the Jubilee year of Queen Elizabeth II who has enjoyed so many happy days, and successes, at the glorious racecourse which gleams like the thoroughbreds it hosts in the beguiling Sussex landscape.

"Surely the most beautiful racetrack in the world," opined an entranced transatlantic visitor - the late, great, US sportswriter Red Smith, writing in the *Herald-Tribune*.

What memories the incomparable setting evokes for this longtime *aficionado* whose earliest viewing site was Trundle Hill, 700 feet above sea level, a wonderful vantage point in the 1930s when the paddock was situated at the foot of this natural grandstand. Here even modest binoculars enabled the racegoer to view the horses, study the colours, and follow every yard of the running until the horses pulled up on the Hill itself.

In 1930 I saw the immensely popular stayer Brown Jack win the Goodwood Cup two years after achieving Champion Hurdle status at Cheltenham. His achievement of eighteen successes on the flat partnered by the legendary Steve Donoghue (who became a good friend), included six consecutive Queen Alexandra Stakes at Ascot and winning prize money aggregating £21,646. Modest enough by twenty-first century standards, but the excellent fruiterer on the Hill, who charged sixpence (5p) for a generous slice of large pineapple and a shilling (10p) for a big bunch of muscat grapes, was widely considered exorbitant.

In 1935 I drove to the course, in my 8hp Morris Minor two-seater for the first time, lodging at The Globe (five shillings b&b) in Chichester - and in the Stewards' Cup, Greenore, of happy memory, funded an upgrade to Tattersall's Enclosure. But I didn't take advantage of it.

'The Trundle' was so appealingly tranquil. Like Birdless Grove, the tall-treed wooded area which lay behind the Stands and in which no bird was ever supposed to have been seen or heard, it had an almost mystical quality. For without a public address system races were run in virtual silence with many unaware of the outcome until the judge's sometimes quixotic verdict was hoisted up the numbers frame.

It was this detail that prompted Goodwood's charming and effective manager and course clerk, Ralph Hubbard, to write to me in July 1952. I had been broadcasting, or trying to, for six years, though not at Goodwood - until that very year.

BBC Radio, for which Raymond Glendenning was chief sports commentator, first broadcast at the Goodwood summer meeting in 1947. Only the Goodwood Cup and Goodwood Stakes were transmitted as it was thought that the six furlongs Stewards' Cup would be far too difficult.

However in 1951 Raymond was requested to have a go at the big sprint handicap and I was employed as 'race reader' for him. It seemed to go reasonably well, while at the same time emphasising the difficulty for an experienced broadcaster, but non-specialist in racing, when the action is short and hectic. The following year I was asked to broadcast the race solo - an assignment which resulted in many hours of expendable homework prompted by the nightmare *débâcle* in 1864. That was the year,

I reflected apprehensively, in which 40 horses and riders, made restive by high temperature and the attention of hyper-active horseflies, defied the starter's attempts to achieve an even break for well over an hour.

I became an instant, if temporary, authority on the contribution of the successive marvellous Dukes of Richmond who have made Goodwood what it is. Notes were prepared and digested on each - like the fifth Duke who had a new grandstand built in 1830 and, thinking of the principal players in the racing game, employed a hundred men and twenty-eight carthorses to haul one hundred tons of tan up to the downs from Chichester as an underlay for fresh turves - a development in which he was much encouraged by his friend and innovator Lord George Bentinck.

In the event, the 3.10 at Goodwood on 29th July 1952 went off at 3.13. The challenger from the North, Vatellus, headed the 18-horse field until the final furlong when Charlie Smirke and Smokey Eyes challenged and went away to win by a length.

No Duke received a mention.

Ralph Hubbard, whom I had interviewed on behalf of the Press Association at Goodwood after the war - before the resumption of racing there - wrote, "I am convinced that only a very small minority of racegoers have a coherent picture of a race as it is run." His idea was to use the public address system to broadcast each race to the crowds at the course. The Jockey Club had given him qualified approval for the innovation.

Would I like to tackle it? Would I indeed. I had learnt that for a commentator there is no substitute for 'live' practice. If I wanted to improve, develop confidence and reduce nervous tension, this was a great opportunity. I suggested that paddock comments might be appropriate also, in which event my colleague Clive Graham would be the perfect choice. Meanwhile I would seek the formality of permission from my principal boss Arthur Christiansen, editor of the *Daily Express*.

I found it hard to believe my eyes when reading the response: "I do not understand the application you make in relation to broadcasting to the Goodwood race crowd. This seems to me to leave pretty well nothing for the *Daily Express* the following day so far as the people at Goodwood are concerned, and I must reluctantly say no." Well, I had obviously expressed myself badly. I wrote back forthwith.

I explained that all I would be doing was reading a race aloud, anonymously, instead of reading it to myself. There was no way this could place me at a disadvantage *vis-à-vis* my work. Anyone might have thought that General de Gaulle himself was handling my modest request. The response was "Non" - qualified by the amazing pronouncement, "It is a question whether any racegoer will buy the *Daily Express* if he can have your views over the loudspeaker system." "I am very sorry," wrote Ralph, "as I reckon we could have put racecourse broadcasting on the map from the outset."

He did. Another first for Goodwood.

It was an inspired decision by the trustees of the Goodwood House Collection to commission the delightful and so very talented sculptress Dame Elizabeth Frink CBE to create a life-size bronze representing the apotheosis of the horse. On a happy, sunny, day (29th July 1980) the Queen - whose great-grandfather, King Edward VII, described Goodwood as "a Garden Party with racing tacked on" - unveiled the sculpture, simultaneously opening the architecturally magnificent new Stand.

The structure, which reflected Edwardian elements with its brick plinth and balustrades, made no concession to tradition via a vaulted parasol roof which has been described as "a minor miracle of modern concrete technology". Instantly award-winning and a delight to the eye it nevertheless had its critics (hands up O'Sullevan) on the grounds that, funded to a degree by a Levy Board loan, it followed the pattern of most post-war developments by benefiting the corporate entertainee at the expense of the *bona fide* enthusiast, the latter being assigned far lower standings beneath the boxes.

The tempo of 'the rot', as punters saw it, was set by Manchester, where redevelopment started in 1955. "Concentrating on creating an entertainment complex," I wrote at the time, "they built steppings which afforded racegoers no better view than the ground-level wearer of stiletto heels." The once fine course was later sold to property developers.

"£1 million take-on" was how readers referred - in a sack of aggrieved mail - to the 1961 creation of Ascot's new Tattersalls Stand. This provided fine viewing at box level but steppings from which races up the straight are virtually unviewable.

In 1982, during a January freeze which curtailed jumping, I reviewed countrywide racecourse renovations in general, like Cheltenham where, following a main stand re-vamp, regular racegoers found their previously uninterrupted view bedevilled by concrete pillars required to support areas to which only box and reserved seat holders had access. Even at ever-progressive Haydock it was a case of 'the old box story'.

"The paradox," I wrote, "is that the only desirable viewing areas are being allocated to those who appreciate them least. Goodwood have proved it with their aesthetically laudable but practically less acceptable grandstand, opened by the Queen in 1980. Here they have sold as many boxes facing the Solent as those looking onto the racecourse."

The piece, which included a very funny letter about Ascot from Robert Morley, the actor, was captioned, "Face-lifts - but at what price?" It was illustrated, inappropriately I thought, by a photo of the densely thronged old Goodwood grandstand and, below, a shot of the new one - empty.

Legitimate grounds, I figured, for an expression of discontent from the Earl of March - as the 10th Duke of Richmond was at that time. It materialised in the form of a characteristically courteous and positive missive from the highly qualified and hands-on operator that he is.

He wrote, "There is one point about boxes on racecourses which seems widely unappreciated. To maintain high quality racing and to provide modern facilities, all racecourses, and especially those in Group 1, must now set out to earn as much revenue as possible. At the same time they must continue to meet the general needs of the racegoers.

"A sensible balance has to be struck between these two objectives. To do so there must be a number of high-earning boxes on all Group 1 racecourses. Otherwise a general decline in standards will be inevitable and racecourses will become even more dependent on subsidies and low-interest loans from the betting levy. In other words, there is a basic point here about the future economics of racing, which the industry ignores at its peril."

The next phase of Goodwood's redevelopment occurred in 1989 with the opening of the new Charlton Stand. Then, in 1990, by which time the Earl had acceded to the Dukedom, there followed the unveiling of the beautiful and immensely racegoer-friendly Sussex Stand, the object of three architectural awards including a commendation from the Royal Fine Arts Commission and largely funded (the 'boss' did not omit to mention!) by revenue from the March Stand boxes.

It was a special privilege for me to have been invited to perform the opening ceremony. The Duke of Richmond and Gordon enjoys great back-up from his equally hands-on son The Earl of March, as well as the support of a fine management team each of whom I have known and admired before and since their appointment: Rod Fabricius, John Thompson and Seamus Buckley. Together they ensure that Goodwood remains both glorious and an ever-progressing centre of excellence.

From sea level the unique grandstand complex creates the illusion of a magnificent liner breasting the rolling Sussex Downs.

To all who sail in her, Happy Anniversary!

Peter O'Sullevan

THE BEAUTIFUL RACECOURSE

If a racegoer at Goodwood in the mid-nineteenth century were by some miracle propelled forward in time to the current July meeting, they would find that the names of many of the races had a very familiar ring. The Goodwood Cup and the Goodwood Stakes, the Stewards' Cup and the Sussex Stakes, for example, were all being run in 1850. It is a remarkable and uplifting thought that there has been this level of continuity across the two hundred years of the racecourse's existence.

Other races recall the role of the Richmond family in founding and nurturing the racecourse since the first organised race meeting held in April 1802, including the Lennox, Gordon and March Stakes, as well - of course - as the Richmond Stakes. It was the 3rd Duke of Richmond who founded the meeting. Two centuries later the present Duke is as enthusiastic about and dedicated to providing high-quality racing as any of his predecessors.

The contemporary visitor to the course will also be able to watch races bearing names that strike a chord with anyone who has spent time in this particular corner of West Sussex. The Molecomb Stakes and the Charlton Hunt Supreme Stakes are survivors of a clutch of races that over the years have acted as a gazetteer of the villages and towns which surround Goodwood (Lavant, Ham, Cowdray, Findon, Singleton and Chichester have all had races named after them in the past), and which evoke reminiscences of leafy lanes, hedgerows and summer sun.

It is this sense of continuity - both of horse racing at Goodwood and of the personal stewardship by the Richmond family - alongside a very specific sense of locality and geography that gives Goodwood such a distinctive character, one that is unmatched by any other British racecourse, or any other racecourse in the world.

Certainly, as far as direct family involvement is concerned, only Ascot, with its royal connections, and Towcester, on Lord Hesketh's Northamptonshire estate, have any similar claims to such longevity.

This may explain in part why Goodwood has survived, when many of the numerous other flat race meetings of the mid-19th century - Abergavenny, Epping, Marlborough and Wrexham among them - failed to last. The delights of Goodwood Racecourse's location are readily appreciated by anyone who has been racing there. The topography is consistently striking, from whichever

Opposite: *Remembrance of summers past - looking south over the old parade ring and winners enclosure from the east corner of the old Weighing Room building.*

GOODWOOD

***Above:** View from the Double Trigger roof terrace (named after the three-time winner of the Goodwood Cup in 1995, 1997 and 1998) towards Chichester and the Isle of Wight.*

direction you approach the course. Heading north from Chichester the road rises gently but steadily past the gates of Goodwood House on the right and heads through shady overhanging trees before reaching an immaculately kept approach with trimmed verges and an avenue of brightly metallic copper beeches which leads upwards to the ridge on which the racecourse stands. As you breast the top, Trundle Hill soars up to the left, while beyond the course to the right, the folds of the Downs roll away in waves of meadows, fields and copses of ancient woodland.

From the other direction, swinging up from Singleton, the approach is even more dramatic. The road climbs steeply after the Weald and Downland Museum, and - tantalisingly - the very tips of the course's tented pavilions peek over the top of the next hill, before disappearing as the escarpment swings round and ever upwards. Suddenly the racecourse unfurls itself, its white rails seeming to work in perfect conjunction with the shape of the terrain, promising heated battles to come and corralling memories of racing highlights of the past.

In fact, those contours were cosmetically enhanced by the imagination of two men and the labours of many others, but the natural amphitheatre up here on top of the Downs quickly proved to be a splendid location for a race meeting. The height of its setting is an essential element of the course's attraction; at 500 feet above sea level - or better still higher again by 200 feet at the top of Trundle Hill - the views are undeniably breathtaking.

Much has been written, and many have eulogised, about those views, but it rarely palls. The aspect to the south-west is particularly stunning, where, as often as not, the vista includes Chichester and its cathedral spire just four miles away, Bosham Creek and - on a clear summer's day - the Isle of Wight stretching beyond the shimmering Solent.

Given the glory of the view, it would be (almost) forgiveable if the standard of racing at Goodwood was no better than average. The fact that it is not is a tribute to the evolution of the course's standards and the owners' commitment to the quality of racing over the past two centuries.

The origins of organised racing at Goodwood can initially be traced to a mercurial decision by 3rd Earl of Egremont. For some years at the end of the 18th century, the Sussex Militia had held a race meeting in the grounds of his house, Petworth Park, but in 1801 he changed his mind about allowing them in to have their fun. The Earl had nothing against racing, far from it. One of the leading owner-breeders of the era, he won the Oaks and the Derby five times each - although it was later revealed that two of those Derby winners (never named) had in fact been four years old at the time they won the race.

Why Lord Egremont decided not to let the officers of the Militia come to Petworth in the spring of 1801 is not recorded. Speculation that over-enthusiastic subalterns had pushed each other into the pond in his grounds once too often seems unconvincing given his sporting interests. Whatever the reasons - and he was by all accounts a capricious character - he said no to the Militia. Deprived of their regular venue, the officers approached their Colonel, the 3rd Duke of Richmond, to see if he could help them out of their predicament.

"Just to look out across those rolling Downs in both directions is a breathtaking sight."

Dick Hern

The Duke was receptive to the idea. At the turn of the eighteenth and nineteenth centuries, Britain was caught up in the Napoleonic wars, and to supply frigates for Horatio Nelson's fleet, the Portsmouth shipyards were hard at work. The 3rd Duke was a military man, who had distinguished himself at the Battle of Minden, and who became a major-general at the age of 26 (he later rose to the rank of Field Marshal). He became Master of the Ordnance in 1782, founded the Royal Horse Artillery and helped to improve the organisation of the Sussex Militia significantly: he felt a natural sense of duty to protect the Sussex coast from the threat of invasion from France. He would therefore have been perfectly aware that the soldiers poised in readiness to prevent such a threat might need to relax with a little R&R. In addition, the Duke himself was at this time in his mid-sixties and had been advised that he was too infirm to continue hunting.

And so the Duke gave his permission for the officers of the Sussex Militia to come to Goodwood, where they held a meeting in conjunction with members of the Goodwood Hunt - of which the Duke was Master - in April 1801. The location chosen was the Harroways, a narrow ridge inside the Duke's own Park. The event was very much a military affair: instead of the conventional saddling bell, a bugler announced the start of the races.

The press picked up on the story swiftly: the *Sporting Magazine* that year reported that "The new racecourse on the Harroway near Goodwood, the seat of His Grace the Duke of Richmond, is now completely formed for sport, and much admired by the acknowledged

***Below:** Looking eastwards down the course from the Members' Lawn, with the March Stand on the right.*

amateurs of the Turf." In the light of such positive feedback, the Duke decided that he would organise another meeting the following year.

The 1802 meeting, which was held over three days, was the first to which the public were admitted, and therefore marks the true start of established racing at Goodwood, and the start of the racecourse infrastructure. In the summer of 1801, the Duke had had a wooden thatched stand constructed for his guests to watch the racing.

During the three-day meeting, which opened on 28th April 1802, sixteen races were run offering prize money of £313, with stakes and matches bringing the total to just over £1000. In comparison, the Goodwood race programme for 2002 consisted of 137 races with total stakes of £2.7 million.

The 1802 racecard included two Hunters' Plates, alongside a Hunting Club Subscription Sweepstake, a number of City of Chichester Plates - one of which was won by the Duke with You Know Me - a Ladies' Plate, two sweepstakes and several matches. One of these head-to-head races proved to be the highlight of the meeting, when Cedar, owned by the Duke, was beaten by Rebel, owned by the Prince of Wales, for 100 guineas (Cedar had, however, won a two-mile sweepstakes on the opening day). In the Duke's stand, various local luminaries, including the Earls of Chichester and Egremont, looked on.

These were the days when races were really tests of strength and stamina - horses might have to run three two-mile heats, with a prize for the horse who won two out of the three. If there was no clear winner, the three winners would be wheeled out again for a tiring fourth heat to decide the issue.

The week after the event, a local newspaper ran a flattering, if not fawning, report of the meeting. "To the efforts of equestrian skill is to be added the princely and almost unprecedented munificence of the noble founder of the Goodwood Races, in providing the newly erected stand with a collation which might be entitled a general refrigarium, for the access was as easy as the reception was elegant and hospitable. We can only add our wish that the illustrious founder may for years enjoy in health and happiness this promising scion, planted his own hand, a wish which we shall be joined in by all Sussex patriots."

The local enthusiasm for racing at Goodwood was not unexpected, as there had long been equestrian activities in the vicinity. In days past, there had been a bridle path running across the terrain of Goduinis - a Saxon laird who was allowed to retain his land by William the Conqueror after the Battle of Hastings and the Norman takeover of England. Local historians and geographical etymologists are undecided about whether the name Godinius transmuted via Godinwood to Goodwood. Suffice to say that by the time that Elizabeth I was on the throne, a survey in 1570 recorded the existence of 'Goodwoode Parke'.

The land passed through various hands before the 13th Earl of Northumberland (nicknamed 'Henry The Wizard' because of his love of scholarship) built himself a house in 1616-17. It was this gentleman's residence that the 1st Duke of Richmond initially rented as a hunting lodge, and then bought from the then owners in order to hunt in the forests of Charlton.

The 1st Duke was the offspring of a liaison between King Charles II and

Right: *Charles, 3rd Duke of Richmond, Lennox and Aubigny, the founder of racing at Goodwood in 1802. He had run a few horses from 1761 onwards and is thought to have been one of the early members of the Jockey Club, which was formed in about 1750. After 1781 he dropped out of ownership for 20 years, but returned to the fray once the Goodwood race meeting came into existence. This portrait was painted by Sir Joshua Reynolds PRA in 1758, when the Duke was 23.*

Above: *On this 1831 plan of Goodwood Racecourse the distinctive loop of the course stands out.*

Louise de Kéroualle, an aristocratic Breton lady-in-waiting to Charles's sister Henrietta, the Duchess of Orléans, who unwittingly effected the introduction between the couple in 1670. Following Henrietta's tragic death at the age of 26, Louise came to the English court in October that year. She withstood the King for a whole year, but nine months after their first union in the autumn of 1671 a boy was born on 29th July 1672. The King gave him one of his own family names of Lennox, and three years later created him Duke of Richmond, Earl of March and Baron Settrington, along with the Scottish titles of Duke of Lennox, Earl of Darnley and Baron Torbolton. All these titles had passed to Charles on the death of James, the last Duke of Richmond and Lennox in the Stuart line.

The 1st Duke loved hunting and gambling, and his decision to buy the hunting lodge at Goodwood was driven by the fact that the nearby Charlton Hunt was one of the most fashionable pack of hounds in England. His heir, the 2nd Duke, was also one of the great sportsmen of his day, and equally passionate about the Charlton. This Duke had developed a fondness for architecture, painting, opera and music during his Grand Tour - he also pioneered organised cricket in Sussex.

When he died in 1750, his son was only 15 years old, but had already acquired a similar appreciation of architecture and the arts. As well as commissioning a then virtually unknown George Stubbs to paint three canvases of equine activity at Goodwood, the 3rd Duke oversaw the expansion of Goodwood House around its Jacobean core. This included two wings, added and designed by James Wyatt - the architect of Fonthill Abbey in Wiltshire - between 1800 and 1806, which were needed in order to house the great art collection after Richmond House, the family's magnificent home on the Thames at Whitehall, had burned down in 1791.

Goodwood was, then, a firm base for the Richmond family in 1802, just as the Duke's role as master of the Charlton Hunt was firmly established. At the time, hunting was the primary horse-related activity of the area. Horse racing in West Sussex was relatively infrequent, although racing was well established at Newmarket, Ascot, Epsom and Doncaster.

The 1802 meeting, like the Sussex Militia's gathering the previous year, had clearly been a success and meetings were planned for the following years. But in this early phase of the course's existence, the meeting had to survive a number of potentially damaging events.

First, the 3rd Duke died in December 1806 - the local newspaper's sycophantic wish four years earlier for his long and healthy enjoyment of the racecourse had not been fulfilled. At his death he owed the then huge amount of £180,000. He had no (legitimate) children, and so the title passed to his brother's son, another military man.

The 4th Duke's career had something of a negative effect on racing at Goodwood. Almost immediately after inheriting the dukedom, he headed off to Ireland as Lord Lieutenant for six years - there was a rumour that this was a convenient way of avoiding his many creditors. Not unnaturally, given the Duke's long absences, the organisation of racing and hunting at Goodwood began to dwindle, and the demands of war with Napoleon also took their toll. Yet the race meeting did not disappear completely - even though one meeting only consisted of a single day's racing with just three events.

Although the Duke was not as involved in either the Goodwood estate or the racecourse as his uncle, he did have some success with his horses, winning a match with Tetuan at the 1807 meeting and later two races with Rosewood.

Despite the patchy state of the meeting during the 4th Duke's tenure, there were, nonetheless, two important events in the course's history and development. One major step forward was the arrival of the Goodwood Cup, first run in 1812 and won by Shoestrings. This Cup (originally known as the Gold Cup) took the place of a Silver Cup which had been won on its first running by Mr Trevanion's Bucephalus - the same horse and owner proceeded to win the race twice more in a row, and the Silver Cup was withdrawn in 1811.

An equally significant event was the decision to move the meeting from April or May to the end of July in 1814, thus gaining the benefit of potentially better weather, and laying the ground for the later emergence of Goodwood's festival week as a major event on the British social calendar. The contemporary racegoer may be surprised to learn that there was only one four-day meeting a

"I never come here without fresh admiration of the beauty and delightfulness of the place, combining everything that is enjoyable in life - large and comfortable house, spacious and beautiful park, extensive views, dry soil, sea air, woods and rides over the downs, and all the facilities of occupation and amusement."

Charles Greville

Left: *Guests leave Goodwood House for the drive up the hill through Birdless Grove to the course for a day's racing.*

year at Goodwood - and at Ascot - until after the Second World War.

Following his time in Ireland, the 4th Duke had been transferred to Brussels as a special envoy, where he was present at, but did not fight in, the Battle of Waterloo. His wife had organised a now legendary ball three nights before the battle, on the eve of Quatre-Bras, an entertainment which was approved by the Duke of Wellington, possibly because it sent a message of disinformation to the approaching Napoleon about the lack of readiness or the frivolity of the British. The 4th Duke's next posting was as the Governor-General of the British settlements in Canada, but while there he was bitten by a pet fox - he contracted rabies and died shortly afterwards.

This personal misfortune and tragedy for the Richmond family had one silver lining as far as the racecourse was concerned. The 4th Duke was succeeded by his 28-year-old son, whose interest in racing - and friendship with Lord George Bentinck - lay behind the transformation of Goodwood from a small, though interesting, local race meeting competing with similar meetings at Brighton and Lewes, into one of the country's top racecourses, able to vie with Ascot, Epsom, Doncaster and Newmarket.

The 5th Duke, like his great uncle, had been advised to give up the exertions of hunting, He had taken a musket ball in the chest while serving with the 52nd Light Infantry at the Peninsular War battle of Orthez in 1814; it was a near fatal injury, and a subsequent heavy fall while hunting had aggravated the wound. The musket ball had not been removed at Orthez,

Below: *Adine wins the Goodwood Stakes in 1853 - this engraving by Hunt shows the excellent view provided by the grandstand's elegant first-floor balcony.*

***Left:** The present, the 10th Duke of Richmond. He first attended the races at Goodwood in July 1946, the first meeting after the Second World War, when he presented Gordon Richards with a cup for the March Stakes, a race which Richards won three times. The Duke has been a member of every syndicate of GROG (the Goodwood Racehorse Owners' Group), created the Richmond-Brissac Trophy for European Amateur Riders with Tim Neligan, and established a twinning arrangement with the Duke of Brissac and Angers Racecourse. Since becoming Chairman of Goodwood Racecourse in 1969, the Duke has overseen the construction of the March, Charlton and Sussex Stands and the New Paddock and Weighing Room.*

and had shifted into a dangerous position. Taking the doctors' counsel to heart, he diverted his energies towards horse racing, and concentrated on making the most of what he realised was a fantastic site for horse racing.

His first success at Goodwood had been in 1817, when his colt Humes beat a gelding of Lord Apsley's in a match. The following year, he won his first public race, in a sweepstakes at Goodwood with Roncesvalles, whose name echoed his experience in the Peninsular War; this horse won twice in 1819, twice more in 1820 (including victory in the Purbrook Stakes) and once more in 1821.

The rise in the fortunes of the racecourse at Goodwood was due not least to the reputation of the Goodwood stables, for which the Duke hired John Kent as his private trainer in 1823. Kent had previously been head lad to R.D. Boyce at Newmarket. The stables, a magnificent hollow square of Sussex knapped flint, had been built between 1757 and 1763 to the design of the Scottish architect William Chambers, one of the greatest architects of the period, who later designed Somerset House and the pagoda at Kew. With Kent in charge, the stables were soon full of horses.

1980

'THE FAMILY HAVE BEEN DIRECTLY INVOLVED WITH THE DAY-TO-DAY RUNNING OF THE RACECOURSE FOR 200 YEARS. I AM SURE THAT THE FACT THAT IT HAS BEEN DEVELOPED OVER THIS TIME FROM A PASSION FOR THE SPORT, RATHER THAN FOR STRICT COMMERCIAL REASONS, HAS MUCH TO DO WITH ITS SUCCESS. IT ALSO HAS A GREAT DEAL TO DO WITH THE OVERALL FEELING OF THE PLACE AND THE SENSE OF CONTINUITY. FEW SPORTING OCCASIONS CAN HAVE HAD SUCH CONTINUITY OF OWNERSHIP AND LEADERSHIP, EVEN FEWER HAVING THE LUXURY OF BEING ABLE TO PLAN FOR THE LONG TERM. EACH DUKE, FROM THE 3RD TO THE 10TH, HAS DONE HIS OWN BIT TO SUPPORT, NURTURE AND DEVELOP - IN A SENSITIVE WAY - THIS EXTRAORDINARY AND UNIQUE PLACE."

THE EARL OF MARCH

The 5th Duke was enjoying his racing. In 1823 the meeting included the inaugural running of the Goodwood Stakes, although a race called the same name had appeared as a one-off twelve years earlier. The Duke's grey filly Dandizette won that initial race.

In 1824, Lord George Bentinck - who was staying nearby at Cowdray Park - visited the races for the first time, and emerged victorious as a rider in the Cocked Hat Stakes on Olive, a mare that belonged to his host at Cowdray, Colonel Poyntz, a Goodwood steward. From then until his death in 1848, he made sure that he attended every Goodwood meeting.

By coincidence this was the same meeting where there was a famous judging error. Posted high above the course, the judge became too engrossed in a battle between Vitinella and Ghost on the far side of the course, and was oblivious to the Duke's Dandizette winning by a good three lengths on the near side, underneath his lofty position. It is reported that Vitinella's owner, Lord Verulam, civilly offered to waive any claim to the victory. The Duke, equally civilly, declined, saying, "The judge's decision is final."

In 1825, the Gold Cup returned after an absence of eight years - it would never again disappear from the racing schedule at Goodwood. On its resumption, the owner of the winning horse Cricketer was none other than Lord Egremont, whose interest in racing continued as strongly as ever.

A golden age of racing at Goodwood was about to begin. That same year, Spree won the City Plate and the Waterloo Plate for the home stable. Two years

***Above:** Frankie Dettori performs another of his trademark dismounts. He rode the first winner of his career as a 16-year-old at Goodwood on Lizzy Hare in the Birdless Grove Handicap on 9th June 1987. By the end of 2001, he had ridden 98 winners at Goodwood, including a double in 2001 with Noverre in the Sussex Stakes and Lailani in the Vodafone Nassau Stakes. On three occasions - in 1997, 1999 and 2001 - Frankie has achieved four winners in a day.*

later, the Duke's Gulnare became the first classic winner to emerge from the Goodwood Stables, winning the 1827 Oaks. Later that same summer, another of the Duke's horses, Link Boy, won the Goodwood Cup. This was an extremely successful year for the 5th Duke: he won 23 races, although only having seven horses in training.

The level of racing, and the solidity of its annual meeting were cementing. Much greater fame came with the success at Goodwood of George IV, who won the Goodwood Cup in 1829 with Fleur de Lis - the horse ran in the colours of and under the name of his racing manager, Mr Delme Radcliffe. The following year, his brother William IV inherited the throne and the King's horses, and won with Fleur de Lis again, under his own name. The new King attempted the hattrick in 1831, but Fleur de Lis was beaten by the previous year's Derby winner Priam, who won again in 1832 and was one of the best horses ever to win the Goodwood Cup.

The 5th Duke and Lord George Bentinck joined forces to continue the racecourse's upward curve. This was a period where trees were felled, earth moved, gallops laid out and the downs levelled - they literally sliced off the top of the Downs - to fulfil the plans of Lord George and the Duke. During the extension of the finishing straight by two and a half furlongs (moving the finishing line much nearer the natural grandstand of the Trundle) they recycled the soil to create an embankment which added much-needed width to the narrow shape of the original Harroways ridge. Even nowadays this would be a gigantic undertaking, with some serious logistical problems.

The shape of the course which resulted - and which was determined to a great degree by the natural rim of the downs - is one of the characteristic features of Goodwood. The straight six-furlong run, down which the field in the Stewards' Cup thunder each summer, is linked to a triangular loop by two bends, known officially as the Top and Lower. This allows for a number of permutations. A race can start on the right-hand side of the triangular loop and take either the Top or Lower bend onto the straight to make a difference of one furlong to the length of the race.

For longer races over two and a half miles, the horses start near the stands and run the reverse way along the course, before turning left, swinging up round the triangular loop and returning to the straight via the Top Bend,

6
8

coming back to the winning post the "correct way". Occasionally this can prove confusing to jockeys unfamiliar with the course and in the past Greville Starkey, for example, has decided to conduct proceedings with hand signals to help his fellow jockeys find the right path.

For many years the run-off after the winning post ran straight up Trundle Hill. The present run-off, on the racecourse side of the public road, was not constructed until after the Second World War. On one occasion, the winner of the Goodwood Cup in 1884, St Simon having defeated the rest of the field by 20 lengths, was so strong and had such momentum that he could not be pulled up and simply kept on running to the top of the Trundle.

Lord George Bentinck had the vision, the Duke had the manpower and - following the unexpected death of his grandfather, the Duke of Gordon, in 1836 - the money. In tandem they must have been a formidable team. There is a story that the Duke, who was something of a stickler for punctuality, appointed his head gardener Henry King to be in charge of timekeeping for the works. One day King was late for work (which began at 7am sharp) by quarter of an hour. He could see that the Duke was already there, so as he approached he adjusted his watch by turning the hands back by 15 minutes. "If they begin 15 minutes late, they finish 15 minutes late. It makes no difference," he said. Apparently the Duke was satisfied with King's explanation.

The innovations included the creation of straw-covered exercise grounds sheltered by a plantation of trees and on the nearby Halnaker gallop. In the particularly harsh winter of 1845, the horses stabled at Goodwood could canter to their, and their trainer's, satisfaction, while elsewhere in the country trainers looked glumly at the frozen ground.

The first private stand built by the 3rd Duke was replaced by a new stand designed by the architect George Draper and opened in 1830. Described as "elegant and commodious", it was 120 feet long and capable of holding 3,000 people. The ground floor contained rooms for retiring and refreshment (always a key ingredient in the enjoyment of racing at Goodwood), while on the first floor arcaded windows ran along the front of a saloon, with adjacent betting rooms. Outside, wide balconies offered good viewing, and above, as was traditional at the time, steeply raked rows of high tiered bench seating were open to the elements.

"Goodwood seems to me the only part of British social life in which the smoothest mixes happily with the roughest, the aristocrat with the urchin, the oldest, staidest money with the newest and brashest. All our tired rules of social stratification are lost in common delight and obsession with the chase of an ancient pastime and the universal human excitement of the gamble against the odds."

Dominic Lawson

In 1841, a weighing room was constructed. Previously, the weighing room had formed part of the grandstand building. As a result, jockeys and trainers had to fight their way to the weighing room past the crowds milling around outside. The new building - in the Grecian style - also contained a small printroom at the back. A local report of the time explained that this was "a neat little room for the use of Mr Mason, the printer, of Chichester, by whom the cards and sheet lists have hitherto been prepared, and who up to the present year, has issued the return lists between every race from a temporary shed erected within the clump of trees, often, from the tempestuous state of the weather, with considerable difficulty."

By the middle of the nineteenth century, Goodwood had taken its place amongst the most significant racecourses in England. The Goodwood Cup, the Richmond Stakes, alongside handicaps like the Stewards' Cup and the Chesterfield Cup, were already renowned (the Sussex Stakes, now the top race of the year at Goodwood, would only start to gain its later significance towards the end of the century).

The racecourse had also proved to be a cradle of international racing. Goodwood's proximity to the English Channel and its aristocratic connections made the journey from the Continent doubly appealing. As early as 1840, the Goodwood Cup had been won by the French-trained Beggarman. This was 20 years before the first French runner in the Derby, and 74 years before the first French-trained winner Durbar II (the French-bred and owned 1865 Gladiateur was trained at Newmarket).

In 1845, one visitor was writing of Goodwood that "an aristocratic atmosphere pervades the whole scene. With magnificent scenery, first-rate racing and the cream of England's best society to inspirit and gratify him, a stranger would indeed be fastidious who did not consider the Goodwood racecourse the perfection and paradise of racegrounds."

1845 marked the zenith of the 5th Duke's fortunes as an owner: he won the Oaks with Refraction, the 1,000 Guineas with Picnic and, as a result of a rare foray to the north, the Liverpool Cup with Lothario. Surprisingly, perhaps, Lord George Bentinck, who had moved his string of horses to the Goodwood stables in 1841, decided to sell them in 1846 and concentrate on politics. The course's nineteenth-century peak had been passed.

"I have read somewhere that perfection is not to be found on this earth; now, with due deference to the uttered judgment, I think I might safely challenge the assertion."

Correspondent of the Sporting Magazine, *on returning from Goodwood, 1840*

After the 5th Duke's death in 1860, the 6th and 7th Dukes continued the racing tradition, and their personal interest in the family estates (the 6th Duke) and entertaining (the 7th Duke) ensured the continuation and increasing reputation of Goodwood, even when the racing was not as well supported: the Goodwood Plate collapsed in 1894 as there were no entries.

In 1886 the 6th Duke - who had ridden four Goodwood winners in 1842 - did not attend as he was in mourning for one of his younger sons. Yet he still made sure that Goodwood House was available for the Prince and Princess of Wales (later King Edward VII and Queen Alexandra). Not surprisingly, the gaiety of that particular meeting was muted. "There was not very much entertainment under the famous trees," wrote one diarist. "A couple of dozen tables perhaps, certainly not more. The Naval Depot had a tent and so had the 5th Lancers, but there was an air of depression over the whole meeting which was not enjoyable."

Just after the 7th Duke succeeded to the title, the 1830 stand was replaced. This stand had a similar high and open seating area, at the back of which was a sheltered, though unglazed arcade. Shortly afterwards a typically Edwardian pavilion - "like an Oxford barge", in Pevsner's words - was put up. Later called the Charlton Building, it contained the Stewards' Balcony on the first floor and a Press balcony alongside. These improvements coincided with the patronage of Edward VII (see the chapter on *The Royal Connection*) which continued to boost Goodwood's fortunes, while successive Dukes made their own impact.

The 8th Duke set the Estate on a somewhat more commercial basis, forming the Goodwood Estate Company in 1931, part of an attempt to cope with the stiff death duties that were a heritage of vastly increased taxation post the First World War, and very poor agricultural returns. On his death in 1935, the title passed to Frederick, the second son (known as Freddie), whose brother Lord Settrington had been killed fighting on the Archangel front in 1919 supporting the White Russians against the Bolsheviks.

Freddie March's first love was horsepower of the automotive kind: out of the wartime aerodrome of RAF Westhampnett he created the Goodwood Motor Circuit which was one of the highlights of British motor racing in the 1950s and early 60s, and which was revived by the current Earl of March in 1998. Yet he still maintained the interest and support of his predecessors for the racecourse - in his time, for example, the brick-built Richmond Stand was constructed.

With the help of the long-time Agent and Clerk of the Course, Ralph Hubbard, the course was nursed back to health after the Second World War, when the grandstand and other buildings on the course had been turned into a billeting centre for the army and (as D-Day loomed) the RAF.

His son, the present, the 10th Duke, has continued to galvanise activity and bring Goodwood into the twentieth, and now the twenty-first century, most recently with the opening of a multi-million pound development which will provide racegoers with views from the new parade ring to that magnificent panorama of Chichester Harbour for years to come.

Right: *The Horseshoe Pavilion roofs looking south, with the Charlton Stand rising above on the left.*

BAR
TEA BAR

THE GOODWOOD CUP

The Goodwood Cup is the second leg of the season's three championship races for stayers, following the Gold Cup at Ascot in the first part of the summer and before the Doncaster Cup in early autumn. The races are strategically placed in the racing calendar to ensure that a horse of class and the necessary robust constitution can be trained for all three with respites between each of the races before being brought back into fast work for the next.

The institution of the Goodwood Cup in 1812 was to ensure that a succession of some of the best long-distance horses that have graced the racecourse during its 200 years have shown their mettle at Goodwood. The list of winners include the superb Priam, who became the first to combine real class with stamina in 1831, the wonderful mare Alice Hawthorn - winner of 52 races in seven seasons before being the dam of a Derby winner Thormanby - and Doncaster, himself a Derby winner, from whom Northern Dancer descended in male line.

An important international flavour was given to the roll call by the Hungarian mare Kincsem, unbeaten in 54 races all over Europe, though the Goodwood Cup of 1878 was the only one in England. In 1884 the winner was St Simon, the most influential stallion of the late Victorian and Edwardian eras.

During the twentieth century more really outstanding stayers maintained the prestige of the Goodwood Cup. The winners included Son-In-Law, an important influence for stamina in his descendants; the legendary Brown Jack; Alycidon, the greatest British stayer of the years following the Second World War; and, in recent times, Double Trigger, the only horse to have won the Goodwood Cup three times with successes in 1995, 1997 and 1998.

The inaugural Goodwood Cup was staged when the only meeting of the year to take place on the course was still held in the spring. It therefore proved a far sterner test of stamina than its present-day counterpart since it was over three miles that Shoestrings, a four-year–old chestnut filly belonging to a Mr Cope, beat four rivals on Monday 4th May 1812.

Having been indirectly responsible for the Goodwood course coming into being, by refusing to allow a meeting to take place in Petworth Park, the unpredictable Lord

Opposite: *The start of the 1955 Goodwood Cup by flag at the foot of Trundle Hill when the race was over two miles and five furlongs. The winner was Double Bore.*

Egremont readily indulged his love of racing by taking advantages of the opportunities, so close to his own splendid property, offered by the Dukes of Richmond. In 1816 he won the Goodwood Cup for the first time, when his three-year-old Scarecrow carried the featherweight of 6st 4lb.

Double Trigger may not have been the best horse in terms of hard talent in the second half of the 1990s, but he was right at the top in terms of popularity with his three wins in the Goodwood Cup, in (from the top) 1985, 1987 and 1988.

In those still formative days of the meeting, the Cup was very much an intermittent attraction. It had not been run in 1815, the year that the Duchess of Richmond gave her celebrated ball on the eve of the battle of Waterloo, nor was the race renewed between 1817 and 1824 inclusive. So it was an interrupted treble in the Cup that Lord Egremont completed by winning it with Cricketer in 1825, when the distance had been reduced to two miles five furlongs, and his grey four-year-old Stumps a year later. Stumps walked over for the Cup, having beaten the Duke of York's Dahlia and two other horses in the Goodwood Stakes earlier in the day.

Lord Egremont may have been capricious on occasion, but he was the most generous of men, thinking nothing of giving away the sum of £20,000 a year to charity. When he died in 1837 he bequeathed his property to his illegitimate son, Colonel George Wyndham.

The Goodwood Stakes, which Lord Egremont won with Stumps in 1825 and again in 1826, had been run for the first time in 1823. Not only was it a weight-for-age, rather than the important handicap that it was to become, but it carried a selling condition, as the winner could be bought for 250 guineas if demanded. All the same it was won by the 5th Duke's very useful grey filly Dandizette, whose only opponent was an unnamed grey colt.

The first royal success in the Goodwood Cup materialised in 1829 when the winner was Fleur de Lis, owned by the elderly King George IV, though running in the name of his racing manager Delme Radcliffe. It was appropriate that that should have been the last of the important races won by the old King, for Goodwood was very much one of his local meetings, by reason of his having spent so much of his time in the exotic Royal Pavilion that he had built in the Oriental style at nearby Brighton.

King George IV died in June 1830, leaving the throne to his brother the Duke of Clarence, who became King William IV. On being asked which of his horses he wished to run at a meeting the new sovereign, a former naval officer with minimal interest in racing, replied, "Why the whole squad, first raters and gun-boats. Some of them, I suppose, must win."

Such must have been the instructions with regard to the Goodwood meeting of 1830, as the royal colours were carried by Fleur de Lis, Zinganee and The Colonel in the Cup. The King's trio dominated the race with Fleur de Lis winning again by beating Zinganee, with The Colonel third in a field of nine.

An interesting innovation at Goodwood in 1830 was a race, once round the course, for which the Members of Parliament for the City of Chichester, seeking to find favour with their electorate, put up the £50 prize money. This was won by Lord Egremont's unnamed bay colt, brother to Grampus, who beat Lord William Lennox's Miss Craven in straight heats.

The Goodwood meeting of 1831 was particularly memorable in as much as Priam, a splendid four-year-old bay colt of ideal proportions, became the first Derby winner to graduate to success in the Goodwood Cup. The colt's owner, the Earl of Chesterfield, had arranged for Priam to complete his preparation for the Cup under the supervision of John Kent, in the Duke of Richmond's private stable on the Goodwood estate, and the trainer's 13-year-old son, John Kent junior, rode Priam in his work.

In due course John Kent junior would take over the Goodwood stable on the retirement of his father, and was to have a succession of high-class horses through his hands. Yet when he was an old man of more than 70 he was to write that "Priam... in my opinion (and I am never tired of repeating it) was the best and most perfectly shaped racehorse I ever saw."

Priam duly justified the enormous confidence reposed in him by beating the King's mare Fleur de Lis, who had been trying to win the Cup for the third year in succession. Twelve months later Priam returned to Goodwood to win the Cup for a second time, beating Lord Exeter's Beiram, with that year's Derby winner St Giles unplaced.

Priam did not run again after crowning his career by winning that second Goodwood Cup, and retired to stud in Bretby Park, near Burton-on-Trent in Staffordshire. George Stanhope, 6th Earl of Chesterfield, was an easy-going man of enormous charm and almost unbelievable extravagance. While Master of the King's Buckhounds in 1835 and 1836, he carried out his duties in truly regal splendour, offering all but unlimited hospitality to followers of the pack. To meet the huge expenditure, 'Chesterfield the Magnificent' was obliged to sell Priam to the United States for 3,500 guineas. Among the stock that Priam left behind him *in utero* was Lord George Bentinck's Crucifix, who won the 2,000 Guineas, the 1,000 Guineas and the Oaks on her only appearances in 1840.

Despite the huge inroads that Lord Chesterfield continuously and carelessly made into his once enormous fortune, he was able to continue racing, deriving particular pleasure from running his horses in the fashionable, yet totally relaxed, atmosphere provided by Goodwood. He won the Goodwood Cup again with Hornsea, who beat Elis into second place in 1836, and for a fourth time with Carew in 1837.

"The Goodwood Cup was always an interesting race to ride in. There are so many turns and corners in the race and there is one point where you can take one of two sections of the track. I recall Greville (Starkey) making the running in the race one time and putting out his hand at the junction as if he was driving a car, to show an Irish jockey who had not had time to walk the course beforehand which way he should go."

Jimmy Lindley

1 ML
1 FUR

In 1831, the year that Priam won his first Goodwood Cup, the Goodwood meeting was extended to four days. Among the races moved to the final day was the Waterloo Plate. In that event, a reminder of the highlight of the 3rd Duke's military service, the runners were ridden by members of the Goodwood Racing Club wearing cocked hats, rather than jockeys' caps, to indicate their amateur status. That year the Waterloo Plate was won in straight heats by Adam Brock, ridden by Major Bouverie, beating the Duke's Wandering Boy in the second.

The first of several outstanding mares to win the Goodwood Cup was Alice Hawthorn in 1844. Ridden by the top northern jockey Sim Templeman, she gave Lord Chesterfield's Prizefighter a stone and a beating of an easy three lengths. She had been bred by John Plummer of Shipton, near York. Plummer was not particularly interested in racing, and having been unable to sell her as a yearling he sent her to be trained by Leonard Hesseltine, whose stables were at Hambleton in the North Riding of Yorkshire, on the understanding they would share any prize money she earned. Later he leased her for a couple of long periods. The action of Alice Hawthorn resembled that of a hare, as she seemed to steal along the ground with her ears pricked. Hailed by her legion of admirers as 'The Queen of the Turf', she was in training for seven seasons.

The savage feud between Lord George Bentinck and John Barham Day and his family - which had been running since Lord George had removed his horses from Day's Danebury stable to have them trained by John Kent junior at Goodwood in September 1841 - reached its climax in the Goodwood Cup of 1845, which Lord George had high hopes of winning with Miss Elis.

Below: *The Goodwood Cup did not have far to travel in 1827, as the winner of the race was the Duke of Richmond's four-year-old Linkboy.*

A three-year-old chestnut filly by Stockport, an own brother to Elis, Miss Elis stood more than 16 hands. Although rather highly strung, she was wonderfully game and liked to make her own running. The day before the Goodwood Cup, she had been ridden by little Kitchener at 5st 7lb to win the Goodwood Stakes very easily indeed. That night, after dining at Goodwood House, Lord George sent for Kent to ask him how Miss Elis had come out of her race, and whether she had eaten up. The trainer replied that she had no more than a good exercise gallop. "In that case," declared Lord George, "I shall back her tonight, as there is sure to be some betting on the Cup, for which Weatherbit has many friends."

On his only previous appearances as a three-year-old Weatherbit had been a very well-backed second favourite for the Derby, in which he was unplaced after jumping a fallen horse. A fortnight later Weatherbit won the Welcome Stakes over a mile an a half at Royal Ascot. Connections had no doubt whatever that Weatherbit would be still better over a longer distance, and to ensure his stamina should be given full play at Goodwood the Danebury Stable also ran St Lawrence, ridden by John Day junior, as pacemaker. Lord George and John Kent, equally anxious that there should be a strong gallop, ran Discord in the same capacity.

Above: *Priam, who had won the Derby in 1830, gave a major boost to the status of the Goodwood Cup with his brace of victories in 1831 and 1832. Lord Chesterfield had bought him for the then considerable sum of 3,000 guineas - the Derby of that year was worth £3,000 - shortly before the first of those two wins.*

Many seasoned racing men and hardened professional backers, who had seen money change hands freely at Royal Ascot or on Derby Day for many a year, were to confess they had never seen such heavy betting as at Goodwood on that last Thursday of July in 1845. Lord George's agents and his friends bet as though defeat was quite out of the question, while John Gully, John Day, his family and their associates took every price they could about Weatherbit. The two horses started joint favourites at 2-1.

Discord, who had won the Great Northamptonshire Stakes, a race of some consequence, at Northampton in March, set off to make strong running for Miss Elis, but was of little use to her, so that she went to the front at the turn on the top of the hill to make the best of her way home. Tension on the stands must have been all but unbearable when Weatherbit ranged within striking distance of her and they raced almost upsides of each other without Lord George's filly losing her marginal edge; then, approaching the stands, she fought her way back into a a decisive lead.

A future Prime Minister won the Goodwood Cup in 1849 when the brown filly Canezou carried the colours of Lord Stanley to beat Chanticleer by a length. Twelve months later Canezou won the Cup a second time, beating Caribou by two lengths, with the Derby winner Cossack in third.

The prestige of winning, no less than the sheer pleasure of watching their horses racing amidst some of the most beautiful countryside in Europe, continually inspired foreign owners to run horses at Goodwood. Back in 1840 the Duke of Orléans had won the Goodwood Cup with the five-year-old Beggarman. Ridden by Jem Robinson, Beggarman won from Lanercost, who had been successful in the first running of the Cambridgeshire the previous year.

French-bred horses dominated the finish of the Goodwood Cup in 1853 when M. Lupin's smart filly Jouvence, ridden by the Epsom jockey Bob Sherwood, beat M. Alexandre Aumont's Hervine by two lengths. Earlier in the summer Jouvence had won the French Oaks.

An even more important French horse won the Goodwood Cup in 1857: Monarque, owned by Count Frédéric de Lagrange, the son of one of Napoleon's generals. Bred by M. Eugène Aumont, all of whose bloodstock was bought by Count de Lagrange in 1857, Monarque was of extremely doubtful paternity, being by Sting, The Baron or The Emperor. On retirement to stud, Monarque became the sire of Gladiateur, who completed the Triple Crown in the 2,000 Guineas, the Derby and the St Leger for Count de Lagrange in 1866, so that yet another victor of the Goodwood Cup became the parent of a classic winner.

As well as those from mainland Europe, horses from across the Atlantic began to intensify international competition at Goodwood in the second half of the 19th century. In 1856 Richard Ten Broeck, a professional gambler of agreeable disposition, sent a contingent of horses to England from the United States, along with their trainer Palmer and jockeys Littlefield and Gilpatrick. Gilpatrick, rated the best jockey in America, looked particularly out of place at Goodwood, and other English courses, by reason of his long Yankee beard.

A good deal of bad feeling was aroused when Ten Broeck's four-year-old chestnut Starke won the Goodwood Stakes in 1859, as Admiral Rous, who combined the roles of Steward of the Jockey Club and Handicapper for many years, had let him into the

Below: *Starke won the Goodwood Cup of 1861 for his owner, the American Richard Ten Broeck, beating The Wizard by a head, and leaving Thormanby - the winner of the previous year's Derby - unplaced.*

race with 7st 7lb, although he was known to have been highly regarded in the United States. Two years later Starke emphasised that class was his strong suit by winning the Goodwood Cup by a head from The Wizard, with the previous year's Derby winner Thormanby unplaced.

Above: *Kincsem was bred in Hungary, but raced all over Europe to record a career tally of 54 wins from 54 starts. On her only appearance on an English racecourse she won the Goodwood Cup of 1878.*

Perhaps the most exciting, and probably the best of the foreign winners of the Goodwood Cup was Kincsem. She started the 5-2 outsider of three and was ridden by Madden, a Manchester man, to beat Pageant by two lengths in 1878.

Although Kincsem had been bred by her owner Ernest de Blascovich, and foaled at the Imperial Stud at Kisber in Hungary, she had a pedigree dominated by English blood, her sire being Cambuscan who had been third to Blair Athol in the St Leger at Doncaster in 1864. In the normal way of things Ernest de Blascovich sold his yearlings, but failing to find a buyer for Kincsem, a liver chestnut, without a trace of white on her, he decided to race her himself.

As a two-year-old she won ten times on ten different courses in Hungary, Austria and Germany. In her second season she won another 17 races, including the equivalents of the 2,000 Guineas, 1,000 Guineas, Oaks and St Leger in Hungary and both the local Derby and the Emperor's Prize in Vienna. As a four-year-old she travelled still further afield to win the Goodwood Cup and the Grand Prix de Deauville on the way home, while the other races she won in 1878 included the Grosser Preis von Baden Baden. In her fourth season she won the Grosser Preis again and eleven other events.

In 1854 the Goodwood Cup had been won by Virago, an English filly of the same remarkable constitution as Kincsem. That year Epsom's two big Spring handicaps, the City and Suburban and the Great Metropolitan, had been run on the same day. Making her seasonal debut in the ten-furlong City and Suburban, Virago won and then defied a penalty in the Great Metropolitan over two and a quarter miles. Within three weeks she had made the long journey up to York, where she won the Great Northern Handicap and the Flying Dutchman Handicap 24 hours later. After success in four handicaps, Virago won the 1,000 Guineas in early May, and was then given a well-earned rest until she beat the older Indian Warrior by 15 lengths in the Goodwood Cup. The next day she won the Nassau Stakes, then over a mile.

Virago was trained by Lord George Bentinck's old adversary, John Barham Day, who had handed over the Danebury establishment to his son John, on taking charge of the private stable of Henry Padwick at Michel Grove in Sussex. Henry Padwick was a solicitor, whose enormous income was derived from lending money at rates of interest that would have made Shylock blush. He raced as 'Mr Howard', perhaps as a delicate

"I love these staying races. They are very much part of our tradition with the treble of the Gold Cup at Ascot and the Cups at Goodwood and Doncaster - great spectacles and betting fun for the punters. One of the intriguing things about the Goodwood Cup is how the horses have to start running away from home."

John Gosden

compliment to his ducal neighbour Henry Howard, 13th Duke of Norfolk of Arundel Castle, on whose estate Michel Grove was situated. Most notorious of the victims of Padwick's usury was the dissolute 4th and last Marquess of Hastings, who won the Goodwood Cup with The Duke, trained by John Day junior and ridden by George Fordham, in 1866. Two years later, worn out by depravity, the Marquess died at the age of only 26.

Baron Meyer de Rothschild's Favonius, triumphant in the Derby of the previous year, was a fitting winner of the Goodwood Cup in 1872. Favonius was trained at Newmarket by Joe Hayhoe in the Palace House Stables, where King Charles had kept his hacks. While Favonius was being led into the unsaddling enclosure after winning the Goodwood Cup in a canter Joe Hayhoe declared "I would not take £1,000 for a hair of that horse's tail!"

Derby form did not work out at all in the Goodwood Cup of 1873. Favonius was opposed by the previous year's Derby winner Cremorne, who had won the Gold Cup at Ascot a month earlier. The only other runner was Flageolet, whom Cremorne had beaten by three lengths into second place in the Gold Cup. Unknown to most Goodwood racegoers, Cremorne had sprung a curb a fortnight earlier, but William Gilbert, who trained him in Newmarket's Nunnery Stable, was unable to contact the owner Henry Savile to obtain permission to scratch him. With Cremorne unable to do justice to himself, the stamina of the three-year-old Flageolet carried the day, and he beat Favonius by 30 lengths.

St Simon, widely regarded as the best horse to have been seen in Britain during the nineteenth century, ran more often at Goodwood than on any other course. Mat Dawson, who was responsible for six Derby winners and many other notable classic winners, always maintained "I have only trained one good horse in my life - St Simon." He maintained that St Simon simply radiated energy, declaring that he had more "electricity about him than any horse I have known". Certainly the colt sweated freely, and was difficult to handle, never allowing himself to be tied up while being dressed over in his box. "Talk about the patience of Job," growled the one-eyed Charlie Fordham, the lad who did him. "Job never did no St Simon!"

Making his racecourse debut at Goodwood, where his owner was generally a member of the Duke of Richmond's house party, on 31st July 1883, St Simon was ridden by Fred Archer to beat Ephrussi by an exceedingly easy six lengths. The following day St Simon ran again, and made equally light work of beating his solitary opponent by a length.

Not only did St Simon have his first race at Goodwood, but he took his leave of racegoers there. As Archer could not ride at the eight stone that three-year-old colts carried in the Goodwood Cup, Charlie Wood, the strongest and much the most competent jockey capable of going to the scale at that weight, had the mount on St Simon again, having won the Gold Cup on him at Ascot the previous month. The only other two runners were owned by the 12th Duke of Hamilton: Ossian, winner of the previous year's St Leger by three lengths, and the older gelding Friday. Once again it was no race, and after St Simon won by 20 lengths, the strength of Wood was, for a considerable time, of no avail in pulling him up.

Above: *St Simon, who won the Cup in 1884, is unarguably one of the best horses ever to race in England; some would put him right at the top of the list.*

During the late Victorian and Edwardian eras, nobody felt more in her element in the brilliant social ambience and relaxed rural atmosphere of Goodwood than the lady known to history as Lillie Langtry. Born on the Island of Jersey, she had become one of the celebrated beauties of her day, and had acquired her enthusiasm for racing from her two most famous lovers, the Prince of Wales, later King Edward VII, and the degenerate millionaire and accomplished amateur jockey George Baird. In 1899 Mrs Langtry won the Goodwood Cup with the Australian-bred Merman, ridden by Charlie Wood. As Mrs Langtry was not yet ready to defy the convention that ladies did not own racehorses, she maintained the myth by running Merman in the name of 'Mr Jersey'.

As the clouds of war gathered over Europe in the summer of 1914, the three-year-old Son-In-Law, owned by the South African industrialist Sir Abe Bailey and trained by Reg Day in the Terrace House Stable at Newmarket, beat the older filly At Last by a head in the Goodwood Cup. Son-In-Law became an outstandingly successful sire of stayers, his offspring including the Ascot Gold Cup winners Bosworth, Foxlaw (also trained by Reg Day), and Trimdon, and was champion sire in 1924 and 1930.

Reg Day had had a stable since the Jockey Club first required trainers to hold licences in 1902. He excelled in the handling of high class stayers like Son-In-Law. Along with his father 'Bushranger' Day and the other trainers of the late Victorian era, amongst whom he had grown up, he believed in giving horses plenty of strong work in order to achieve maximum fitness. To the younger school of Newmarket trainers, a good half-speed gallop was known as "One of Reg Day's canters". Reg Day did not retire until 1968, and died aged 89 four years later.

Sir Harold Wernher's Brown Jack was by far and away the most popular stayer to race in Britain between the World Wars. He won the Queen Alexandra Stakes at Ascot six years in succession, and appeared almost as regularly at Goodwood, where he ran in the Cup five times. On arrival from Ireland, Brown Jack was sent to Wroughton in Wiltshire

to be trained by the Hon. Aubrey Hastings, on whose death in May 1929 he and the other horses at Wroughton were taken over by Hastings's former assistant Ivor Anthony.

Brown Jack, with whom the former champion jockey Steve Donoghue struck up a memorable partnership based on mutual confidence and affection, was not only a horse of remarkable ability and consistency, but a great character. He so easily became bored by the routine at Wroughton that he refused to put his back into his work, making it extremely difficult to bring him to peak fitness.

Above: Brown Jack, winner of the Goodwood Cup of 1930 and the Champion Hurdle of 1928, is principally remembered, however, for his six consecutive wins in the Queen Alexandra Stakes at Royal Ascot, the last of which came in 1934 when he was ten years old.

While he had no liking for the magnificent open landscape of Newmarket Heath, on which he was twice beaten in the Cesarewitch, Brown Jack thoroughly enjoyed galloping up and down the gradients and around the turns of the Sussex downland. When he turned out for the Goodwood Cup for the first time in 1929, he was ridden by Joe Childs, Donoghue being on the sidelines with a broken knee. Throughout the final three furlongs there was nothing to choose between Brown Jack and his longstanding rival Old Orkney, neither giving an inch, until the judge awarded the verdict of a short head to Old Orkney.

Reunited with Steve Donoghue 12 months later, Brown Jack had his lead horse Mailed Fist, the mount of Charlie Elliott, to make the pace for him in the Goodwood Cup. Mailed Fist set a sensible gallop ahead of the strongly fancied French challenger Monsieur le Marechal, with Brown Jack third of five. Mailed Fist still led when they reappeared at the top of the hill. Shortly afterwards Mailed Fist dropped back as Brown Jack was moving up to join Monsieur le Marechal, who was coming under pressure. Once in the straight Brown Jack became engaged in a duel with Jugo, ridden by Bobby Dick. Ominously Donoghue was the first to flourish his whip, though that was seen to be no sign of despair as Brown Jack fought on to secure an advantage of a length over Jugo at the finish.

Brown Jack went close to giving an encore in 1931, being beaten by only a neck by Salmon Leap, with Trimdon four lengths away third. Classic form proved too good for him in the Goodwood Cup of 1932 and he was beaten by four lengths by Brulette, winner of the Oaks the previous year, ridden by Gordon Richards for Fred Darling's Beckhampton Stable. Contesting the Goodwood Cup for a fifth time as a nine-year-old in 1933 Brown Jack was beaten by four lengths by the six years younger Sans Peine, to whom he was giving two stone.

One of the dourest stayers of the mid-twentieth century won the Goodwood Cup in 1938. That was Epigram, ridden by the veteran Australian 'Brownie' Carslake to beat Senor by half a length. Another of the sons of Son-In-Law, Epigram carried the colours of J.V. Rank, whose wealth came from the milling of flour in Hull, and was trained by Noel Cannon at Druid's Lodge, the owner's private stable on Salisbury Plain. Epigram

***Above:** Double Bore (Tommy Gosling) gives his owner Jeremy Tree his first big success as a trainer by beating hot favourite Elpenor (Manny Mercer) in the Goodwood Cup of 1955. Tree had inherited the winner's dam on the death of his uncle Peter Beatty, owner of the 1938 Derby winner Bois Roussel.*

had also won the Goodwood Stakes in 1937. The threat of war with Germany, duly declared less than six weeks later, was again cast over Europe when racing was staged at Goodwood in 1939, and Colonel J.P. Hornung's Dubonnet, ridden by Tommy Lowrey for Basil Jarvis's Newmarket stable, beat Senor by a length in the Goodwood Cup.

Although the Second World War ended on 8th May 1945, racing at Goodwood did not resume until 1946, when there were two meetings. As well as the traditional four days from Tuesday 30th July until Friday 2nd August, there was racing on the last two days of August. At the longer fixture the Goodwood Cup became one of the first of many valuable long-distance races in post-war England to be won by French horses when M. Marcel Boussac's Marsyas II, trained by Charles Semblat and ridden by Charlie Elliott, justified favouritism by beating the King's Kingstone.

Another French horse landed the Goodwood Cup in 1947, when Monsieur l'Amiral, ridden by Charlie Smirke for E. Charlier's stable, readily justified his hot favouritism in a field of four. Further evidence of the Goodwood Cup having regained its international importance was forthcoming in 1948, when Tenerani carried the colours of that great Italian breeder Federico Tesio to win by a length and a half from the French-trained Arbar, who had won the Gold Cup in a canter on his previous appearance, but pulled up lame at Goodwood.

The season of 1949 was in no small part notable for the four-year-old Alycidon proving that England could still produce stayers of the very highest calibre. A chestnut colt by Donatello II out of the Hyperion mare Aurora, Alycidon was owned by the 18th Earl of Derby, great-great-grandson of the 14th Earl, who had won the Goodwood Cup with Canezou in 1849 and 1850.

Alycidon had given a broad hint of the heights to which he might aspire given an exacting test of stamina by finishing second to Black Tarquin in the previous season's St Leger. Over the extra six furlongs of the Gold Cup of 1949 he had taken his revenge by beating Black Tarquin by a convincing five lengths. On that Ascot form Alycidon seemed certain to win the Goodwood Cup. Backers who so readily laid the odds of 100-30 on being asked by the bookmakers at Goodwood, though, took no account of Alycidon being totally unsuited to the hard going or that he had already jarred his shoulders in a gallop on ground that he detested. In the circumstances, Doug Smith, Lord Derby's retained jockey, was far from confident even though Alycidon had both Benny Lynch and Stockbridge to make the pace for him as they had done at Ascot, while Black Tarquin did not take the field again.

Stockbridge jumped off in front and made strong running until Benny Lynch took over at the halfway stage. Alycidon was never striding out freely, so that, as Doug Smith recalled in his memoirs, he was "merely hobbling at the top of the hill, six furlongs from home". Benny Lynch was hating the ground just as much. In consequence Doug Smith had to go to the front earlier than he wanted to do and Alycidon, rallying with the utmost courage under the whip, went away to beat Riding Mill by two lengths.

"I have never been more relieved to reach the winning post in my life," Doug Smith was to recall. On his only subsequent appearance Alycidon completed the stayers' Triple Crown in the Doncaster Cup.

The Goodwood Cup was among the first important races won by Vincent O'Brien when he was engaged in the arduous process of proving that he could do as much

Left: *Using the word 'never' is invariably a risky business, but is it wrong to say that no one will ever emulate the training feats of Vincent O'Brien? He won just about every top-level race on the flat and in jumping - classics, Grand Nationals, and Gold Cups at Cheltenham and Ascot all fell to horses from his yard in Co. Tipperary.*

Above: *"Hats off for The Queen", as Her Majesty's Gaulois (Ron Hutchinson) wins the 1966 Goodwood Cup from Vivat Rex (Bill Williamson).*

justice to good-class horses on the flat as he could to the steeplechasers, with whom he had won three Grand Nationals and four Cheltenham Gold Cups. That was in 1958, when Lester Piggott had the mount on Gladness at Goodwood, and she made nearly all the running to beat the French horse Ranchiquito by a length and a half. On her previous appearance Gladness (owned by the American builder John McShain, whose firm undertook the construction of The Pentagon in Washington) had won the Gold Cup at Ascot, and next time out she defied top weight in the Ebor Handicap at York.

During that era no stayer had a more loyal following at Goodwood than Predominate, a rangy chestnut gelding with large generous ears, owned by Jim Joel, who had interests in diamond mines and other investments in South Africa. Joel, a lavish supporter of racing under both rules, had bought Predominate for hurdling, but as the gelding showed a lack of enthusiasm for hurdling, Mr Joel sent him to his private trainer Ted Leader, who was established in the Sefton Lodge Stable at Newmarket.

On coming under the care of Leader as a six-year-old in 1958, Predominate revealed appreciable improvement on the flat, and that year he beat The Tuscar by an easy six lengths at the end of the two miles and three furlongs of the Goodwood Stakes. Twelve months later Predominate was again the comfortable winner of the Goodwood Stakes, although he beat All Serene (owned by The Queen's late aunt the Princess Royal) by only a length. To complete the hat-trick in the Goodwood Stakes in

1960, Predominate took the lead approaching the final furlong, and went away to beat Freelight by four lengths without being extended.

Wilful crime deprived the Goodwood meeting of a high class runner in 1961. Pandofell, from Freddie Maxwell's Lambourn stable, had won the Gold Cup at Ascot unchallenged. On the morning that he was to have returned to Ascot for the Sunninghill Park Stakes, he was found to have been nobbled with a large dose of phenobarbitone. As a result Pandofell had to miss the Ascot race and the Goodwood Cup as well. With the withdrawal of Pandofell, the Goodwood Cup was left wide open, and it was decided that Predominate would bid for the £3,222 first prize that it carried rather than bid for a fourth success in the Goodwood Stakes, which was worth £1,620 that year.

That Goodwood Cup of 1961 proved to be a severe test of the courage of Predominate, as well as calling for the stamina that had already won him three races on the course. Throughout the final furlong Predominate was engaged in a hard fought duel with Shatter, and almost on the post got up to beat Shatter by a short head, with The Queen's Agreement, twice winner of the Doncaster Cup, three lengths away third. At nine years of age, Predominate was the oldest horse ever to have won the Goodwood Cup.

In each of those four races that he won at Goodwood, Predominate was ridden by Jim Joel's retained jockey Eph Smith, elder brother of Doug. Today Predominate is commemorated by the Derby Trial - the Predominate Stakes, first run in 1970. It was won in 1979 by Troy, who went on to triumph in the Derby. In 1988 the distance of the Predominate Stakes was reduced from its original mile and a half to a mile and a quarter. Today the race is run over one mile and three furlongs.

In 1965 The Queen won the Goodwood Cup with Apprentice, who was ridden by Stan Clayton to beat Soderini in impressive fashion by two and a half lengths. The following season The Queen won the race again, as Gaulois ran on resolutely in the hands of the Australian Ron Hutchinson to come home three lengths clear of Vivat

Left: *Another Goodwood Cup for Jeremy Tree. This time, 30 years after his win with Double Bore, it is Valuable Witness (Pat Eddery), with a resounding success over Kublai (Taffy Thomas) in 1985.*

Overleaf: *Le Moss (left in picture) was one of the outstanding long-distance horses of the second half of the twentieth century when he became the only horse to win the stayers' Triple Crown - the Gold Cup at Ascot and the Goodwood and Doncaster Cups - on two occasions, as he did in 1979 and 1980.*

Rex. Both Apprentice and Gaulois were homebred at Sandringham, and trained by Captain Cecil Boyd-Rochfort, who was to receive a knighthood in the New Year's Honours List of 1968.

When starting stalls came into almost universal use for races run under Jockey Club Rules in 1967, an exception was made for the Goodwood Cup, as it was thought inadvisable to prejudice the condition of the ground in the straight by having the mechanism hauled up it for a long-distance race for which the manner of the start was of little consequence. The winner that year was Wrekin Rambler, the best stayer trained by Sir Gordon Richards.

In 1971 the Pattern was introduced to identify the most prestigious races, divided into three Groups or categories. Group 1 events were of international championship status, Group 2 races of slightly lower calibre though still of international importance, and Group 3 races of domestic, rather than international, significance. The Goodwood Cup was originally in Group 3 but was raised to Group 2 when Le Moss, ridden by Joe Mercer, made all the running to win by an easy seven lengths in 1979, before making forcing tactics pay off again the following season.

In 1986 the Goodwood Cup reverted to Group 3, though the outcome suggested it was still regarded as highly as before, as the winner was Mr Dick Hollingsworth's Longboat, bred by his owner at the Arches Hall Stud in Hertfordshire. On his previous appearance Longboat had shown that he was a stayer of the highest class by the readiness with which he had justified favouritism in the Gold Cup at Ascot.

Below: *Lucky Moon began his three-year-old season by finishing sixth in a run-of-the-mill maiden race at Salisbury. Yet such was his progress that only three months later he romped home in the Goodwood Cup.*

The distance of the Goodwood Cup, as well as its status, was subject to change during the last two decades of the twentieth century. The race was run over two miles and five furlongs for the last time when Mr A.P. Ward's Mazzacano, trained locally to the course by Guy Harwood at Pulborough, beat his far better backed stable companion Sadeem by a neck in 1989; Sadeem, owned by Sheikh Mohammed, had been trying to win the race for the second year in succession.

Above: Only two three-year-olds have won the Goodwood Cup since the mid-1970s, and both of them, Lucky Moon and Sergeyevich, were trained by John Dunlop. Based only a short distance from Goodwood at Arundel, and a director of the Racecourse, he has trained more than 150 Goodwood winners.

There was a still more popular local success in the Goodwood Cup when the trip was reduced to two and a half miles in 1990, as the winner was Lucky Moon, owned by Lavinia, Duchess of Norfolk, and trained by John Dunlop in the Castle Stables at Arundel. At the time that Dunlop took charge of that establishment in 1966, it was still the private stable of the Duchess and her husband. For many years the Duke and Duchess of Norfolk were strong supporters of Goodwood, where their runners commanded a big public following. The great achievement of John Dunlop, who is a Director of Goodwood Racecourse, has been to transform the small private stable, in which he began his career, into one of the largest and most successful in the country, to such effect that he was leading trainer in 1995. Despite the heavy calls that a long string of horses make upon him, John Dunlop still finds time to do a great deal for the Stable Lads Welfare Trust and other voluntary organisations - charity work that was recognised when he was awarded the O.B.E. in The Queen's Birthday Honours List of 1996.

When the Goodwood Cup was run over two miles for the first time in 1991, the winner was Further Flight, trained by Barry Hills at Lambourn, and ridden by his son Michael, for Mr Simon Wingfield Digby, the Dorset landowner and Civil Lord of the Admiralty from 1951 to 1957 in the Conservative Government. Further Flight, who won the Goodwood Cup again in 1992, was another of those stayers in the mould of Predominate, who earn popularity amongst racegoers by their consistency throughout long careers: the most remarkable achievement of Further Flight was to win the Jockey Club Cup at Newmarket in five consecutive seasons.

The Goodwood Cup was reinstated in Group 2 in 1995 when the race became a family affair, with Double Trigger, a chestnut horse with a big white blaze, trained by Mark Johnston, beating his full brother, and stablemate, Double Eclipse. Johnston, a qualified veterinary surgeon who has the Kingsley House stable at Middleham, Yorkshire, had no runner in the Goodwood Cup in 1996, but in 1997 he saddled both Double Trigger and Double Eclipse again. As Double Trigger had disappointed by finishing last of eight in Ascot's Sagaro Stakes and last again in the Gold Cup on his only two previous races of the season, and also performed poorly in the Prix du Cadran at the back end of 1996, he was deserted by the stable jockey Jason Weaver, who rode Double Eclipse.

More or less neglected in the market at 16-1, Double Trigger was ridden by the South African jockey Michael Roberts, and made all the running to beat Classic Cliche by a length and a half, with Double Eclipse half a length away third. Mark Johnston

"Two of Double Trigger's Goodwood Cups stand out for different reasons. The first time, when he beat his full brother Double Eclipse, was very, very special. It was a wonderful race, one of the best I have ever been associated with, and I think it may have been the only time that two brothers were first and second in a Group 1 race. That unique third win was equally memorable. I have listened to the commentary of the race many times, and the commentator is saying, 'Double Trigger is fading out of it' about three furlongs from home, but then he rallied and went on to win. I have never seen a crowd reacting like they did that day - they were running from the stands to get round the winner's enclosure. It was very, very emotional. Goodwood and Royal Ascot are the two festival meetings I plan for months in advance. Obviously Trigger has played his part in making it like that; the Goodwood Cup is a bit special."

MARK JOHNSTON,
TRAINER, DOUBLE TRIGGER

"This was only the second time I had ever ridden Double Trigger. The first was in the Gold Cup at Ascot. After he had run so well there, we knew we were going to Goodwood with a big chance. We had decided at Ascot that we would not try to make all the running as had been the normal thing to do with him, but just to let him go out and enjoy himself."

DARRYLL HOLLAND,
JOCKEY, DOUBLE TRIGGER

Above: *Even the most ardent of his admirers would have to admit that Royal Rebel has his good days and his bad ones. Here, in the Goodwood Cup of 2000, he was very much on song as Mick Kinane rode him to get the better of a sustained battle with Far Cry.*

was not surprised. "I have maintained that Double Trigger always had too much class to be written off because of three bad runs," he said, going on to explain that the horse been beset by a series of minor problems like pus in his foot. Of the other brother, the trainer said "I feel sorry for Double Eclipse. What a superstar he might have been if he had four good legs. He has had only one proper gallop in the last 14 months."

Double Trigger took the field for the Goodwood Cup again in 1998, and made history by becoming the first horse to win the race three times. Rather surprisingly he was not prominent from the start, and actually seemed to come under pressure five furlongs from home, only to rally absolutely splendidly rather more than a furlong from home, and getting up inside the distance he beat Canon Can by three parts of a length. Two years later Mark Johnston won the Goodwood Cup for the fourth time in six years when Mick Kinane drove Royal Rebel (owned by Peter Savill, Chairman of the British Horseracing Board) past the post half a length ahead of Far Cry.

Like so many other features of the racing on the course, the Goodwood Cup maintains a long and unbroken tradition. Yet Goodwood has always been ready to move with the times to ensure that its institutions are never in danger of becoming moribund. Hence the reduction of the distance of the Cup to two miles to ensure that Goodwood's richest prize for stayers attracts a strongly competitive field in these days when the international bloodstock industry puts less emphasis on extreme stamina than it did 70 years ago.

Whereas the Gold Cup is over Ascot's right hand course, and the Doncaster Cup is run on a left-handed circuit, the runners for the Goodwood Cup have to turn both left and right, thus bringing an element of variation into one of the season's greatest tests of the best of the long distance horses.

SUMMER AT GOODWOOD

When the Sussex Militia, no longer allowed to hold their annual sporting day in the grounds of Petworth Park, received permission from their Colonel-in-Chief, the 3rd Duke of Richmond, to race on top of the Downs above Goodwood House, they decided to make something more of it than just racing. So they put up some tents, where "collations, consisting of every dainty in season, were profusely served up". Racing at Goodwood started as it meant to go on.

Although the Duke had initially seen that meeting for the Sussex Militia as a one-off event, they proved so popular with his family and local landowning friends that it was decided to continue and develop the meeting. Its popularity was not, however, confined to that small corner of Sussex. In *The Times* of 8th May 1801, the newspaper reported that "the races set on foot this year by the Duke of Richmond at Goodwood have been very well attended and afforded good sport. Next year they are to last three days."

The following year a makeshift stand was erected, The Duke put an announcement in *The Times* heralding the date (in a canny piece of PR he also added that the Prince of Wales had "signified his intention of honouring the meeting"), and the promised three-day meeting was held.

During the early years of the meeting, there were fluctuations in both its duration and the time of year that it was held. In 1805 it moved to early May and five years later to late May. Finally, in 1814, the (then two-day) meeting was moved to the last week of July, the week that is now simply known as 'Goodwood week'. In 1825 the racing was extended back to three days, in 1835 to four days and in 1970 further lengthened to five days of racing, to include the Saturday.

Although it was the 3rd Duke who had built the racecourse, it was his great-nephew, the 5th Duke, who turned Goodwood into the racecourse and the social event, that it is today. Through a combination of enthusiastic house-building, the 3rd Duke had managed to go through the Richmond fortune, and it was largely for this reason that his nephew, the 4th Duke, did not live at Goodwood.

However, it was eventually possible for the 4th Duke's son to indulge his passion for horses and racing, thanks to the entirely unexpected inheritance of Charlotte, the 4th Duke's wife and the 5th Duke's mother. Charlotte was the daughter of the 4th Duke of Gordon; on the his death in 1836 the huge Gordon wealth passed to his daughter and the Richmond fortunes were restored and the ducal name extended.

Since 1814 the last week of July has been raceweek at Goodwood, the event that has come to mark the end of the social season.

***Above:** A holiday atmosphere is always present on the course. Between races the crowds can wander around in the summer Sussex sun being serenaded by one of the many bands imported for the week, while feasting on strawberries and Pimms.*

The 5th Duke formed a racing partnership with Lord George Bentinck, the second son of the Duke of Portland. Lord George was passionate about racing and a vastly influential figure in the racing world (see the chapter on *Characters Of The Course*) As a duo they proved a formidable force and Goodwood racecourse became the epitome of the cutting edge of racing, a position that it has been able to maintain through the centuries. By 1830 the *Sporting Magazine* was reporting that "the Duke seems determined to leave no stone unturned to make this eventually the very 1st meeting in the kingdom."

As the 1830s progressed, so Goodwood flourished: the meeting grew in both size and prestige. One of the major problems for racegoers was getting to this hitherto fairly unreachable corner of the country. It could easily involve a day's travelling, which proved acceptable only to either the very local, or very hardened, racegoer. In the 1840s these logistical difficulties were vastly reduced when, probably through what is now known as lobbying, the owners of the South Great Western Railway were 'persuaded' to ferry people from the capital, via a combination of steam and wheels, to Goodwood - London to Fareham by train, and Fareham to Goodwood by coach and horses. This meant that going to the races at Goodwood could be a day trip from London (albeit a long one), and so Londoners flooded to West Sussex.

Long before its sustained royal patronage Goodwood had become an absolute must in the social calendar. When, in 1814, the week was moved to the last week of July, it formed a natural end to 'The Season' - the social season for the aristocracy that started with the debutantes' presentation at court in March. Goodwood was the final date in the diary before 'society' upped sticks and headed north for the Scottish balls, fishing, and the grouse season.

By the 1830s, every day during festival week *The Times* would publish a number of names of the 'great and the good' who had been spotted in the stand at Goodwood, a convention that, surprisingly, has not entirely died out nearly two centuries later. Being printed in this list obviously carried a certain amount of social kudos, the obverse of which is that it caused indignation to those who were not mentioned, but sincerely felt that they should have been. Certain people must have kicked up a right aristocratic fuss as there was often a subsequent list of names along the lines of "Among those mentioned in our report on Thursday as having been present in the Grand Stand on Wednesday, there should have been included..."

Goodwood has always attracted the social commentators. The editor of *Pathé News* annually requested permission to shoot cine film that could be shown in 400 cinemas around the country. She was, annually, politely refused. This might have been because the social editors could be somewhat more blunt than their modern counterparts. In one gossip column in 1886 there was a report on the presence of "the Marquis (sic) and Marchioness of Londonderry, Lady Ormonde and Caroline, Duchess of Montrose, who was, to use a modern vulgarism, 'going strong' and wearing one day sky-blue satin and the next scarlet poplin."

On another occasion, in 1883, the *West Sussex Gazette* commented that "The Princess of Wales... engaged for the greater part of the time in conversation with the fair young Princess of Saxe-Meiningen, and the Princess Helena, whose matronly figure is not often seen at Goodwood."

The 7th Duke adored racing and entertaining, and it was this combination that put Goodwood firmly at the top of the social calendar. He always entertained lavishly

Below: *Stage coaches gather at the cross in Chichester in the early 1900s, ready to take punters to the racecourse.*

Overleaf: *Picnicking in the late 1920s.* The Sporting Life *wrote of Goodwood, "Here at the meeting is the microcosm of English sporting people. Thousands of holiday makers take advantage of its spacious stands and picnicking. As likely as not they will have caught a glimpse of the King or his family, who, like the rest of the visitors, discard all formality, and enjoy themselves in the same happy way as the humblest of their subjects."*

GU 2527

"As I drive in, I often see the same people in the same place having the same picnic, day after day, year after year. Some people take a picnic and never go inside the course. They just spend the day eating and drinking. There really is no accounting for taste."

Peter Willett

during the week, and was a great friend of both Edward VII and his son, George V who, as a result, both stayed at Goodwood every year for the racing. It was during this time that the new stand was built and the very fact that a large part of this new stand was The Royal Pavilion spoke loudly about Goodwood's popularity and status.

This social interest gave rise in some instances to a certain amount of snobbery and the same local newspaper was to report that "The Lawn on a fine day is certainly one of the prettiest sights that can be seen, but of late years the company frequenting it has become sadly promiscuous; and last year especially the complaint among the ladies was very general of being in such close quarters with those who, by their glaring display of jewellery, left no doubt to which world they belonged." However, Goodwood has always been much more than just the aristocrat's racecourse.

With the advent of the motor car, access to Goodwood became even easier, and the crowds grew and grew. By the 1950s there were up to 50,000 racecard-clutching punters attending the course every day during festival week, so it is therefore unsurprising that Goodwood races made such an impact on the locality. The social influence of Goodwood went far beyond the privileged few who were invited to be part of the party in the main house.

Above: *As cars became more prevalent, Goodwood became increasingly accessible, and by 1925 the sight of the local roads flooded with motoring racegoers became a normal one. Cars are now as much a part of the special character of Goodwood as horses, with the revival of the Motor Circuit and the huge success of the Festival of Speed.*

The financial importance of the festival week on the area around Goodwood was significant. From the very earliest days that horses raced at the course, the innkeepers of Chichester - who at the time were known as the 'Shylocks of Chichester' - recognised the commercial opportunities of having such a racecourse on their doorstep. As early as 1802 one indignant reporter on the *Sussex Chronicle* bemoaned the fact that "All lodgings and beds are in a state of close siege and provisions have very handsomely risen in price, as duty bounds."

The Swan, the biggest inn in Chichester, was re-named 'The Shark' (not entirely affectionately). For one week, the town was an entirely different place. All manner of folk descended on West Sussex: "ostlers, stable-helps, race-card men, queer hangers-on of the race meeting, all of them, with wonderful clothes, and still more wonderful swagger", wrote J. Low Warren in *Chichester Past & Present*. For the people in the town and the surrounding villages the racing was a major income-provider. Shops, pubs and hotels all relied heavily on the four days of the meeting. The revenues that they generated during that one week of the year could sustain their businesses for the other 51 weeks of the year.

It was not only the commercial enterprises that profited. The financial difference that it could make to individuals and families was such that the sawmill at Charlton (a significant local employer) closed for the week, so that the mill's employees could earn the much-needed supplement to their income. This tradition continued well into the twentieth century. When Archie Long was put on the gate of the racecourse to collect the ticket money, he was paid five shillings for the week, which in turn paid his annual rent.

"In my book *The Racing Tribe*, I divided racegoers into two broad categories: Enthusiasts and Socials. Socials are primarily concerned with the establishment and maintenance of relationships and the social micro-climate of the racecourse - characterised by a highly unusual combination of relaxed inhibitions and exceptionally good manners - provides ideal conditions for social bonding. Goodwood, despite the high quality of the racing, is the natural habitat of the Social racegoer. The 'Glorious Goodwood' meeting has a particular appeal for a sub-species of Social that I call the Be-seens. To 'see and be seen' is one of the many social motives for racegoing. I found that almost all Socials - and a significant proportion of Enthusiasts - showed a keen interest in the dress and appearance of other racegoers and in their own self-preservation. Even those who professed indifference to such frivolities had no difficulty, when questioned, in parsing the sartorial statements of their fellow racegoers. For the Be-seens - who, incidentally, come from all types of social background and are to be found in all three enclosures at the racecourse - this form of non-verbal communication is a prime source of entertainment and gratification. And Goodwood provides the perfect setting for their displays."

KATE FOX, SOCIAL ANTHROPOLOGIST

In the 1800s and into the 1900s local residents would give up their cottages and go to stay with relatives so they could collect a rent from 'the Gentlemen' who needed housing for the week. 'The Gentlemen' were essentially the workers for the week: the bookmakers, the number board men, the fruit stall owners, the farriers and many others. Normally it was not the whole household who moved out (the cost of moving would have dented the rental income), but simply the children. They were sometimes farmed out and sent away, but often they were not dispatched very far at all: they would sleep in the woodshed. There is even one account in the parish magazine of children sleeping in the little cottage pigsties so that their bed could be filled by a bookie or a trainer. Goodwood was good business. However there was no implication that the 'woodshed' children felt that they had been hard done by.

After the train line had been extended, the majority of racegoers arrived at Singleton station, from where they would walk up Town Lane to the top of Trundle Hill. Alternatively they could take a carriage, for which they would be charged 'arf a dollar', although certain parts of the journey were so steep that they had to walk at least part of the way. Children would station themselves at various points along the route and skip around the walkers chanting a ditty in the hope that they could relieve the racegoers of their ha'pennies: "Goodwood races just begun, You've got money, we got none. Now's the time to have some fun, Up goes the donkey, down goes his tail!" The other lucrative hunting ground was beside the church. If anyone had decided to have a sharpener to ease the walk, they then had to pass the church after they had left the pub. Before beginning the march up Lamb Down they had to run the gauntlet of the local boys and girls with a hand out and an eye on the main chance.

***Below:** Thankfully rain is not a huge problem on the racecourse, although when it does rain, it comes down in spades and tends to be of the horizontal variety. If the weather looks stormy, it is always worth coming prepared, advice that The Queen took to heart. If the skies were grey, she would be discreetly followed at all times by an attendant carrying a raincoat and a more practical pair of all-weather shoes.*

The week also attracted large numbers of gypsies, for whom the week became as important a part of their calendar as that of anyone else. Their brightly painted vans camped at Cadger's Corner were an expected part of raceweek, but were not popular in all quarters. The local gamekeepers and foresters would despair as suddenly, in the space of five days, the hazel would all be cut (to make clothes-pegs) and poaching hit new heights. Rabbits were the favourite quarry, with the meat providing dinner and the skins making their way to the fur trade in Russia.

The Goodwood meeting turned into such a popular reunion week for the gypsies that their presence eventually became a problem - and in the 1920s a ban was effected. Although this was not officially directed at the travellers, the official line was that there were to be no 'sleeping caravans' within two miles of the course and no dogs within one mile. History does not relate if this proved effective...

Most of the people walking up Town Lane were heading for what is sometimes referred to as the social, if not geographical centre of West Sussex. Trundle Hill (or the Trundle, as it is also known) is without doubt the most beautiful natural grandstand on any racecourse, anywhere in the world. When Lord George Bentinck re-laid parts of the course, he added an extra 400 yards to the finishing straight. Previously, being on Trundle Hill meant that you were well away from the action, but those additional yards meant that the Trundle became the ideal vantage point. From the top of this remarkably symmetrical hill there was a clear view of the paddock and the finishing line. And it was here that the picnicking racers flocked. In 1953, there was a record crowd of 55,000 people in one day. Of those, 21,000 were on Trundle Hill: it was said to resemble a human ant hill.

It was a very different world to the sedate life on the Lawn or in the Grand Stand. This was not a scene of bustles and parasols, but of shirt-sleeves, flat caps, and braces, and it was the day out of the year. The racing added an extra dimension to the day, but for many was not the primary motivation for going. Whether they saw a horse or not, it was still 'Glorious Goodwood'. In the 1850s a racegoer was overheard justifying his merriment - "Let us be jolly. I don't suppose if we deny ourselves the vulgar pleasures of the day we shall be invited to Goodwood House."

People would arrive in coaches with picnics precariously balanced on the roof or carrying their hampers, but a particular favourite was to cram all the food, bottles and all into an old pram and push it up the chalky lane. The picnics would consist of glasses of 'homemade', of the non-alcoholic variety, and 'home-brewed', of the rocket-fuel variety, along with whole hams and plum cake wrapped in newspaper. If you did not wish to bring your own, there were always travelling vendors and hawkers ready to slake your thirst or hunger. You could breakfast on cockles, mussels and jellied eels, and wash it down with a cup of tea from the nearest knapsack tea-vendor. Or you could go to the men who sold pickled salmon and oysters, the ones who offered nuts, crabs and pickled whelks, or the hawker who always conducted a cracking trade offering three large oysters for a penny - a bargain considering that your penny included vinegar and pepper! Local merchants also set up temporary shops (known as food booths) at the foot of the hill; course favourites included Payne's from Midhurst, Goatches from Petworth and Trim from Arundel.

"I shall never forget seeing, on a ghastly water-logged day, an elderly Countess sitting on a shooting stick at the bottom of the slope watching the start with her glasses glued to her face. On the slope behind her an obese Duchess started to slip. She charged down on the unsuspecting Countess, seized her round the waist and adroitly saved herself getting muddy by throwing the Countess to the ground and kneeling on her. The Countess was taken to the ladies cloakroom and careened with a bread knife."

Major Geoffrey Harbord in the Sunday Express, *July 1949*

10

Above: *A practical alternative to the hats in the main enclosures. Although Goodwood has the informality of the panama hat and the linen suit, the ladies always dress up and don hats for the meeting.*

By the end of the nineteenth century, the competition for booth space was fierce, and was orchestrated in a sergeant-major fashion by the then clerk of the course, Mr W. F. Forbes. In response to a Miss R. Russell he wrote, "Madam. You can have number 2 toy stall: ground, 20 feet for £1. You will come next to Lieutenant Carter. David Lee used to take 44 feet of ground and pay £2, which included his living van. But I cannot include your living van, for 20 feet you must pay the men in charge of the ground for it."

The most popular booth, certainly the most frequented, was owned by a character called Mant. So loved and revered was this booth that it became known as 'Mant's Temple'. This shrine at which the racegoers worshipped was in effect a mobile pub, where Mant sold gin and water from primitive tea pots with their lids tied onto the handles. He was nicknamed the 'Friar Tuck' of Goodwood and his booth was always filled with course entertainers: it was the centre for music and dancing, tumbling and drinking.

The entertainment at Goodwood was not only in equine form. All around the racecourse strolled players who would entertain the punters between races in an attempt to ease their winnings from them. Every year the same faces would be seen. A typical cross-section of these performers in the 1850s was described by the *West Sussex Gazette*, including the "elegantly dressed lady with the harp accompaniment, warbling sweetly to the delicious disgust of all married females, who entertain very prejudiced estimates of her charms", the "dark" banjo player and the "rough-headed" character who imitated the bray of a donkey. There were strolling musicians, normally ladies with mouth organs and tambourines, and not forgetting the Highland piper. There was a handicapped man whose trick was to write names (his handicap being that he did not have any limbs) and an elderly acrobat who "performed wonders on a slack rope" while wearing wellies. The acrobat's closest competition was from the "greasy tumbler", or the fiddle-playing monkey whose most frequently performed trick was to sweep coins from the outstretched hands of his audience.

"Milliners agree that an Ascot hat will just not do for Goodwood. I feel hats worn at Goodwood should have a classical line, ideally tailored and close-fitting."

Country Life, *July 1961*

Not surprisingly the course had a holiday feel (in fact, Cup Day *was* a holiday for many, as the majority of local employers gave everyone a half-day off). Of course it was a racecourse, but parts were also a fairground, with shooting galleries where one could try and win nuts, Punch and Judy shows, and skittle alleys, which were also known as 'knock-em-downs'.

Mant's Booth was not the only famed partying spot. Some people preferred the 'van parties'. Just as today, when you know where the best parties are to be found in the car park, so racegoers knew where the best van parties were to be found. There was one in particular that even made it into the national press and was a Goodwood institution for many years. The van itself was a horse-drawn, round-bender Sussex van, and was known for the most raucous on-course parties. As the *West Sussex Gazette* reporter found, "it contains one of the nicest, free and easy parties there is to be seen".

With all of this free and easy partying there needed to be an element of restraint on the course. This came in the form of the police, although certain wrongdoers were subjected to the crowd's own brand of justice. For example, if a bookie could not pay his losses (winnings to the successful punters) he was "shorn of coat and garments". This was a polite way of saying that he was stripped stark naked and thrown over the railings to make his own, lonely, and probably chilly way off the course.

The course was policed by the Metropolitan force, who were ably assisted by a band of huntsmen and whips. To mete out justice a special police station and court was constructed, hidden away under the beech trees. Both these facilities were used to deal with opportunistic pickpockets, for whom Goodwood was a lucrative annual outing. The police would catch the light-fingered punter and steer him to the 'station'. This would normally be accompanied by numerous protestations of innocence, peppered with a lot of "Gawd forgive you, Guv'nor". This was not deemed to be an effective defence and a magistrate would be found on the course and sentence passed. The pickpocket's gamble had not paid off.

The Goodwood festival of racing has always been about more than just racing. It is, and has always been, an integral and pivotal part of life in West Sussex, but its place in

"Since the barbarous practice of wearing crushed birds disappeared, nothing so ridiculous in the way of millinery has been imagined."
West Sussex Gazette, *July 1880*

history will show that its influence spread far outside the county. Racing at Goodwood has maintained a prominent and unchanging place in British social history.

In the days when society was governed by an extremely rigid set of rules, these included where one went, with whom, and when. By 1814 the annual week for the Goodwood festival had been established; its place in the year is unchanged to this day. The last week of July proved to be the ideal end of 'the Season' and remained so throughout the twentieth century.

Because of the relaxed holiday atmosphere on the course, Goodwood raceweek was the perfect antidote to the rigours of a season of socialising; it also signalled the start of the holidays - which lasted all through August and September when one's season was officially over. The whole of London society would arrive for the races and then decamp to Scotland - maybe via Cowes - for two months of shooting and fishing and the Perth and Skye balls. Being seen in London after Goodwood was certain social death. It meant that one did not know 'the right people' to be asked to a house party for Goodwood, and had no one to stay with in Scotland.

At the racecourse, not everyone could simply turn up; who was allowed into certain parts of the course was closely monitored. To watch the racing in what was then called His Grace's Private Stand, one had to apply to be a member and complete an application form.

The present Duke, remembers, "Once I went with my father to Weatherby's to watch him go through this vetting process. You didn't have to say much about yourself on this form, but at the bottom it said, 'Clubs'. It was there that you had to write down what clubs you were a member of, and there was evidently at that time a rather disreputable club called The Albany Club. Every now and again the clerk would say, "I would like to draw Your Grace's attention to the fact that this gentleman is a member of The Albany Club", at which point the application would be turned down; it was definitely not on."

No private dances were held after Goodwood, so any of the local hostesses who wanted to organise a dance or cocktail party and did not want to do so in London, had to hold it during Goodwood week. In addition, there was frequently a ball at Goodwood itself, and every alternate year the Duchess of Norfolk would host a ball at Arundel in aid of one of her charities.

Each night there would be at least two cocktail parties to go to, a dinner before a dance, and then one, or sometimes two, dances to attend; Sussex was heaving with dancing debutantes. This was the week that kept the ubiquitous Jennifer of *Jennifer's Diary* (the late Mrs Kenward) as busy as she was throughout the whole year - and that is really saying something for a woman who once flew to South America simply to attend a dinner party.

By the 1960s the press was beginning to lament the dearth of debutantes at the racecourse. Indeed, it was the start of the demise of the debutante and 'the Season'. There was no longer such an inflexible social calendar for the year, but this did not stop anyone racing at Goodwood. Whether it is because of its long history or simply because of the time of year, Goodwood continues to mean a great day out and still seems to mark the start of the holidays.

GOODWOOD

THE STEWARDS' CUP

For reasons clear to anyone watching, the race for the Stewards' Cup has been dubbed 'The Finest Cavalry Charge'. As the field of some 30 runners sweeps along Goodwood's straight six-furlong course, the jockeys seem determined to maintain line abreast as if under strict orders. Yet it is not in obedience to some latter-day Earl of Cardigan - the military martinet who led the Charge of the Light Brigade in 1854 - that the jockeys have their mounts racing head to head.

The spectacle of this line of horses at full gallop, with the multicoloured silks of their jockeys generally shimmering in the afternoon sun, is due to the skill of the handicapper who has allotted the weights to the horses so as to give each, as near as possible, an equal chance.

Even as the leaders pass the winning post there is, as often as not, almost nothing to choose between them, thus ensuring that the Stewards' Cup is one of the most exciting races of the season.

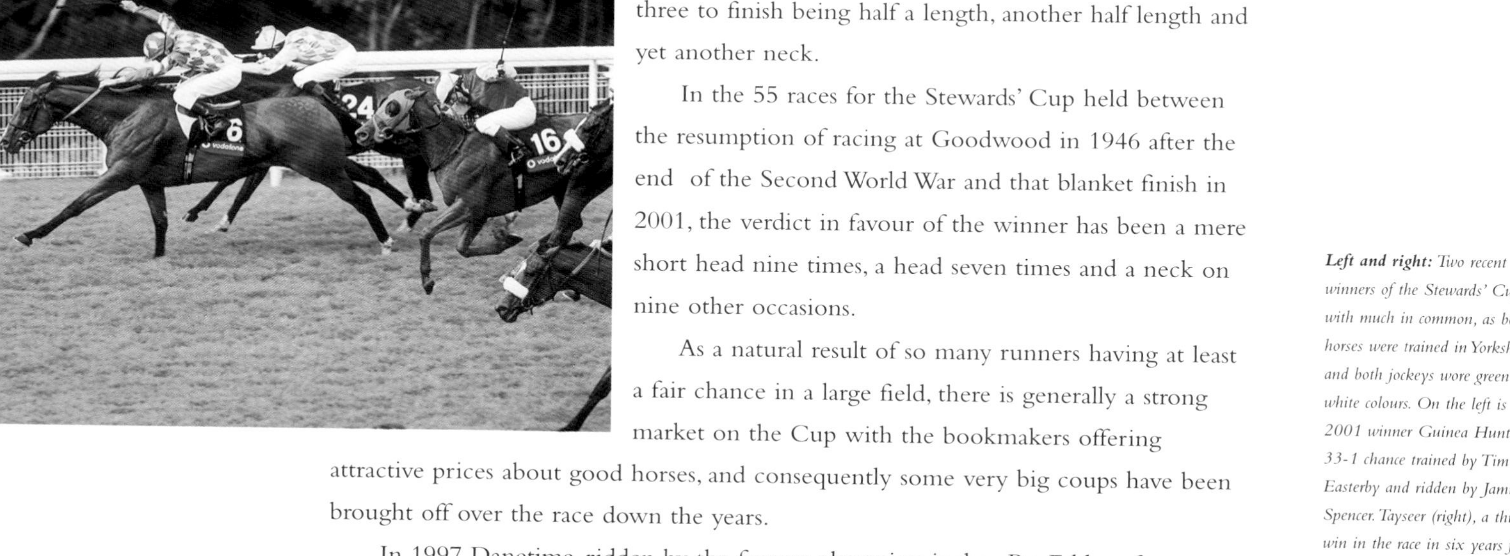

There was a real blanket finish in 2001, when Guinea Hunter won by a neck from Halmahera, with Undeterred another neck away in third, the distances between the next three to finish being half a length, another half length and yet another neck.

In the 55 races for the Stewards' Cup held between the resumption of racing at Goodwood in 1946 after the end of the Second World War and that blanket finish in 2001, the verdict in favour of the winner has been a mere short head nine times, a head seven times and a neck on nine other occasions.

As a natural result of so many runners having at least a fair chance in a large field, there is generally a strong market on the Cup with the bookmakers offering attractive prices about good horses, and consequently some very big coups have been brought off over the race down the years.

In 1997 Danetime, ridden by the former champion jockey Pat Eddery for Neville Callaghan's Newmarket Stable, landed some huge wagers when he justified being backed down to clear favouritism at 5/1. Despite having twisted a shoe during

Left and right: *Two recent winners of the Stewards' Cup with much in common, as both horses were trained in Yorkshire and both jockeys wore green and white colours. On the left is the 2001 winner Guinea Hunter, a 33-1 chance trained by Tim Easterby and ridden by Jamie Spencer. Tayseer (right), a third win in the race in six years for Richard Hughes when he won in 2000, was trained by David ('Dandy') Nicholls, who rode Soba to victory 18 years earlier.*

Above: The prize given to the winning owner after the cavalry charge of the Stewards' Cup, which for many years was held on the first day of the Glorious Goodwood meeting, but which now takes place on the Saturday.

Below: Lord George Bentinck was the dominant figure in British flat racing towards the end of the first half of the nineteenth century. He was determined to rid the sport of its army of villains and was successful to a certain extent, though it would be overstating the case to say that he himself was whiter than white.

running, Danetime held off the late, strong challenge of My Best Valentine by a neck. Among the bets on Danetime had been one of £30,000 to £5,000 each way; winning owner Michael Tabor, a former bookmaker, was reported to have won some £200,000.

The origins of the Stewards' Cup as we know it can be found in a decision made by the 5th Duke of Richmond and Lord George Bentinck to revive a race for which Mr T. P. Cosby, while one of the two Stewards of the Goodwood meeting, had given a cup worth £100 some six years earlier. That race had been run over a mile and a half and won by Baleine, owned by the Goodwood trainer John Kent, from three of the other ten entries to go to the post.

In the hopes of attracting a larger entry, the distance was reduced to six furlongs and the prize money increased to £300. On 31st July 1840 the Duke and Lord George had the satisfaction of seeing 22 runners go to the post for the first running of the new race. The winner was the chestnut six-year-old Epirus, owned by the John Bowes (son of the Earl and Countess of Strathmore), trained by John Scott in the historic Whitewall Stable at Malton in North Yorkshire, and ridden by the trainer's brother Bill. The runner-up was the Duke of Richmond's Mus. Lord March's Guava was left at the post along with the runners of the Duke of Bedford and Lord Exeter - all the same it was declared a good start.

Increasingly heavy drinking obliged Bill Scott to give up riding in 1847. On his deathbed the following year the rider of the first winner of the Stewards' Cup told the clergyman who was attending him, "Three things I can confess to. Since I was 21, I've been drunk almost every night. I never sold a race, which is more than some can say, and I never kissed a lass against her will."

Above: *George Fordham rode the winners of 16 classics during a career which began in 1851 when he was 14 and continued, with one brief and unhappy spell of retirement, until 1883. He rode much shorter than most of his contemporaries and was much less vigorous with his whip.*

"He was 'cluck-clucking' at his mount all the way. I thought I had him beaten two or three times. But with his infernal 'cluck-cluck' he was always coming again. Still 200 yards from home I thought I had him dead settled. I'll 'cluck-cluck' you I thought, but at that moment he swoops, and beats me easily!"

Fred Archer on a clash with George Fordham

For the second time in the first four years of the race's existence, the Duke of Richmond came close to winning the Stewards' Cup in 1843. His filly Balaena was beaten by half a length by Lord George Bentinck's Yorkshire Lady, ridden by the jockey Kitchener, who weighed in at 6st 4lb. In having first claim on Kitchener, a man who was able to ride at a boy's weight, and someone of absolute loyalty, Lord George had an invaluable asset. When this diminutive specimen of humanity was presented to Queen Victoria, the Queen enquired his weight. "Please, Ma'am," Kitchener replied, "my master told me not to tell *anyone* my weight!"

A notable feature of the Goodwood meeting of 1850 was the first success for German-bred horses in England. On the Wednesday of the meeting Count Hahn's Turnus justified 3-1 favouritism in the Stewards' Cup, beating The White Lady by a decisive three lengths, with the Duke of Richmond's four-year-old Ploughboy, ridden by Kitchener, third in a field of 25. Two days later Turnus carried a penalty in the Chesterfield Cup, but still beat the Duke of Richmond's filly Officious by a length. Count Hahn had also won a race on the opening day of the meeting as his five-year-old Meridian beat Vigilant a decisive four lengths in the Innkeepers' Plate.

Turnus and Meridian were successful three years before any French horse won in England, but, as Peter Willett wrote in his book *The Thoroughbred*, German breeders failed to build on those achievements, not least because they insisted that their stallions should have the strength and substance of halfbreds combined with the action of an Arab.

George Fordham, who had become champion jockey in 1855, obtained his first success in the Stewards' Cup on Tournament two years later. Still able to go to the scales at seven stone, Fordham forced Tournament home by a head from Unexpected, with Theodore just a neck away third.

Overleaf: *A Stewards' Cup field makes its way to the stalls at the six furlong marker.*

20
19
18
17
16
13
12
11
30

23
4

***Above:** Fred Archer was the most amazing jockey of his day and would have been exceptional in any era. Despite the fact that he fought a constant battle with his weight, and at various stages lived on some repulsive concoction called 'Archer's Mixture', he rode 2,748 winners and was champion jockey thirteen times before he shot himself in a fit of delirium and depression at the age of 29 in 1886.*

Born of poor parents in Cambridge in 1837, George Fordham had completed his apprenticeship with Richard Drewitt at Lewes in Sussex. Fordham rode far shorter than his contemporaries, as he slewed his body round to one side, and with his shoulders hunched high as he cantered to the start he looked almost slovenly. Among his many assets, however, were really beautiful hands, the gift of keeping his mounts perfectly balanced, and the ability to deceive his rivals as to how well he was going.

As well as on Tournament, Fordham won the Stewards' Cup on Lady Clifden in 1862 and by a head on Elf King in 1880. A dead-heat would probably have been the verdict in the latter year if Fred Archer, still only 23, had not been obliged to put up one pound overweight at eight stone on Lord Hastings' Hackthorpe.

By way of contrast to George Fordham, Fred Archer came of racing stock. In 1858, the year after Fred was born, his father - Billy Archer - won the Grand National on Little Charlie. Fred was apprenticed to Mat Dawson at Heath House, Newmarket, and rode his first winner under Jockey Club rules on Athol Daisy at Chesterfield in 1870.

At the age of only 17 in 1874, Archer was on the way to his first jockeys' championship, when he took Lord Wilton's Modena to the post for the start of the Stewards' Cup early, so that he could obtain the most favourable position. Fourth favourite at 10-1, Modena won by a convincing four lengths. The following day, Archer appeared before the stewards, and was reprimanded for riding through the crowd before the order to clear the course had been given.

Twelve months later Archer won the Stewards' Cup again on Trappist, beating Coomassie, one of the Rothschild horses, by two lengths. This was very much a local success as Trappist was owned by Captain Arthur Prime, formerly of the 5th Dragoon Guards, who lived at Walberton House in Arundel. Captain Prime was a brother-in-law of Captain James Machell, who was the owner and manager of the Bedford Cottage establishment at Newmarket, the most successful gambling stable of the mid-Victorian era, for whom Archer rode many other winners.

The Stewards' Cup of 1883 was a desperately close run affair. The previous year's Oaks winner Geheimniss, ridden by Fred Archer, was in a clear lead approaching the post, with Sir George Chetwynd's well-backed Hornpipe, the mount of Charlie Wood, badly shut in on the rails. Wood managed to extricate Hornpipe just in time, and got up to beat Geheimniss by a head.

Although Senior Steward of the Jockey Club in 1880, Sir George was really no more than a professional gambler, reliant on successful punting to maintain an extravagant style of living. He and Wood, the real owner of most of the horses at Chetwynd House (now Machell Place, Newmarket), played fast and loose with the Rules of Racing that Chetwynd was honour-bound to enforce.

Chetwynd and Wood continued to run their horses to suit their betting until Lord Durham's made a thinly veiled denouncement of them at the Gimcrack Dinner at York in 1887. Sir George Chetwynd sued Lord Durham for damages. By mutual agreement the case was heard by the Stewards of the Jockey Club, James Lowther, the Earl of March - son and heir of the Duke of Richmond and future 7th Duke - and Prince Soltykoff, as it was feared that no High Court judge would have the necessary knowledge of racing.

Chetwynd claimed £20,000 damages, and won his case. The arbitrators, though, made plain their opinions of his character by awarding him a mere farthing in damages. Sir George Chetwynd resigned from the Jockey Club. Through the good offices of Leopold de Rothschild, a reconciliation between Chetwynd and Lord Durham was effected at Newmarket - Sir George never lost his interest in racing, and died at Monte Carlo in 1917.

A thorough rogue, this time of the equine variety, let his supporters down badly in the Stewards' Cup in 1888. This was Bismarck, owned by the professional backer Arthur Cooper. He was trained by Alfred Day at Fontwell Park, on what is now the jumping course, which was laid out by Day, a nephew of Lord George Bentinck's adversary John Barham Day.

While trained by Charlie Morton at Wantage, Bismarck proved exasperating - a real morning glory, who was brilliant on the gallops and all too often proved to be a bitter disappointment on the course.

"You probably never go faster than in this race all season. With the field splitting into two groups as it always does, you have the one side trying to catch up with the other. It is practically impossible to win from the front, as when you approach the final furlong the horses who have been up there hit a brick wall."

Richard Hughes

"THE STEWARDS' CUP IS A VERY EXCITING RACE TO RIDE IN WITH ITS BIG FIELD. WHEN YOU ARE DOWN AT THE START IN THE DIP YOU CAN'T REALLY SEE THE STANDS, AND THEN YOU COME OVER THE BROW OF THE HILL AND THERE IT ALL IS BEFORE YOU. I HAVE RIDDEN IN THE RACE FOURTEEN OR FIFTEEN TIMES, AND WHEN I WON THE RACE ON REPETITIOUS IN 1980, IT WAS ONLY MY FIFTH OR SIXTH WINNER. THE RACE WAS RUN IN FOG WHICH CAME AND WENT ON DIFFERENT PARTS OF THE COURSE. I WAS RACING ON THE FAR SIDE, AND I COULD SEE THE DANGER TO ME OVER BY THE STANDS RAILS. GUY HARWOOD HAD TWO RUNNERS IN THE RACE AND GREVILLE STARKEY WAS ON THE MORE FANCIED ONE CALLED PACE JEAN. I WON BY A SHORT HEAD, AND GREVILLE ASKED ME WHEN WE WERE PULLING UP IF I HAD WON. I SAID THAT I WASN'T SURE, BUT I THOUGHT SO, AND HE SAID THAT I DEFINITELY HAD."

TONY CLARK

"It is a unique sprint. The adrenalin rush you receive in calling the Stewards' Cup is like nothing else on the flat. The fact that you cannot see the horses with the naked eye makes the sight of them coming over the brow of the hill even more dramatic. You have to be really alert and aware. Anything can happen."

JIM MCGRATH

One day at Windsor in the middle of May 1888, Charlie Morton learned through an intermediary that 'Mr Abington' would like to ride Bismarck in the five furlong handicap. Morton agreed, and much to his surprise Bismarck won.

'Mr Abington' was the *nom de course* of the 26-year-old George Alexander Baird, the immensely wealthy - and utterly irresponsible - member of a family of Glasgow ironmasters, whose only redeeming talent seemed to be to ride as well as all but the best professionals on the flat. After Baird had won on him at Windsor, Bismarck won in the hands of Sammy Loates at Bath next time out, and then in those of Billy Warne at Sandown Park in late June.

On the strength of those performances Bismarck became strongly fancied for the 1888 Stewards' Cup, for which he started third favourite at 8-1, with Billy Warne up again. By this time Bismarck had been sent to Alf Day at Fontwell as a result of Charlie Morton having become private trainer to George Baird at Newmarket.

Bismarck came over the hill in solitary splendour at the end of the first furlong of the Stewards' Cup, and with less than a furlong to run he held a lead of ten lengths. The race seemed as good as over when, all of a sudden, Bismarck swerved so violently to the right that he went straight across the course and had put his head over the far rails before Billy Warne had him on an even keel again, and Tib, ridden by little Blake for Tom Cannon, got up to beat him by a head.

Alf Day may have been robbed of a Stewards' Cup victory by an arrant rogue - Bismarck was subsequently sent to Buenos Aires in disgrace at the end of the season - but he did win a number of notable races at Goodwood with the inmates of his small stable. He won the Goodwood Cup with Barmecide in 1893, the Goodwood Stakes with Ignition in 1911, and obtained some measure of compensation for the ignominious failure of Bismarck in the Stewards' Cup by winning the great Goodwood sprint with Romney in 1907.

When Britain celebrated the Golden Jubilee of Queen Victoria in 1887, the Cannon family more or less dominated the Stewards' Cup, with 14-year-old Mornington Cannon riding Upset at 6st 3lb to win by three lengths from his elder brother, Tom Cannon junior, on Tib.

Tib was owned and trained by the brothers' father, Tom Cannon senior, who had taken over the Danebury Stable from his father-in-law, John Day the younger. Upset was an appropriate winner of an important event during Jubilee Year as he was trained at Kingsclere by John Porter, whose patrons included the Prince of Wales.

In a further family saga, Bill Jarvis became the first of three generations of Newmarket's famous Jarvis racing clan to train the winner of the Stewards' Cup when Mr Arthur James's Dog Rose, ridden by Jim Woodburn, got home by a neck from Amphion in 1889. Bill, who died in 1921, had three sons to train at Newmarket - Willie, Basil and Jack. Towards the end of his career Jack (later Sir Jack) won the Stewards' Cup with the 6th Earl of Rosebery's Creole in 1963 and again with Mr Tom Blackwell's Potier in 1965.

The member of the third generation of the Jarvis family to win the Stewards' Cup was Ryan Jarvis, the son of Willie. One of his earliest achievements had been to send out Smokey Eyes, the mount of Charlie Smirke, to beat Vatellus by a length in the

__Left:__ Sir Jack Jarvis began his racing life as an apprentice with his father William and weighed only 6st 10lb when he rode Hackler's Pride to land a major gamble in the Cambridgeshire of 1903. He trained for some 50 years and had a very successful association with the 5th and 6th Earls of Rosebery, for whom he trained classic winners in Blue Peter, Ellangowan, Sandwich, Plack and Ocean Swell.

Stewards' Cup of 1952. Ryan Jarvis died in 1991; his son William succeeded him at the Phantom House stable in Newmarket.

There was a local success in the Stewards' Cup in 1899, when Horatio Bottomley's Northern Farmer got home by a neck from Nun Nicer, the winner of the previous season's 1,000 Guineas. The winner was trained by Harry Batho in the owner's private stable at Alfriston, near The Dicker, Bottomley's country house in Sussex.

The success of Northern Farmer enabled Bottomley to take some £50,000 (about four million pounds in today's money) out of the ring. The orphaned son of a London tailor, Horatio Bottomley had accumulated much wealth by floating a series of public companies, from which investors rarely saw so much as a pittance by way of return, before becoming Member of Parliament for South Hackney in 1906.

While providing great scope for his natural wit, a seat in the House of Commons did little to alter his way of life, or his method of underwriting it, until his conviction at the Old Bailey for fraudulent conversion in 1922, when he was sentenced to seven years' imprisonment.

__Overleaf:__ You might think that number 9 My Best Valentine (ridden by Ray Cochrane) has won the 1997 Stewards' Cup and that it is close for second between number 4 Dashing Blue (Frankie Dettori) and number 7 Danetime (Pat Eddery) - which just goes to show how angles can deceive, as Danetime won and landed a massive gamble for owner Michael Tabor.

9
ODAFONE
GROUP

27

During one of the many court cases in which he had been involved Counsel asked him, "You keep racehorses, Mr Bottomley?" - "No, sir," he replied. "They keep me." He died a pauper in the Middlesex Hospital, London in 1933, aged 73.

The success of the leaders of the American invasion, and the brothers Lester and Johnny Reiff, two of the jockeys they had brought with them, was the feature of the Goodwood Meeting of 1900. With complete indifference to any elements of sportsmanship or fair play, James Drake, 'Boss' Croker and William 'Betchamillion' Gates had their jockeys stop their runners to suit their betting, while being perfectly confident that those riders would be able to do full justice to their mounts when the money was down. Worse still, those American owners and their trainers introduced the pernicious practice of doping horses, to enable them to show form far better than they had ever done before.

While trained in the North in 1899, Royal Flush had won in decidedly moderate company at Carlisle, Manchester, Newcastle and Pontefract. On being acquired by James Drake he was sent to his new owner's compatriot Enoch Wishard, who trained in the Red House Stable near St Mary's Square in Newmarket, and who brought the administration of stimulants to a fine art.

Having been runner-up in a minor event at Alexandra Park since landing the Royal Hunt Cup, Royal Flush was again ridden by Johnny Reiff in the Stewards' Cup and won the usually wide open handicap by an almost unbelievable six lengths from 'Boss' Croker's Americus.

A pair of brothers have probably never have been in greater ascendancy at an important meeting than Johnny and Lester Reiff at Goodwood in 1900. As well as victory in the Stewards' Cup on Royal Push, Johnny Reiff won the Charlton Welter Handicap on Spectrum - owned by the one-time US Secretary of the Navy W. C. Whitney - and other events on Armful and Free Companion on the opening day, while brother Lester was successful in the Richmond Stakes on Handicapper, who was to land the 2,000 Guineas of 1901.

On the Wednesday Johnny Reiff won the Goodwood Plate on Jiffy II and Lester the Sussex Stakes on the Raft. The following day Johnny landed the Rous Memorial Stakes on Volodyovski, on whom Lester would win the Derby of the following season. Finally, on the Friday, Johnny enabled W. C. Whitney's Spectrum to notch up his second success of the meeting, in the Chesterfield Cup, and won the Chichester Stakes on Horton, while Lester also landed a double - on Princess Melton in the Molecomb Stakes and Merry Gal in the Nassau Stakes. Between them the Reiff brothers had ridden a dozen winners at the Goodwood meeting of 1900.

At season's end Lester Reiff was Champion Jockey. By the end of the following season he had been warned off. Riding De Lacy on the old New Barns course at Manchester on 27th September 1901, Lester was beaten by a head by his brother on 'Boss' Croker's Minnie Dee. The stewards reported Lester Reiff to the Stewards of the Jockey Club, who decided that he had not done his best to win. For his part, Johnny Reiff prudently retired to the less demanding atmosphere of France, only returning to England for major races like the Derby of 1907, which he won on Orby, and that of 1912, in which he was successful on Tagalie.

Above: Jack Barnato Joel made a fortune from the diamond fields of South Africa in the later years of the nineteenth century. His vast investment into racing yielded at least one winner of every classic, with Sunstar and Humorist successful in the Derby in 1911 and 1921 respectively. His son Jim more than maintained the family tradition.

The inevitably strong market on the Stewards' Cup ensured that it was one of the favourite races of the Joel brothers, Jack and Solly, who were betting very heavily indeed during the first 30 years of the twentieth century. They emerged from poverty in the East End of London by making huge fortunes from the diamond fields in the Kimberley area of South Africa, and both began racing in about 1900.

Jack (the elder of the brothers, born in 1862) was a man of enormous energy and remarkable intellect, and owed his success on the racecourse very largely to the horses he bred at the Childwick Bury Stud in Hertfordshire. The more flamboyant Solly, with his sweeping moustaches and neat grey beard, was to a large extent reliant upon the horses that he bought, as yearlings or as proven performers.

Their interest clashed over the Stewards' Cup of 1908, for which Solly backed his three-year-old Poor Boy down to clear favouritism at 9-2, while Jack's Elmstead figured amongst the 20-1 outsiders. In a close finish Elmstead, ridden by the immensely strong lightweight Joe Plant at 7st, prevailed by a neck over Poor Boy, the mount of the future champion jockey Frank Wootton.

Poor Boy simply seemed to have a jinx on him in the Stewards' Cup. After being runner-up in 1908, he was unplaced in 1909, second again in 1910, down the field in 1911, runner-up again in 1912, second for yet a fourth time in 1913 and finally unplaced to Jack Joel's Gold Sun, who ran a dead heat with Walter Raphael's Lord Annandale in 1914.

GOOD
STRAIGHT
COURSE
ROUND
COURSE
GOOD
GOOD TO FIRM
IN PLACES

Sol Joel did eventually win the Stewards' Cup with Fleeting Memory in 1929. A trifle ironically, a few weeks after Solly Joel died in July 1931, the race was won by Poor Lad, who was trained at Lambourn by Ossie Bell for the tobacco magnate Sir Hugo Cunliffe Owen.

Soon after racing at Goodwood was resumed after the end of the First World War, the good French three-year-old Epinard brought off a huge gamble in the Stewards' Cup under 8st 6 lb, which was 6 lbs more than any other horse of his age had ever previously carried successfully in the race. Trained by the American Eugene Leigh, Epinard was backed from 100-8 to 7-2 favourite, and won in a canter by two lengths from Jarvie, ridden by 16-year-old Charlie Smirke at 7st 6lb.

Jack Leach, one of the most successful and stylish jockeys in the decade which followed the First World War, had been obliged to retire from the saddle because of increasing weight at the end of 1930, and began training in the Graham Place Stable at Newmarket. In 1934 he obtained his first important success in his second profession when he brought off a gamble with Figaro in the Stewards' Cup. Starting at 100-7 and carrying Leach's own colours - Eton blue with red striped sleeves - Figaro was ridden by Tommy Weston. After joining the leaders about a furlong from home, Figaro finished very strongly to beat Alluvial, the mount of the veteran 'Brownie' Carslake, by a decisive length.

For the second time within half a century the course at Goodwood was closed due to the exigencies of World War between 1940 and 1945. With the resumption of racing amidst an atmosphere of restriction and shortages in 1946, the Stewards' Cup was won in an old-fashioned blanket finish by the six-year-old chestnut Commissar, a gelding owned in partnership by the brothers Arthur and Alan Budgett. As Major Arthur Budgett had not had time to re-open a stable since leaving the army, Commissar was trained by Major Eric Stedall at West Ilsley in Berkshire. Soon afterwards Budgett was able to resume his career in the Whatcombe Stable, and the greatest of his many achievements was to be the only man to breed, own and train two Derby winners during the last century, being responsible for triumphs of Blakeney in 1969 and that horse's half-brother Morston in 1973.

Twelve months after Commissar had won for for Arthur and Alan Budgett, Noel (later Sir Noel) Murless obtained his first important success in the south when Closeburn, ridden by Gordon Richards, beat Commissar by a length, with Fairey Fulmar (winner of the Cambridgeshire a few weeks later) in third.

In 1948 the Stewards' Cup was won by Dramatic, ridden by Eph Smith and trained by George Todd at Manton. Although George Todd, a veteran of the First World War, was already 54 at the time, it was still later that he was to emerge as a specialist trainer of staying handicappers, the first of which was French Design, who won the Goodwood Stakes in 1952, the Cesarewitch in 1954 and the Goodwood Stakes again as an eight-year-old in 1955.

After the Stewards' Cup had been won in the two years immediately after the war by Arthur Budgett and Noel Murless, very much men of the future, memories of the distant past were revived when The Bite, ridden by Bert Packham, won the race in 1949. The Bite was trained at Downs House, Epsom, by James Wood, whose father

"By and large, things have gone pretty well when I have been starting the race. Like all the big races, the Stewards' Cup is exciting. You have good years and bad years, but these senior and experienced sprinters know all about going into the stalls, and they also know that they are about to be in a race going as fast as they can."

Simon Morant

Overleaf: *Willie Carson with (inset) King's Signet and (main picture) Julian Wilson.*

"The ground was a big factor in King's Signet winning. 1993 was the first time that the Stewards' Cup had been run on a Saturday, and a lot of the track had become well chewed up throughout the meeting. But it was drawn to my attention - maybe by the trainer or the groundsman - that there was this little green strip about two yards wide on the far side which had been saved for the day. Having had discussions with John Gosden it must have been decided that we should go over to the far side and to take the chance, even with that big weight. Only three horses went down it, including me, thank God. It was a landmark to get past by riding my 3,500th winner, but I don't recall getting home and throwing my hands in the air. It was always a good race to win, and another of my tactical triumphs."

WILLIE CARSON, JOCKEY, KING'S SIGNET

"Willie was always a terrific interviewee. After Troy won the 1979 Derby he came out of the weighing room to talk to me and put on my top hat, which went straight down over his ears. 'Just to show that I'm not getting big-headed,' he said. I persuaded him to join the BBC team after retiring, and he made the transition to TV punditry very successfully."

JULIAN WILSON

4th

Charlie had won the race on Peter in 1879 and again on Sir George Chetwynd's Hornpipe in 1883, before being warned off for ten years in the aftermath of Sir George's suing of Lord Durham for libel. Because of what he saw as his own misfortunes, Charlie Wood could never countenance his son becoming a jockey, but rode the first winner trained by Jim, which was Auroscope at Alexandra Park in 1899.

Memories of the rivalry of the brothers Jack and Solly Joel in the Stewards' Cup were revived in 1956 when Matador won the race under 9st 2lb, a new record for a three-year-old. Matador was owned by Solly Joel's son Stanhope Joel. He was trained in the Heath House stable at Newmarket by Jack Waugh, whose great-grandfather Joe Hayhoe had trained Favonius to triumph in the 1872 Goodwood Cup.

Perhaps the most popular winner of the Stewards' Cup of all time was Sir Winston Churchill's Tudor Monarch. Ridden by Geoff Lewis, and trained by Walter Nightingall in the South Hatch stable at Epsom, Tudor Monarch beat Deer Leap by a neck in 1959. Sir Winston's father, Lord Randolph Churchill, also owned racehorses. They included L'Abbesse de Jouarre, known to the less cultured bookmakers as 'Abcess On The Jaw'. She won the Oaks in 1889, but was unplaced in the Stewards' Cup in 1890. When he began racing Sir Winston revived his father's colours - pink jacket, chocolate sleeves and cap.

***Above:** Soba was one of the romantic stories of the 1980s. From a small stable and with a humble pedigree, she was unsuccessful at rock-bottom level as a two-year-old; yet over the next two years she established herself at the top of the sprinting ranks. This win in the King George Stakes followed her success in the 1982 Stewards' Cup twelve months earlier.*

Calibina, trained by Paul Cole at Lambourn, became the first horse to complete a notable double in 1977. After winning the Wokingham Stakes at Royal Ascot, she followed up by beating Briarvanter by three parts of a length in the Stewards' Cup, being ridden by Geoff Baxter in both races. Cole, whose horses have won regularly at Goodwood, moved from Lambourn to the historic Whatcombe Stable in 1985. He won the Derby with Generous in 1991, and was champion trainer that season.

Mrs Muriel Hills's splendid homebred filly Soba won the Stewards' Cup in the course of her remarkable progress through 1982. Trained near Stillington in Yorkshire by David Chapman, she was out of Mild Wind, whom Chapman had bought for a mere 360 guineas as a yearling at Doncaster. Embarking upon 1982 as a maiden three-year-old, Soba won at Thirsk on her first appearance of the season, and was winning for the seventh time when successful at Goodwood. She was ridden by David Nicholls, and made all the running to beat Bracadale by a perfectly effortless two and a half lengths. In all Soba won 11 races in 1982, retaining her form until she beat the older

Scarrowmanwick at York in the last of them that October. Since turning to training, David Nicholls has had a number of smart sprinters through his hands. In the season of 2000 he had six runners in the Stewards' Cup, winning with Tayseer, the mount of Richard Hughes, with his son Adrian Nicholls fourth on Royal Result.

More than a century and a half after its institution by Lord George Bentinck, the Stewards' Cup remains amongst the most popular betting handicaps of the season. With the field spread across the course almost throughout running the winner can come from the runners drawn high on the far rails, the runners in the middle of the course, or those drawn low on the stands side rails.

When Willie Carson had been booked to ride Sheikh Mohammed's King's Signet for John Gosden's stable in 1993, he was pleased to be drawn high at number 21. Bringing King's Signet home a length and a half clear of Hard To Figure, Carson obtained his 3,500th success under Jockey Club Rules. By complete contrast to King's Signet, Soba had been drawn number one, against the stands rails, when winning in 1982, showing that there is no hard and fast rule as to where the winners of the Stewards' Cup come from.

Below: *Not quite into the valley of death, but the cavalry charge at the start of the Stewards' Cup in 1999, a race won by Harmonic Way, ridden by Richard Hughes.*

THE ROYAL CONNECTION

The royal history of Goodwood Racecourse goes back to its inception in 1802. It was only by a whisker that Goodwood missed having the Prince of Wales at the inaugural private meeting. He was staying at nearby Uppark when he was summoned away minutes before the sport was due to begin. It was such a close-run thing that all the riders hung around for some time before it became apparent that they would not be watched over by the Prince.

The man who was to become George IV loved everything about racing. He adored the sport itself and was a very successful owner. Being the hedonist that he was, he especially loved the inevitable partying that accompanied it all. The 3rd Duke invited him to the 1802 meeting; again he had to change his plans at the last minute.

***Above:** George IV was a very knowledgeable and successful owner, and indeed won the Goodwood Cup in 1829.*

***Right:** The Queen was such a regular visitor to Goodwood in the 1950s that racing became renamed 'the sport of queens'.*

There were further royal near-misses to come before Goodwood was to become a royal course. George IV's private secretary, Lord Errol, replied to the 3rd Duke's invitation: "It will not be in his power to accept your kind invitation as the Duke and Duchess of Cambridge are to arrive at Windsor on the 10th. His Majesty really seemed quite disappointed at not being able to go to Goodwood."

However, by the 1820s he was a regular at the meeting, which had proved to be a triumphant one for him as an owner. In 1829 he won the Goodwood Cup with Fleur de Lis, which was a fitting end to his racing career, as this was to be the last year that he was able to race. During raceweek the following year he was at Windsor Castle on what he thought was his deathbed. George's fear of death was obviously second only to a fear of dying without knowing the latest Goodwood results, and so a relay of post boys ran between Windsor and Goodwood to convey the race results as they came through. There was, in the end, no need for such drastic measures, as he survived the end of the meeting (although he did die not long afterwards).

Goodwood was clearly jinxed as far as first royal visits were concerned: William IV also failed to make it to the first meeting that he tried to attend. He had inherited his brother's impressive stables and was very keen to see if the horses could repeat their Goodwood victories under his colours. He was therefore distinctly unimpressed when his father-in-law, the Duke of Saxe-Coburg-Meiningen, decided to drop in to Windsor

unannounced and caused him to cancel his forthcoming racing trip. He did however, go on to emulate his brother's victory in the Goodwood Cup, but in a slightly more cavalier fashion. Although he inherited the horses, he did not inherit the accompanying level of knowledge and so, when asked by his racing manager which horse the King would like to run in the Goodwood Cup, he naively replied that they should run the whole lot. This uninformed approach proved ultimately an intelligent decision, as the royal horses came in first, second and third in 1830.

After the death of William IV, there was a hiatus of royals at Goodwood. Although the 5th Duke was a firm favourite with Queen Victoria she never came to stay at Goodwood: she was not amused by racing. In spite of the absence of royal patronage Goodwood was by now confirmed as one of the most fashionable racecourses in England. Going to Goodwood at the end of 'The Season' was an absolute must before the mass exodus up north. "One can't possibly be seen in London after Goodwood," was very much the view.

Goodwood had not only become the racecourse of choice for the punter, it was very firmly the racecourse of choice for the aristocrat. All the large houses in the area would be filled with Dukes, Duchesses, Marquesses and Princes, and a whole week of partying and racing would ensue. There is a painting by Walter Wilson and Frank Walton of 'The Lawn At Goodwood' during raceweek which depicts the very cream of English society: it is cheek by jowl peers and peeresses. On view are four Princes, nine Dukes, sixteen Earls and eighteen Barons. Goodwood was certainly the smart place to be.

Right: *Ever since man realised he could dominate and control the power of a horse, racing has been a favoured sport of the aristocracy and gentry. This painting, which is attributed to Judith Lewis, a follower of John Wootton, may show the 2nd Duke of Richmond in blue, with his nephew, the future 3rd Earl of Albemarle, standing with his back to the viewer. This would date the painting in the 1740s and make it the first depiction of racing at Goodwood.*

Above: *Gordon Castle.*
The day after the races ended, the 7th Duke would move the household north and depart for his beloved Gordon Castle on the banks of the River Spey. This was no mean feat, and involved taking a whole train to carry the Richmond party (which included 70 servants) to Scotland, where the Duke and his guests would indulge in a month of salmon fishing and grouse shooting.

There would of course be a large party in the house itself with at least 20 or 30 guests, while other annual house parties were hosted at Stansted, Uppark, West Dean, Cowdray Park, Petworth House, Slindon and Arundel Castle. The house parties of the 6th Duke are remembered by his granddaughter, Lady Muriel Beckwith. "In a sense he (the 6th Duke) was a working man, and had less time for sport than my father. But at Goodwood week, he gave himself to entertaining in the Grand Manner. I can think of the great rooms and the desultory gathering of guests who strolled in one after another, foraging happily to find a pre-war breakfast in all its succulence in the Egyptian dining room. Then in the great hall, the people who had breakfasted gathered for a gossip. Beneath the hanging banners and granite columns people walked idly to and fro, reading papers and looking over race cards. Enthusiasts would stroll to the stables, or to those at Waterbeach, to cast a critical eye over the favourites."

If entertaining in the 'Grand Manner' was beyond one's means, there were always the 'pay parties', that were exactly as they sound. One went to stay in a house party and one paid. Lady Nellie Wyckham was one lady who always had such a party, which although practical were somewhat frowned upon by many of the society ladies. No one seemed very impressed by this form of entertaining - even the media was dismissive. "I always think pay parties are such a mistake. Nobody is pleased, very few are even satisfied. It costs the hostess a great deal more than she receives; while she has not even the credit of having done a more or less generous thing," wrote one observer.

The 6th Duke of Richmond was much more interested in country sports than the sport of racing, and although he entertained during raceweek, it was his son who so loved the racing and always filled the house during raceweek. The twice-widowed 7th Duke lived in great state and style and, even when alone, would dine in true solitary

Overleaf: *'The Lawn At Goodwood', by Walter Wilson and Frank Walton, 1886. Although this painting is not an actual reproduction of any specific year at Goodwood, the artists have featured all of the people who could have been there in any one year. This collection of aristocrats and a few celebrities of the day is, of course, headed by HRH the Prince of Wales (later to be Edward VII) who takes centre stage.*

IN
OUT

***Above:** During the Victorian era, Queen Victoria and Prince Albert presided over a reluctantly pious nation. The royal couple imposed their strict moral code on their subjects, for whom the new-found austerity was hard to accept after the frivolity of the Regency period. Therefore, when Prince Albert died and Queen Victoria plunged herself into mourning, the country looked to their young Prince of Wales to lead society back into more hedonistic days. They were not to be disappointed: the young, profligate Prince (far right in photograph) steered society to a life of cocktails, house parties, mistresses, extravagance and disrepute.*

splendour in the State Dining Room. During raceweek he would hire an orchestra and every evening after dinner the house would fill with the guests of the nearby households all coming to dance. This could cause such chaos that the police had to be brought in to sort out the parking. His youngest daughter Helen, later to become the Duchess of Northumberland, or his sister Lady Caroline (Aunt Lina) would act as hostess, even when the Duke had his bachelor raceweek parties. The day after racing finished, everything that could possibly be needed for his Scottish holiday - servants, furniture, food and all - was put on to a special private train from Chichester to Carlisle and then taken on to Gordon Castle.

All this activity created a logistical nightmare for the staff. One particularly onerous problems was that of airing the beds before raceweek. The only way to do this was to lug all of them up to the roof; they would then have to be turned at midday and once again at teatime before being brought back down. The following day, the whole process would have to be repeated and the next load of mattresses taken onto the roof. With the number of guests and servants staying in the house for raceweek, this single chore could take weeks.

During July the kitchens catered for exactly the same number of people as they would during every other month of the year. However, the food bill was exactly double, since the raceweek guests were fed as if they were kings. And in fact, they normally were. Edward VII's attitude to the sport of kings could not have been more different to that of his mother: he adored racing, and especially racing at Goodwood.

He started coming to Goodwood as Prince of Wales and came practically every year until his death. Very little was allowed to come between this king and his week in West Sussex. It was during this time that it was considered so normal to find a coterie of royals at the house that Viscountess Chelsea noted in her diary on arrival, "The usual party at Goodwood. Prince and Princess, 2 princesses etc, etc."

When entertaining their Majesties (he was normally accompanied by Queen Alexandra and the Prince of Wales, the future George V), observing royal etiquette was obligatory. Edward greatly enjoyed the privilege that his rank afforded him, and so royal etiquette had to be strictly adhered to. Thankfully, little was left to guesswork: there were fairly stringent guidelines for a host to follow. The host must always be at the railway station to meet the royal train, and there could be a guard of honour made up of local volunteers. However, there was not to be a band or procession. There would need to be a carriage (with four horses and postilions) which would carry the royal party and the host, and there would be other carriages to convey the luggage and the other guests who had also travelled on the 'Royal Special' train. The royal carriage would then journey to the residence, where the hostess was to be waiting in the entrance to welcome her regal guests.

The Duke went one step further and would ensure that the road to Goodwood was watered immediately before the King's arrival, thereby ensuring that the drive was not a dusty and unpleasant one. The Duke was not the only one who would spare no detail when it came to the comfort of the royal party. The tender of the Royal Special train would always be full of white-washed coal so that no black coal dust would trouble their Majesties.

The state apartments at the back of Goodwood House, built by James Wyatt in the 1770s, were where the royals always slept. They certainly met with George V's approval: "I have the same comfortable rooms," he noted in his diary entry for 26th July 1920. The royal suite had French windows opening onto the lawn; the Drawing Room was hung with the Gobelin tapestries which had been presented to the 3rd Duke when he was Ambassador to the court of France. The King's room was on the ground floor, the centrepiece of which was a carved four poster bed surmounted by the royal arms.

There were many legacies that Edward VII left to Goodwood, one of which is the dress code. He felt that his beloved Goodwood was being taken over by the young dandies and fops who were attempting to turn it into a fashion show and saw this as a total disaster undermining the enjoyment of the week. How could you really enjoy your racing if your main concern was the perfect crease down your trouser or the line of your tails?

He started with a roundabout approach by sending a message to the Turf Club the week before the races asking them to inform their members to come in 'pot hats' or straw hats. The members failed to comply. A couple of years later he decided that more direct action was necessary and himself wore a 'pot hat' and a shooting coat. This was commented upon, but nothing changed.

In 1904 he took advantage of the custom that male fashion would follow the King and turned up with a white silk topper instead of the regulation black one. Male followers of fashion were sent scurrying back to the capital as London hatters were

***Overleaf:** Edward VII was Goodwood's biggest royal fan. As Prince of Wales and King, he never missed a July meeting, and affectionately dubbed it "a garden party with racing tacked on". To reflect this more relaxed atmosphere he single-handedly managed to switch the dress code from the rigid formality of stiff collars and morning suits to the linen suits and panamas still worn today.*

***Overleaf, inset:** The first fine day of the race meeting offered an opportunity to take the 'house party' photograph.*

"The Royals always came to Goodwood for pleasure. They were cocooned by the private house party, emerging daily to the Duke's own enclosure at the racecourse, where they came as near as they ever could to mixing with crowds of people similarly enjoying a sport. I think it must have been very relaxing for them, a sort of holiday at the end of the summer season. Kings and Queens are

used to a very high level of entertainment and, although they never show it, are probably easily bored. At Goodwood there was no problem of that. People who do not know Goodwood often think the racecourse may be rather grand and overwhelming because of its royal history and because it is owned by a Duke. In fact it has always had a very happy and relaxed atmosphere. Racegoers are smart but never uncomfortable. Definitely linen rather than silk."

ROSEMARY BAIRD, CURATOR OF THE GOODWOOD COLLECTION

begged to supply the 'royal model' overnight. Two years later he completed the sartorial downgrade with a switch from morning suit to suit, with the choice of a white bowler/derby, a panama or an ordinary straw hat. Being freed of the stiff collar and long skirts gave Goodwood a much more relaxed holiday feel than any other racecourse, an atmosphere that it has retained to this day. This is probably what prompted Edward to dub his favourite race meeting, "a garden party with racing tacked on".

The Queen did not share her husband's passion for racing and seemed to endure rather than enjoy her husband's hobby. This was one of the reasons why the new stand (built in 1903) housed such a sumptuous royal pavilion: at least the Queen could be comfortable while on the course if nothing else. No expense was spared. Even the standard of convenience was worthy of the royal seat. The King's lavatory was made of monogrammed marble with a marble frieze and a thick mahogany seat. Even the royal flush was given a blue-blooded make-over: the chain itself was silver-plated.

Despite these fittings, the standard was still not quite high enough for our fastidious Queen, who suggested certain *minor* improvements. These included enlarging the window at the end of the her private room and turning the whole pavilion around on its axis so that she could look out over the picnicking area. She gave much more detailed instructions as to how she would prefer her ladies' room. In the 'Account of Works' submitted by the builder, the changes to what was now referred to as 'the Queen's Pavilion' included "To preparing, supplying and fixing mahogany shelf and mirror with mahogany frames in WC and French-polished paper box and fixing WC and 1 electro-plated towel rail and brackets in lavatory." The cost of the 'tweaks' suggested by Her Majesty cost the Duke the queenly sum of £6,400.

There was also an underground subway that ran from one end of the pavilion to the other. The main box was located at one end, the ladies' box at the other. The Queen did not like being constantly surrounded by chattering people as she had problems with her hearing, which may have been the reason for having two boxes. However it also gave Queen Alexandra the added bonus of being able to sweep down the subway and escape another bout of socialising with her husband's mistresses.

Lillie Langtry and Alice Keppel would frequently join the Goodwood party. Mrs Keppel was especially popular with everyone and was described by Lady Muriel Beckwith as having "a wonderful way with her, a pleasant word for everyone and gracious to all." She was full of charm and fun. One year she retired to her room only to find the place filled with bats. She commandeered some members of the party and asked them to deal with them in any way they saw fit. For most of them this involved wielding a tennis racquet, although one young gent attempted to fight them off with a croquet mallet.

If it had not been for Lillie Langtry, the story of Edward VII's racing career could have been very different. She was not only a beautiful woman, but a clever one - in her days as his mistress she used to advise Edward on his stables. Long after she had stopped being his mistress, Edward would still rely on her racing advice and would go and have tea with her in the garden of the cottage in Singleton that she used to rent for Goodwood week.

__Above:__ The strictly private balcony of the Royal Pavilion, from where the Duke of Richmond and his royal guests could watch the racing, with Edward VII in top hat and Queen Alexandra next to him.

She was no passive observer of the racing world, though, as she was a well-respected owner. However it was not thought feminine to own horses, so Lillie would race her horses under the pseudonym of 'Mr Jersey'. It was as Mr Jersey that she scored a double at Goodwood in 1899 with Merman, winning both the Goodwood Stakes and the Goodwood Cup. She was not, however on the course that day: she was in Jersey becoming Lady de Bathe, having met her future husband at Goodwood two years previously.

The King and Queen would stay in the royal apartments (which would have been partly furnished with furniture that they themselves brought from Windsor) for breakfast and would not normally appear downstairs until it was time to leave for the racecourse. The rest of the houseparty, however, was more active and would take off for a walk along Bognor beach. Sometimes they simply walked along the pebbles, but when it was hot the ladies' long skirts would be lifted, and the men would roll up the trouser legs of their tweed suits to indulge in a paddle. Those who did not feel like the sea air could take their exercise on the golf course, or go for a ride in order to fill the time before the carriages would be waiting in the drive to convey the noble party to the grandstand.

After racing there were more sporting activities. Most evenings featured a mixed tennis match on the grass and a rival croquet match. The demon croquet player of the party was always the King himself, so he generally opted for the more sedate game. The guests reconvened for cocktails before dinner and headed into a sumptuous feast of every conceivable delicacy. The table would be covered in silver, down the middle of which were placed the Duke's racing cups and trophies.

__Overleaf:__ On the stroke of twelve noon the cars would be brought around to the front door to convey the Goodwood house party to the racecourse. Edward VII (far left) and the Prince of Wales, the future George V (second from left), are accompanied by the 7th Duke of Richmond (fourth from left).

"AS AN EIGHT-YEAR-OLD CHILD, IT WAS A VERY EXCITING EXPERIENCE HAVING THE ROYAL FAMILY TO STAY. ENORMOUS ENERGY WENT INTO THE PREPARATIONS AND STAFF NUMBERS SEEMED TO ZOOM FROM THREE TO THIRTY-THREE. THERE WAS BUSTLE AND BUSYNESS EVERYWHERE, WITH EVERYONE SINGLE-MINDEDLY TRYING TO ATTAIN ABSOLUTE PERFECTION IN WHATEVER THEY DID - NOTHING LESS WOULD DO. I SAW MOST OF THE VISIT FROM THE TOP OF THE STAIRS. THERE WERE RED COATS, WHITE GLOVES AND BLACK SHINY SHOES EVERYWHERE. IT WAS VERY EXHILARATING - EVEN THE HELICOPTER WAS RED. ONE OF MY EARLIEST MEMORIES WAS MY WHOLE FAMILY STANDING IN THE FRONT HALL WAITING FOR THE GREAT NOISE OF THE ROTORS, WHICH SIGNIFIED THE ROYAL ARRIVAL. FOR A SMALL CHILD THE FEELING OF ANTICIPATION WAS OVERWHELMING."

THE EARL OF MARCH

Previous pages: *The 7th Duke of Richmond escorts Queen Alexandra (main picture, arriving at the station) and Queen Mary (inset) en route to the racecourse.*

Following dinner there would be dancing for those who still had the energy and more gambling for those who did not. The gambling was in the form of bridge or poker and the stakes were high. On 2nd August 1906 Viscountess Chelsea wrote, "A lovely day. Played at croquet in the evening with His Majesty and Mr Keppel. Played bridge in the evening and ended having won £14." This was the equivalent of the annual agricultural wage of the time.

There was one year when the King (when he was Prince of Wales) did not stay at Goodwood. Instead, he went to stay down the road at West Dean with some of his great friends, the Jameses. Evie James was beautiful, she was charming, she was the toast of English society. She also had the approval of Queen Alexandra, which was no mean feat. Alexandra had a rule that she would not stay in the house of a commoner: the only person for whom she ever broke this rule was Evie James, and Edward and Alexandra were frequent visitors to West Dean. There is also some confusion as to the role Evie James played in the King's life. There is no doubt that there was great affection between them, but no one is quite sure if Evie was his mistress or his daughter.

There is little conclusive evidence either way. Whatever the relationship between the King and Evie James, they were certainly close. When the 6th Duke intimated that there were a couple of ladies on Edward's list whom he did not wish to have in his house, Edward took umbrage and asked himself to stay with the Jameses down the road. The Duke was then most upset that they would not be staying at Goodwood and fired off a letter to Windsor to that effect. He received a very apologetic reply, but Edward and Alexandra nonetheless went to West Dean. To show his displeasure the Duke did not offer Edward the privilege of entering by the private gate and did not ask him into the Richmond Enclosure. For one year the Prince had to race with his future subjects.

Evie and Willie James had four daughters and then they had a son. The long-awaited heir was born in 1907, his name was Edward and his godfather was King Edward. For the year prior to the boy's birth, Willie James had been extremely ill and bedridden, and it was generally presumed that this was the natural child of the King. However, the present Duke of Richmond asked the late Edward James if what he had read in the *Times* newspaper about him being the son of Edward VII was true. The eccentric Mr James replied, "No, no, no, you are quite wrong, it is my mother who was his daughter."

George V shared his father's passions for racing and for Goodwood. As Prince of Wales he always accompanied his father and as King he continued the annual pilgrimage until his death. There was little that could put him off his racing stride, although there was one year that he was unable to make it. He wrote and apologised to the Duke that he would not be with them that year. "I very much regret to say that I find it impossible to leave London for my promised visit to Goodwood." He then went on to explain what was probably one of the few things that had the power to keep him away: "the probability of war with Europe." The year was 1914.

When he was staying at Goodwood, George would rise and go for a pre-breakfast ride along the course. He obviously enjoyed this early morning ritual with his two riding companions (the Earl of Lonsdale and his equerry, Wigram) as his diary entries

Above: *A houseparty at Molecomb in the 1920s. From left to right: the Earl of March (the future 8th Duke), the Countess of March, Arthur Penn, Lord Settrington (the future 9th Duke), Lady Elizabeth Bowes Lyon (the future Queen Elizabeth the Queen Mother), Lady Katherine Hamilton, Bobby Somerset, 'G' and Lady Doris Gordon Lennox. Although her late Majesty the Queen Mother had not yet discovered her passion for racing, she was a frequent guest at Molecomb. She was a great friend of the daughter of the 8th Duke of Richmond, Lady Doris Gordon Lennox. The Queen Mother's brother David was up at Oxford with the 9th Duke, and through this connection the Queen Mother and the Duke became lifetime friends.*

always referred to "a capital ride". Whether he went for a ride would often depend on whether he was accompanied by the Queen, as did his wake-up call. A member of the household wrote in her memoirs that "when the Queen came, the King shared her room and was called with tea, but when he came alone, he slept in a little iron bedstead in his dressing room and was called with whiskey."

Sport however, was not allowed to interrupt royal business completely, so George would secrete himself in the royal apartments before the races and spend the morning reading and writing letters and "doing boxes with Wigram". While on the racecourse his interest in his own horses and betting was fierce. Goodwood was kind on the royal purse and it was not unheard of for the King to win £25 on one race. Where he was impeccably careful in all other aspects of his life, he was a cavalier punter on the course.

Finally, there is another monarch who adores Goodwood - our Queen. Indeed, she was such a frequent visitor that during the 1950s it began to be known as 'the sport of queens'. For many years she stayed alternately at Goodwood itself or with the Duke and Duchess of Norfolk at nearby Arundel Castle. Sadly this all came to an enforced end when school holidays had to take priority over racing and polo and the Queen's raceweek at Goodwood could not be fitted into her diary and that of her children.

Official business, however, did not bring a halt to her racing and as a result, there have been more meetings of the Privy Council in Goodwood House than in any other privately-owned house in the country (other than royal residences, of course). Race week often coincided with the end of the parliamentary session and so a Privy Council had to be held quickly. Logistically this could have been a nightmare but was always

made somewhat simpler by the fact that most of the Privy Councillors were already in the area. When the Queen called her first one in 1953 (the last Privy Council held in a private house had been convened at Goodwood by George V nearly thirty years earlier), only the clerk and two councillors had to drive from London - the other five were already on the course. Business was then conducted swiftly and efficiently in the Tapestry Drawing Room, so much so that on leaving the room Prince Philip commented, "Not bad: 35 items in 12 minutes."

On another occasion, the Queen and the present Duke drove over to Arundel stables one evening. They arrived to find Lord Scarborough, who was Lord Chamberlain at the time, waiting in the yard with a great scroll under his arm. When asked if she could sign the document, she rolled it down the back of the Duke of Norfolk, signed it with a flourish and went off to conduct her tour of the stables.

Although the Queen would "intently follow each race through field glasses," according to the *Daily Mail*, the Duke of Edinburgh's passion was polo. After the fourth race of the day, the Prince would disappear off to Cowdray to play polo where the Queen would join him when the races had ended. It was then back to Goodwood for croquet before cocktails, a feast fit for a queen and a quick round of The Game (a formalised version of charades) before retiring. All this activity did nothing to tire Prince Philip, who would organise a ducal cricket match for the end of the week. It would be the Duke of Edinburgh's XI versus the Duke of Norfolk's and was a fiercely contested duel.

One year when the Duke of Edinburgh wanted to get in some pre-match batting practice he enlisted the help of the present Duke and asked if he could set up a net in the park. Having telephoned the local cricket club, a net was duly produced and the Duke and his brother, Lord Nicholas Gordon-Lennox, prepared to bowl at the Prince. In order to harness the fitness of the batting Duke, they decided to produce only two cricket balls. This way they could have some kind of breather as they sauntered over to retrieve the hit balls. This was fine in theory, but was destroyed in practice when the Duke of Edinburgh appeared with a whole bag of brand-new composite cricket balls, which he then proceeded to whack around the park. Total exhaustion was only saved by the detective who was standing out of the grounds on the other side of the hedge and could throw the balls back to the two weary fielders.

It was not only the Queen and Prince Philip who loved the week: it was a favourite of the whole royal household. One day during a royal visit, the 9th Duchess picked up the telephone to overhear a member of the royal staff on the line to Buckingham Palace saying, "George, you had better come down with the others, it is good grub." George obviously passed the word around: the following day three more members of the royal staff arrived on the Goodwood doorstep. You see, Goodwood has always been popular with everyone.

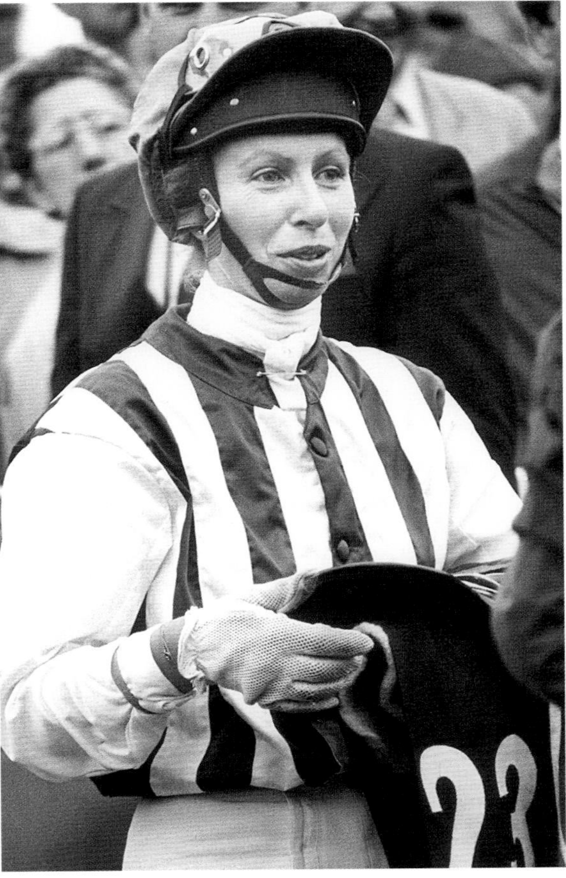

Above: *The Princess Royal almost did not ride at Goodwood in September 1985. The previous year she had ridden at Epsom and publicly said it was quite the most terrifying experience of her life and one she did not want to repeat. After her ride at Goodwood (on Little Sloop in the Oxo Stakes - they finished sixth), she was reminded of this. "Oh no," she said. "I didn't say that I definitely wouldn't. I said that I* probably *wouldn't."*

Left: *The house party at Goodwood for raceweek in 1957. From left to right - back row: Lady Alice Egerton, Lord Astor, Lord Plunkett, Lady Astor, Major R. Seymour. Middle row: The Countess of Euston, Miss M. Hudson, the Duke of Northumberland, Mrs Mary Finnis, the Earl of Euston. Front row: The Duchess of Richmond and Lady Ellinor Gordon-Lennox, HRH the Duke of Edinburgh, HM the Queen, the Duke of Richmond, the Earl of March and Lord Settrington and the Duchess of Northumberland.*

STARS OF THE FUTURE

Two-year-old racing is the nursery ground for the classics the following season and all the big prizes after that, as potential stars are brought along to learn gradually what racing is all about over increasingly long distances. The Glorious Goodwood meeting stages two of the most important two-year-old races of the season, the six-furlong Gerrard Richmond Stakes, and the Vintage Stakes, the first two-year-old Pattern race over seven furlongs.

The Richmond is much the older of the pair as it was first held in 1877, while the Vintage is a comparative newcomer since it was not introduced until 1975, reflecting the general trend to provide two-year-olds with longer distance races in which to compete earlier in the season.

However, even the Richmond Stakes has to give way in terms of seniority to the Molecomb Stakes, which takes place on the Thursday and was first run in 1833. For much of its existence the Molecomb was confined to fillies and was won by some of the speediest of their times - including La Tendresse, Abelia, Tessa Gillian (who went on to be second in the 1,000 Guineas), Cawston's Pride and Queensberry - but that level of quality has not, generally speaking, been maintained since the race was opened up to colts as well as fillies in 1981.

Curiously, though, the Molecomb Stakes has one particular landmark to its name which occurred after it was opened up to both sexes. In 1985, when it was the very first race of the meeting and was run in driving rain, it provided one of the longest-priced winners in Goodwood's entire history with victory for the 100-1 chance Hotbee, a filly who had run seven times before that without success. Her win defied logical explanation.

Eight years earlier the Molecomb had a significance of which most people, if not all, were unaware at the time. The winner of the race in 1977 was a filly called Hatta, trained by John Dunlop and ridden by Ron Hutchinson, who upset Lester Piggott on the 7-2 on Amaranda. Hatta was the first horse to run in this country for Sheikh Mohammed of the Maktoum family from Dubai, who are now such powerful players in Britain and the rest of the world. It is interesting to speculate what might have happened with the Maktoums had Hatta not been any good.

Opposite: *There is nothing like encouraging them young... Sheikh Mohammed al Maktoum and three sons in the Sheikh's box with Trundle Hill in the background. It was at Goodwood that Sheikh Mohammed had his first important success in Britain, only a few months after he had started having horses in training here. This came when Hatta, trained by John Dunlop, won the Molecomb Stakes of 1977. Since then, he and his Godolphin team have had major two-year-old wins at the course with horses like Naheef and Aljabr in the Vintage Stakes and Bachir in the Richmond.*

CITROEN

During his long and successful association with Fred Darling - you could hardly use the word 'happy' about the arrangement because happiness and Darling seemed poles apart - Sir Gordon Richards observed the many foibles of that brilliant trainer.

One of Fred Darling's rigid principles, from which he would never be diverted, was how to campaign his two-year-olds. There were, as Sir Gordon related in his book *My Story*, three categories of youngster in Darling's stable - "the Ascot horses, the Goodwood horses, and the rest, which he did not bother very much about."

This shows in what regard the trainer held the two-year-old races at Goodwood, and among his top horses subsequent Derby winners Coronach and Manna won the Richmond and the (now defunct) Rous Memorial Stakes respectively. It seems safe to speculate that the two Royal horses with which he did so spectacularly well during the Second World War, Big Game and Sun Chariot, would have run at Goodwood had the course been in operation.

The Richmond Stakes, though, was established as an event of serious significance long before Fred Darling gave it that accolade, as in only its second year, 1878, it was won by the top-class filly Wheel Of Fortune, trained for Lord Falmouth by Mathew Dawson at Newmarket.

Right: *Fred Archer on Bend Or, on whom he won the Richmond Stakes at Goodwood in 1879 and whom he rode to one of his most brilliantly effective finishes to win the Derby the following the season. With one arm strapped to his body after it had been savaged by a horse at Newmarket less than a month before Epsom, Archer rode a finish of immense power to get Bend Or up to beat Robert The Devil by a head.*

Above: *Persimmon (John Watts) was the best horse to race for the Prince of Wales, who was to become King Edward VII. He won the Derby and the St Leger of 1896 and the Gold Cup at Ascot and the Eclipse Stakes the following year before becoming a very successful sire.*

Wheel Of Fortune went on to win the 1,000 Guineas and the Oaks, and was described by Fred Archer as the best filly he ever rode. As she stood just over 15 hands high, Wheel Of Fortune - who loved eating oranges and once consumed an entire bag of meat pies - must have looked a comical sight when Archer was on her. His long legs must almost have touched the ground!

Twelve months later the Richmond went to an even better horse. This was the first Duke of Westminster's home-bred colt Bend Or, who went on to win one of the most dramatic of Derbys in 1880. Fred Archer had been badly injured a few weeks before the Derby when he was attacked by a horse at Newmarket, so that not only was his arm seriously damaged, but he also put on so much weight through the enforced inactivity that he had to lose a stone in four days to make the weight for Epsom. In spite of all this Archer was able to ride one of his most powerful finishes to force Bend Or in front near the line to beat Robert The Devil by a head, though even then the drama was not yet over.

Robert The Devil's owner, Mr Brewer, lodged an objection with the Jockey Club claiming that the horse who finished first at Epsom was not Bend Or, but a different colt named Tadcaster. This was rejected, but the doubts have never been fully eradicated and on his deathbed Mr Brewer's 'mole' at the Duke of Westminster's stud remained adamant that his story was true.

There is an interesting indication of the way in which society worked in those days in connection with this objection. It appears that when Mr Brewer planned to lodge his plea he mentioned this to the Senior Steward of the

Overleaf: *Flat racing is so much dominated by the big, powerful stables nowadays that Group race successes for smaller yards are especially welcome. In 2001 there was just such a moment when Whitbarrow's success in the Molecomb Stakes was the first at Group level for Rod Millman. Both he and Jamie Osborne, trainer of the runner-up Irony, were jump jockeys before they turned to training.*

1
CANTOR
SPORT

Above: *Sri Pekan (Richard Quinn) was one of the top juveniles of 1994 when his record of five wins from six starts included the Richmond Stakes and the Champagne Stakes at Doncaster. Unfortunately he was unable to run as a three-year-old before going to stud in Ireland.*

Jockey Club, Sir George Chetwynd. Sir George suggested that Mr Brewer should speak to the Duke of Westminster in the first instance, but Mr Brewer was horrified at the idea of such presumption on his part and knew his place far too well to speak to a Duke in such a, or indeed any, way.

The winner of the Richmond in 1895 was owned by the Prince of Wales (later King Edward VII). His home-bred colt Persimmon went on to take the Derby and the St Leger the following season, and this trend of top-level winners of the race was maintained through at least the first half of the twentieth century. Bayardo (1908), Manna (1924), Colombo (1933), Mahmoud (1935), Petition (1946) and Palestine (1949) all continued on to classic or the equivalent of Group 1 success in later years.

The 1954 winner, Eubulides, was one of the first good horses to carry the colours of Phil Bull, the sometime teacher of mathematics who went on to become the founder of the Timeform organisation and act as a lifetime scourge of the Jockey Club, of whom he was constantly critical. Eubulides also won the Chesham Stakes at Ascot, but at the end of 1954 Bull sold him to interests in the USA - almost the only bright spot as far as he was concerned in a year when his betting cost him about £14,000 (around £190,000 in today's terms). Which just goes to show that when such a well-informed racing man can lose there will always be men standing on boxes with a broad smile and a hodful of cash longing to add yours to their roll.

Perhaps rather surprisingly in view of his remarkable career - the likelihood of there ever being another trainer of such brilliant versatility seems non-existent - Vincent O'Brien never won a Richmond, but his compatriot Paddy Prendergast, who was the first of the pair really to hit the flat race headlines, had three successes in the race with Artane in 1952, The Pie King a year later and Typhoon in 1960.

One of the most dramatic and controversial runnings of the race took place in 1983 when Vacarme, racing for the all-powerful combination of Daniel Wildenstein, Henry Cecil and Lester Piggott, started at 3-1 on and won by three-quarters of a length and a length from Creag-an-Sgor and Godstone. However, he had had a far from trouble-free run, and when the stewards found Piggott guilty of careless riding on his way through, Vacarme - inevitably, under the rules as they then stood - was disqualified.

Thus Creag-an-Sgor became the winner, but not for long. Godstone's rider Graham Sexton objected to him for bumping and boring and Godstone emerged the winner. Whether he would have done so had the current less rigid rules been in force is debateable, but that is how things worked at the time.

Daniel Wildenstein was not renowned for taking defeat well, and even less so when his horse, as in this instance, should have won easily. He took against Piggott in a major way and later in the year, following a row about Piggott riding or not riding another of his horses, he produced the oft-used - and in this case accurate - line of "Piggott, you will never ride for me again." On this particular occasion the jockey chose not to utter his stock riposte of "Oh well, I'd better retire then."

Piggott later described the Wildenstein family as "inveterate bad losers". A couple of years later they gave Henry Cecil the sack as well. Cecil was only one of a number of trainers to incur Wildenstein's displeasure.

Godstone's owners were a company called Esal Commodities Ltd., who had won the Richmond Stakes with Tender King a couple of years before. They shared the same name as Esal Bookmakers, who made a name in a very big way when they offered 33-1 for the 2,000 Guineas about a colt called Gorytus after he had made a winning debut at York in the summer of 1982. Esal were knocked over in the rush to take that price, but Gorytus finished a distant fourth in a field of four in the Dewhurst Stakes at Newmarket two races later. No one was ever able to explain this unexpected loss of form and he never came anywhere near to his early promise.

"The Vintage was introduced in 1975 when it became clear that there was a niche for it, and is the first Pattern race for two-year-olds over seven furlongs. It has been a great success, producing two Derby winners in Troy and Dr Devious, and many of its winners have gone on to achieve major results as three-year-olds."

Peter Willett, director of Goodwood Racecourse and former member of the Flat Race Pattern Committee

There was a long gap after Palestine's victory in the Richmond Stakes of 1949 until the next subsequent classic winner was successful, but this should not imply that the winners in that period were nonentities. Horses like Tudor Music, Sallust, Swing Easy, Primo Dominie and Sri Pekan were all high-class performers, and if things had worked out differently the 1987 winner Warning might well have added his name to the classic roll of honour.

Warning ended the year as the top two-year-old colt in Europe, having followed his Goodwood success with a win in the Champagne Stakes at Doncaster, and he headed into the winter as the ante-post favourite for the 2,000 Guineas of 1988.

As things turned out, Warning was beaten in the Craven Stakes by the subsequent Guineas winner Doyoun and he was not able to run in the classic. He came back in style later in the year, winning the Sussex Stakes and putting up a magnificent display in the Queen Elizabeth II Stakes at Ascot, What might have happened had he been able to run at Newmarket?

In any event the classic-winning tradition was picked up again in 2000 when the previous year's Richmond Stakes winner, Bachir, took the Irish 2,000 Guineas and the equivalent race in France, the Poule d'Essai des Poulains at Longchamp. When he won at the Curragh he beat no less a rival than Giant's Causeway and, in view of what Giant's Causeway did later on, Bachir could not have performed much better.

The second of Goodwood's major two-year-old races, the Vintage Stakes, has been a serious pointer to the following year's classics almost from its first running in 1975. It was the sort of race at which Dick Hern would aim his potential top-level winners and, with six wins apiece, he and Henry Cecil have won getting on for half the runnings to date.

Hern was landing the prize for the third time in four years, and with only his third runner, when Troy was successful in 1978. The following year Troy won the Derby by the massive margin of seven lengths, as well as taking the King George VI and Queen Elizabeth Diamond Stakes, the Irish Derby, the Benson and Hedges Gold Cup and the Predominate Stakes at Goodwood. He also came third in the Prix de l'Arc de Triomphe and, as far as Timeform at least were concerned, was the Horse of the Year in Europe.

Willie Carson, Troy's regular partner, finds it very difficult to decide which was the best middle-distance flat horse that he rode, but he has no doubt that Troy is right up with the best of them. He also feels that the colt was given far less credit than he deserved and, after Troy had won the Benson and Hedges Gold Cup at York, he lambasted members of the press for not, in his view, doing Troy justice.

Hern and Carson, who won the race six times, were also on the mark with The Queen's Church Parade in 1980, but Carson was on the sidelines with a broken wrist when Petoski, who was to beat the Triple Crown winner Oh So Sharp in the King George the following season, got the better of 16-race winner Provideo in 1984. Joe Mercer, Carson's predecessor as Dick Hern's stable jockey, was the man on top that year.

Above: *The brilliant training career of Sir Noel Murless came to an end when he retired at the end of 1976. In that final season he trained the top two-year-old in Britain and Ireland in JO Tobin (here with Lester Piggott up) who was rated 5lb and more clear of his contemporaries. However, he did not get the chance to prove that rating the next year as he was sent to race in his native United States.*

Pat Eddery gained the first of his four wins in the Vintage Stakes in 1986, when Don't Forget Me became the longest-priced winner of the race at the time (at 7-1!), and the colt maintained the Vintage's classic-pointing reputation by winning the 2,000 Guineas at Newmarket and the Curragh the following year.

Don't Forget Me's victory had been one of only two years in which the favourite or joint favourite failed to win the Vintage Stakes, and the race has had a highly impressive strike rate for market leaders. No fewer than 18 favourites, including one joint favourite, were successful in the first 27 runnings of the race: a rate of more than 66%.

On a cautionary note, though, the first two runnings of the new century produced two of the three longest-priced winners in the race's history, with the 8-1 victory of Naheef in 2001 following the 12-1 success of No Excuse Needed the previous season. Since both of those winners were racing for members of the Maktoum family they were remarkable SPs, and suggested that the price worm might well be turning.

Pat Eddery has ridden 262 winners at Goodwood, more than double the tally of any of his contemporaries, with the first of them coming more than 30 years ago, when he was still a 3lb claimer and rode Mrs Hauksbee, trained by George Todd, to win a maiden race at the September 1970 meeting.

"I was always a big fan of Goodwood and the two-year-old races there. And I was always very keen on the Champagne Lanson Vintage Stakes because there was a case of champagne for the winning trainer - that was the chief incentive! We always thought of Troy as being a very good horse and, to an extent, we had already been thinking of him as a Derby horse. When he won the Vintage Stakes in 1978 he beat Ela-Mana-Mou, whom I trained later on when he won the King George. On Derby Day Troy was pretty well unbeatable, and he certainly looked it. He won very well in the King George and was a horse who needed a fair bit of work - that is why we ran him in the Benson & Hedges at York. I remember that I pretty well had to give the Weinstocks a written guarantee that he would win. But the horse needed the run and he won, so everyone was happy in the end. Well, everyone apart from the second.

DICK HERN, TRAINER, TROY

"Troy won the Vintage Stakes as a two-year-old, but I especially recall him winning at Goodwood in the Predominate Stakes before he won the Derby. It was my first ride back after twelve days off with a broken collarbone. I was grimacing with a bit of pain, but Troy was such a good horse that I had to get back for him, and I had a figure-of-eight bandage to hold my bone in position - the sort of thing you would not get away with nowadays."

WILLIE CARSON, JOCKEY, TROY

When Pat Eddery gained his second Vintage win on Undercut in 1987 he was in his first season as retained jockey for Prince Khalid Abdullah, a role which came to him, at least in part, after the controversial defeat of Dancing Brave in the 1986 Derby. Greville Starkey was widely - though in some views very unfairly - criticised for his riding of Dancing Brave at Epsom, and within not much more than two months Eddery had signed up for the Abdullah job.

The Vintage Stakes' second Derby winner was Dr Devious, who won the race for Robert Sangster, Peter Chapple-Hyam and Willie Carson in 1991. There had, though, been a major change of personnel by the time of Epsom the following summer with only Chapple-Hyam still involved.

Robert Sangster, who always takes a realistic view about the value of his horses and is prepared to sell if he is offered what he considers an acceptable price, had sold Dr Devious to the Italian owner Luciano Gaucci following Goodwood, and later Gaucci in turn passed the colt on to the American Jenny Craig. Mrs Craig was the owner of a very successful health food company and bought Dr Devious as a birthday present for her husband Sidney.

At Epsom, Willie Carson was claimed to ride Muhtarram for his retaining owner Sheikh Hamdan al Maktoum and so it was John Reid who came in for his first and, as it turned out, only Derby winner.

Sadly, by the end of the 1990s Sangster and Chapple-Hyam had gone their separate ways, with the trainer leaving Sangster's superb estate at Manton in Wiltshire and trying his hand in Hong Kong.

Mark Johnston has been a major fan of Goodwood since the start of his training career and his three Goodwood Cup victories with Double Trigger have to be high in everyone's memory. He had his first winner at the course with The Can Can Man in the SIS Handicap in May 1991 and his first big race victory when Mister Baileys won the Vintage Stakes two years later.

Mister Baileys went on to give Johnston his first classic victory when he won the 2,000 Guineas the next season, and many felt that they had seen another future Newmarket and/or Epsom hero when Alhaarth won in 1995, providing a final Vintage strike for Dick Hern and Willie Carson. Alhaarth, though, did not live up to those expectations the following year when his form was good rather than brilliant and he had to wait until his seventh run of the year before his first win.

To end on a somewhat off-beat note, you would not normally go to Goodwood in July expecting to see a future Grand National winner taking part, but those who went to the 1960 meeting had just such an opportunity.

At that time the last race on the Thursday was the Arundel Castle Private Sweepstakes, which soon became known - jokingly, and rather unjustly - as the Arundel Castle Private Carve-Up, in spite of the fact that in its short existence it produced at least its fair share of shock results.

The race was first run in 1947, when owners qualified to have runners if they had ever been the guests of the Duke and Duchess of Norfolk at Arundel Castle for the four days of the meeting. The race was for two-year-olds who had cost not more than 500 guineas at auction, and it was discontinued after

Above: *Goodwood is not normally a rehearsal stage for future Grand National winners. Those who saw Flag Of Convenience finish third in the now defunct Arundel Castle Private Sweepstakes of 1960 may not have anticipated him changing his name to Anglo and becoming the Grand National winner six years later, when he was ridden by Tim Norman.*

1965 when the chances of buying a reasonable horse for such a modest sum were regarded as too unlikely to be feasible.

Major-General Sir Randle Feilden, who was for many years one of racing's top administrators, ran his horse Flag Of Convenience in the 1960 race. Flag Of Convenience ran respectably to finish third, but clearly was not very good and, having been beaten in a selling race later in the year, was sold to John Nichols, who trained jumpers under permit on his Huntingdon farm. Flag of Convenience ran once for his new owner-trainer, finishing unplaced in a novice hurdle in June 1962, but he must have shown something to somebody as the next time he appeared he was owned by the film-making team of Nat Cohen and Stuart Levy and was trained by Ryan Price.

As well as having new owners and trainer, he also had a new name and was now known as Anglo. In those days, and until 1969, it was permitted to change a horse's name, the only stipulation being that Anglo had to be identified as 'Anglo (late Flag of Convenience)' on the first two occasions that he ran under his new name.

Anglo progressed through the jumping ranks and, one dreary afternoon in March 1966, now trained by Ryan Price's former stable jockey Fred Winter and ridden by Tim Norman, he dominated the racing headlines as the 50-1 winner of the Grand National. A far cry from the Arundel Castle Private Carve-Up!

CHARACTERS OF THE COURSE

In the two hundred years of its existence, the Goodwood Racecourse has attracted its fair share of personalities - both equine and human. The latter category includes a number of people who brought along with them a wide variety of talents, energies, virtues and vices, and who made significant contributions to the colour and individuality of proceedings at the course. They are as much a part of Goodwood as panamas and Pimm's.

One of the most influential reformers of the turf that we have ever seen was a man once described in the *West Sussex Gazette* as "a model of manly beauty, quick of eye and action". He was Lord George Bentinck, the younger son of the Duke of Portland, and he was born in 1802, the year that Goodwood held its inaugural race meeting - a fitting start in life for a man who played such a large part in the development of the racecourse.

He was passionate about racing, a passion neither shared nor appreciated by his autocratic father, who tried in vain to keep the young Lord George from the turf. After a disastrously expensive St Leger (he managed to lose £26,000), his father bought him an estate in Ayrshire in the hope that he would retire quietly to the Borders.

However, this simply was not going to happen and Lord George went on to be a highly influential senior steward of the Jockey Club as well as following a successful career as a politician. In his early twenties he was private secretary to his uncle, George Canning (who was then foreign secretary and later, for a handful of months in 1827, Prime Minister). Bentinck entered parliament in 1828 and in the 1840s - with the support of Benjamin Disraeli - led Tory opposition to Sir Robert Peel.

Lord George's racing debut was at Goodwood when, aged 22, he rode his first winner, in the Cocked Hat Stakes. In this, not the most serious of races, the riders were required to start the race wearing silk jackets (which the unprepared novice had hastily run up by a ladies' maid at Cowdray) and a military hat of the day – they were also required to finish the race thus attired. The first three riders past the post had to still be wearing their hats and, on this occasion, it took Lord George three attempts to secure a win. The race was run in three heats and he won the third, and deciding, heat on Olive.

Left: *Lord George Bentinck was one of the most powerful and authoritative figures in British racing in the nineteenth century. His racing partnership with the 5th Duke, and his patronage of the Goodwood stables, largely contributed to making Goodwood the racecourse it is today.*

Above: *The 5th Duke of Richmond (1791-1860) made wide-ranging and beneficial changes to the course. It was during his tenure that Goodwood gained its respect as a course. This was largely through an extensive knowledge and love of racing, as well as the financial windfall to the family that came from his maternal grandfather, the Duke of Gordon.*

As senior steward of the Jockey Club Lord George made it his personal mission to oust all villainy and dodgy dealings from the turf (although he was happy to pull a stroke himself if it suited him). He tightened up all the rules surrounding weighing in and weighing out and even turned detective himself when he felt that the winner of the Derby was not all that he seemed. The 1844 Derby had been officially won by the three-year-old Running Rein - all Derby entrants, of course, must be three-year-olds. Lord George's instincts proved to be correct. Running Rein was in fact a four-year-old ringer named Maccabaeus who had been dyed to assume the guise of a three-year-old contender.

In a weak attempt to disguise the depth of his involvement from his father, Lord George formed racing partnerships, so that many of his horses ran under someone else's colours. The two most famous of these partners were Charles Greville (who was a cousin of Lord George's and the Duke of York's racing manager) and the 5th Duke of Richmond. In 1836 there was a spectacular falling out with Greville when Lord George believed that his cousin had sabotaged a horse that they jointly owned in favour of a horse that Greville owned outright. This feud was to last for a decade; it was during this time that he formed a very close partnership with the 5th Duke. Between the two of them they put Goodwood at the very cutting edge of racing.

Lord George is responsible for a great many innovations in racing that are taken for granted today, including the parade ring and public saddling, and it was his idea to have numbers on racecards and a number board. He also significantly improved starting techniques. In earlier days the starter would simply yell "Go!" and the horses would be off - rarely at the same time. Lord George introduced the use of the starting flag, which must have come as a relief to the Goodwood starter, who suffered from a speech impediment. He introduced different priced enclosures (including a roped-off smoking area "lest it offended the ladies") and fined the clerk of the course if the races did not start on time. This string of innovations shook up the racing world and due to Lord George's association with Goodwood, these reforms were always seen first there.

In 1841 he decided to move his horses to Goodwood and turned his not inconsiderable energies to improving the stables. He laid the Halnaker gallops (still in use today) with the nineteenth-century equivalent of all-weather terrain. In pursuit of the perfect gallops he spent £2,000 on bone dust alone, but it was money well spent as this meant that horses could train all year round while other stables were at the mercy of the vagaries of the English weather.

Left: *Charles Greville was a cousin of Lord George Bentinck, and one of the friends with whom he formed an owning partnership. That was until they had a ferocious row that turned into a vitriolic feud which lasted for the next ten years.*

Bentinck was instrumental in re-laying parts of the racecourse and adding 400 yards to the finishing straight. Apart from the racing advantages of this, it put Trundle Hill right in the action and made it the perfect vantage point from which to watch the racing. This was the true birth of the Trundle. The Duke was running the meetings at a loss and so it is possible that Lord George either paid for many of these improvements or lent the Duke the money. It would have made no odds to him. He was an extremely wealthy man, and he adored Goodwood.

The Richmond/Bentinck owning partnership was a phenomenal success. At their peak in 1845 they recorded 82 winners, although much to Lord George's chagrin the Derby eluded him. It was at this time that Lord George felt it was time to devote himself solely to politics. Having been the MP for King's Lynn for some time, he was asked to become leader of the Protectionists and knew that the post would allow no other mistress. Bentinck offered his horses to anyone at the Goodwood house party who would pay £10,000. George Payne took out an option to buy for £300, to expire at noon the next day. Not recognising the racing bargain of the century, he paid the forfeit, and Edward Mostyn, another guest at the house, stepped in and bought the horses.

Overleaf: *George Stubbs' painting from the Goodwood collection: 'Racehorses Exercising on the Downs at Goodwood'. It is a measure of the 3rd Duke's precocious interest in art, science and horses that he was only 24 when he commissioned Stubbs to paint three canvases in 1759-60; the others depict 'Shooting At Goodwood' and 'The Charlton Hunt'. Until the publication of Eadweard Muybridge's* Animal Locomotion *in 1887, artists were unable to visualise the action of galloping, hence the rocking-horse posture of the three horses on the left, which are carrying the yellow and red livery of the Duke of Richmond.*

By buying Bentinck's string of horses, Mostyn had - at one fell swoop - acquired some of the most impressive horses of the time, including Surplice who went on to win the Derby in 1848 (although by then he had sold the horse to Lord Clifton). On the evening of Surplice's victory, Disraeli found Lord George slumped in the House of Commons. He explained that his horror came from missing out on winning the Derby and asked if Disraeli knew what the Derby was. Disraeli replied, "It is the blue riband of the turf." The dejected Lord George corrected him. "No, it is the blue riband of life."

Probably the most telling story about the colourful Lord George was of how Elis won the 1836 St Leger at very long odds, ensuring that, as his owner, Bentinck pocketed not only the purse but £12,000 from his bet. Horses had to travel to the race meeting on foot, so everyone always knew which horse was on the move and when. When Elis did not appear to have left Goodwood a mere four days before the St Leger, it seemed that the horse would not have a prayer of walking the 200 miles and then being a contender. As the race drew nearer, the odds lengthened to 12-1 – extremely long odds considering that Elis was such a good horse. The day arrived, and Elis looked fresh as a daisy and, much to everyone's amazement, waltzed the race. This had been achieved with what was probably the prototype of the first-ever horsebox. A box of sorts, constructed by a local coachbuilder had been pulled north by alternative horsepower, leaving Elis ready to race and a bamboozled betting public and racing fraternity none the wiser.

Below: *'Elis' by Abraham Cooper. When Lord George Bentinck wanted to sneak his horse, Elis, up to the St Leger, he had built what was probably the prototype of the horse box. Elis became the first horse to be chauffeured to a race, rather than being walked there, and so arrived in peak condition, going on to trounce the opposition.*

Left: *Caroline, Duchess of Richmond was the daughter of the 1st Marquess of Anglesey. It was said that Lord George Bentinck's bachelor status was attributable to the fact that he had always been secretly in love with the wife of his best friend, the 5th Duke, and no other woman had ever matched up to her.*

This great reformer of the turf died of a heart attack aged 46 while in the garden of Welbeck, his father's house. He had never married, and it was always rumoured that his one true love was the wife of his friend the Duke: Caroline, Duchess of Richmond. After his death Greville confirmed this in his diaries by saying that Lord George had "confessed his sentiments without disguise".

Unfortunately Bentinck was an unbearably arrogant and hypocritical man; consequently his reputation was much reviled in the racing world. This seems somewhat unfair, as he certainly did more good than bad, and something was irrevocably lost from Goodwood when Lord George Bentinck died.

For many years there was one particular character who was as familiar a face at Goodwood (and indeed at many other racecourses) as the Prince of Wales himself. He was Hugh Lowther, the 5th Earl of Lonsdale. That was his formal title, but he was also known as 'the Sporting Earl' or 'the Yellow Earl'.

Overleaf: *Lillie Langtry, who won the Goodwood Cup as an owner with Merman (inset) in 1899. She used the pseudonym 'Mr Jersey', as the convention of the time was that ladies did not own racehorses.*

The most beautiful girl in Jersey also became known as 'The Goddess of Goodwood'. With her perfect classic features, tiny waist and impeccably contrived hats, Lillie Langtry was a great favourite at Goodwood Racecourse, where in the late 1870s the Prince of Wales paraded her quite openly: she was his first recognised mistress. A dark, smouldering and violet-eyed beauty, Lillie was also intelligent and humorous, so that people flocked to meet her. It is extraordinary to think of this free and relaxed behaviour happening in contrast to Queen Victoria's serious and moralistic court. Even Princess Alexandra put up with her from afar.

However, the 6th Duke was quite strict and we do not know if she ever came into Goodwood House; we do not think that she ever stayed here. She was obviously happy about the arrangements because long after her affair with the Prince was over, she came back to race at Goodwood, now as the owner 'Mr Jersey'. She remained friends with the Prince and even attended his Coronation.

ROSEMARY BAIRD

***Above:** The Earl of Lonsdale was a great lover of both racing and boxing. Sadly his love of the former also extended to a passion for spending money on it, and given the exuberance of his extravagances he managed to drain away the Lowther fortune during his lifetime.*

Lord Lonsdale was a highly colourful character in more ways than one. Canary yellow was his colour and he painted all his possessions in the vibrant shade. His racing colours were canary yellow, his tie was always canary yellow, his carriages were canary yellow, and of course, his liveried servants were always resplendent in canary yellow. Boxing was his first sporting love (hence the Lonsdale belts, which he created as president of the National Sporting Club), with racing running a close second. He was senior steward of the Jockey Club towards the end of his life, although while on the course, he never placed a bet. This showed remarkable restraint in a man who was totally over-the-top in all other areas of his life, and stemmed from an experience early in his life. As a young man he had managed to lose the huge sum of £18,000 in one single card game. This was before he inherited the vast Lowther fortunes and he was in no position to get his hands on that kind of money. Defaulting on this debt would have meant certain and irrevocable social death, but he was bailed out by Lord Calthorpe and the Yellow Earl's honour was rescued. He never bet again.

The Lowther fortune was one of the most substantial in the country and when he inherited, his disposable income was the equivalent of £3.5 million per year. The dissipated Earl set about spending it with great style and flourish. He always had to have the biggest and best of everything, and he generally got it. When he travelled, he would have two first class carriages in the train reserved - one would be for him, the other for his dogs. Even his trademark cigar had to be fatter and longer than anyone else's. To that end he had six-inch cigars handcrafted especially for him and named 'Lonsdales', a vanity that cost him £3,000 a year. Even the Lowther monies could not keep pace with the spendthrift Earl and it was during his life that the family estates were steadily sold off. Even the hub of the family, Lowther Castle, was forced to close.

Lonsdale was a close friend of George V's, and with his love of horses, was an ideal candidate to be of Master of the Horse, a position he coveted. However, his friend's famed caution blocked the appointment and George was to lament, "I should really like to have Hugh, the only trouble is that I could never afford him."

The Earl shared a slightly more complex relationship with George's father, Edward VII – they also shared Lillie Langtry. There is a much-repeated story that the two paramours are purported to have bumped into each other in the darkened corridors at Goodwood while both were trying to find the rooms of the notorious actress (although the anecdote has never been substantiated). Lillie was also the cause of a very public and humiliating incident that took place in Hyde Park. Mrs Langtry was riding with Lord Lonsdale when she stopped to talk to another 'suitor', Sir George Chetwynd. Lord Lonsdale took great exception to this, and insults and whip lashes were traded. The sparring rivals fell from their horses and continued their unseemly scuffle in the park dust before the pair were pulled apart by the Duke of Portland and Sir William Gordon Cumming.

The Yellow Earl's antics and extravagances were the lifeblood of society gossip, but his charm always won through for him in the end. One year while staying at Goodwood (he would always demand the royal apartments if no member of the royal family were staying) he received a telegram from his wife. The telegram was terse, simply stating "Will meet the 11.45am train - be on it!" The Duchess slipped it under the door of the tapestry drawing room having already read the telegram and so was surprised to be told by the ever-winsome Earl, "I have had a communication from my wife, in which she particularly requests to be remembered to you." Racecourses were a much paler and more subdued place when the Earl died in 1944.

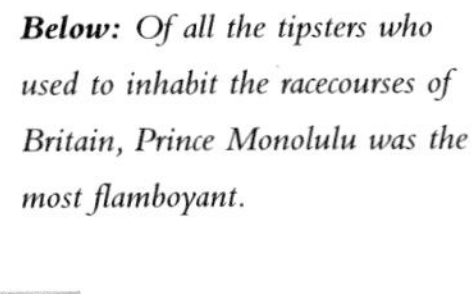

***Below:** Of all the tipsters who used to inhabit the racecourses of Britain, Prince Monolulu was the most flamboyant.*

Tipsters have always been an integral part of racing and, before the days of newspaper and radio tipsters, the tipsters themselves would travel from course to course. They were as much a part of any race day as the bookies or the jockeys and would roam the enclosures touting for business and selling their tips for tuppence a time. During the first half of the twentieth century the most colourful of these was a giant of a man: a self-styled prince who stood over seven feet tall and was a familiar figure towering over eager punters as he cried "I gotta horse."

He went by the name of Prince Monolulu and proclaimed himself an Abyssinian prince who had been born on the banks of the Zambezi. His real name was Peter Carl McKay and the story

goes that he was born on the less exotic banks of the Thames. Whatever, he was a stylish, larger-than-life figure whose clothes certainly helped him stand out from his fellow tipsters. On his head he would wear an outrageous feathered headdress (which seemed to have taken its fashion influence from the American Indians) which he matched with jodhpurs and spats and finished off with a variety of colourful capes. His favoured accessory was his ubiquitous umbrella. Although his tips were as hit and miss as the next man's, he was a born showman and each punter would be given a full spiel of amusing nonsense that came free with each tip. Archie Long, whose brother was a groom at Goodwood, thought that it was the other way around. "He certainly could talk, and he sold a lot of tips with his stories." Monolulu soon became a household name (which without the help of radio and television was quite something) and the Prince with his ringing cry of "Roast beef of old England" became a much-loved regular at Goodwood. His appearance would even merit a mention in the local press. In 1928, the *West Sussex Gazette* reported that "the Abyssinian Prince whose tall, black figure with a crown of fuzzy hair is the most picturesque among the tipsters, was on the hill in form, ready to offer advice in English or French indiscriminately." He was thought to be in his eighties when he died in 1965.

***Above:** Bernard, the 16th Duke of Norfolk, managed to persuade the 9th Duke of Richmond to allow him to hold a race called the Arundel Castle Private Sweepstakes, a rather elite affair open only to guests of the Arundel house party.*

Arundel Castle is a stone's throw from Goodwood and Arundel and the Norfolk family have always played an active part in Goodwood's history. This was especially true during the life of Bernard, the 16th Duke of Norfolk. He almost felt that Goodwood was his own private course - it was nearly in his backyard after all - and every year he would telephone Freddie, the 9th Duke of Richmond, and arrange to come over the week before the festival in order to walk the course. As the two Dukes walked and talked, the Duke of Norfolk would advise the 9th Duke on how the following week's races should be run, and he certainly had quite a say in one of the races. In 1947 he managed to persuade the 9th Duke to allow him to have his own race at the July meeting. The Arundel Castle Private Sweepstakes was only open to those who were part of the Arundel house party. There were a number of other restrictions: the race was only for two-year-olds, which had to have been bought as yearlings at private auction and not one was allowed to cost a penny over 500 guineas. The race was a particular favourite with the punters as, barring an act of God, the most expensive horse in the field generally romped home first.

The Norfolks were very successful owners and had a famed set of stables at Arundel. Indeed, being an owner once left the Duchess of Norfolk with an interesting dilemma of etiquette. The Duchess was watching the Gordon Stakes with the Queen. Gordon Richards was riding Gay Time for Her Majesty (it was on this occasion that commentators swore that Richards lowered his head in a neat little bow as he thundered passed the royal box) and no doubt the Duchess felt that she should cheer on - albeit demurely! - her companion's horse. This must have been somewhat frustrating for her as the horse that Gay Time was beating and did beat was Tarr Steps, the Duchess's own horse.

The Queen and Prince Philip used to stay at Arundel for the races every alternate year. During the week of Glorious Goodwood, the Norfolks would hold a huge charity ball at the castle that became a fixture of the racing week. The castle would be floodlit and thrown open to some 1,500 guests - the event was always a successful fundraiser for one of the Duchess's charities, especially in the years when the young Queen was staying at the castle. Tickets were meant to be sold at £4, but due to an impromptu black market they were changing hands for £10 a piece. Partying aside, the racing remained the most important part of the week. When Prince Philip was staying at Goodwood one year he remarked, "You know, the difference between staying here and at Arundel is a remarkable thing. When we stay at Arundel and you arrive down at breakfast, you can read any paper you like, except the *Sporting Life* as everybody is reading the *Sporting Life*. When you come to Goodwood, you can only have the *Sporting Life* as everybody is reading all the other papers."

The name of Macdonald-Buchanan is another that was associated with Goodwood throughout the twentieth century, with three generations of Macdonald-Buchanans serving as stewards. The family's connection with Goodwood started one generation further back with Lord Woolavington.

***Below:** Sir Reginald Macdonald-Buchancan. For three generations there have been Macdonald-Buchanans stewarding at Goodwood, a tradition that was started by Sir Reginald. With his wife Catherine, he created the influential Lavington stud.*

Above: *Assistant Clerk of the Course Seamus Buckley was previously at Epsom, where he saw 14 Derbys. Although he lived on the Goodwood course itself for six years, he still finds that the sheer beauty of the place can take him by surprise. "There is nowhere like Goodwood on a fine day - it is certainly the most beautiful racecourse in Europe, and probably the world."*

Previous pages: *Trundle Hill is a magnificent natural grandstand. For two centuries, racegoers have packed their picnics and walked up the hill to set up camp and watch the racing from their elevated vantage point.*

Lord Woolavington lived at Lavington Park, the beautiful Palladian house just over the hill from Goodwood. In the 1920s, when there was a small but powerful coterie of owners, Lord Woolavington was one of the most influential. His stud at Graffham was highly successful and he bred numerous good horses over the years (including two Derby winners). He passed his love of horses onto his only child Catherine; when she married Sir Reginald Macdonald-Buchanan the couple became a formidable racing duo, and Lavington was one of the country's leading studs. Their box at Goodwood was enormous (second in size only to the Richmond box) and was always filled with the very great and good of the racing world. It was in fact the box that Queen Alexandra and her ladies had escaped to during the reign of Edward VII, and sat at the furthest end of the grandstand. Sir Reginald and Lady Macdonald-Buchanan did not live at Lavington, but at Cottesbroke Hall in Northamptonshire. Therefore, for one week every July they would pack up their racing lives and move to Lavington for their famed racing house parties. After Goodwood, they transferred their retinue onto Cowes before heading north to Scotland.

There is one other character of the course that has looked over and participated in all the proceedings for the last two hundred years. This is Trundle Hill, the most glorious free grandstand in the history of racing. When Lord George Bentinck added the extra 400 yards to the finishing straight in the 1830s, the Trundle came into its own with its marvellous view overlooking the entire racecourse, especially the parade ring and the winner's enclosure (this was true up until 1967 when the parade ring was moved). Racegoers and holidaymakers visiting the Sussex coast would stream up there and set up camp, with all manner of small businesses seeing an opportunity to make a few bob. In 1948 a local farrier, Tom Hood, took advantage of the impracticability of female footwear and rather than re-shoeing horses spent the week re-shoeing women whose heels had snapped off on the rough ground. He found that he was most in demand from those women who had naively chosen to wear "the wedge-heeled type".

During its heyday, the Trundle was *the* place to be. When Goodwood's record one-day crowd of 55,000 turned up in 1953, well over a third were up on the hill. One observer commented, "You couldn't have dropped a pin on there without it falling on someone's head." Although in the last 20 years the majority of racegoers have upgraded themselves, and attendance on the Trundle is now numbered in hundreds rather than thousands, the Trundle is as much a part of the character of Goodwood as linen suits, strawberries and champagne.

Right: *Ralph Hubbard (left in photograph) was the highly respected and popular Clerk of the Course and agent at Goodwood from 1939 to 1978. He was no stranger to the course, having been brought up there as his father Gerald was also clerk of the course. As a boy he was sent to Eton, where he excelled both in his studies and his sport: he was* victor ludorum *and keeper of the field. Although he hankered after being a land agent he briefly became a stockbroker. The world of finance proved not to be for him, so he began to study under his father. When his father had to have a leg amputated, Ralph succeeded him in the job and played an instrumental role in moulding Goodwood into the racecourse it is today.*

THE SUSSEX STAKES

The Sussex Stakes, run on the second day of the Glorious Goodwood meeting, is one of the major mile races of the year and has enjoyed Group 1 status since the Pattern of Racing was introduced in 1971. The midsummer mile championship of Great Britain, it links in with the Prix Jacques le Marois at Deauville which takes place two or three weeks later, and with the Prix du Moulin de Longchamp and the Queen Elizabeth II Stakes at Ascot later in the year.

The Sussex Stakes of today is a significantly different event from the version first staged in 1841. In fact, had the race continued in its initial guise it is highly unlikely that it would have reached its current status.

When first introduced over a century and a half ago, the Sussex Stakes was a race for two-year-olds, but it was received with a marked lack of enthusiasm by both owners and trainers. During its 37-year existence under the original format the race was uncontested on no fewer than 25 occasions, and on 14 of those when a horse *did* turn up for the race there was only one runner and so the result was a walkover. Even allowing for the fact that walkovers are much more unusual nowadays than they were in the nineteenth century, that still represents a huge proportion.

***Above:** Another major success for Michael Tabor and Mick Kinane as Among Men takes the Sussex Stakes of 1998.*

Consequently, the format was changed in 1878 and the Sussex Stakes became a mile race for three-year-olds. It was not long before the race started to attract the quality of horses with which it is now associated as a Group 1 event. In 1885 the winner was Paradox, owned by the American Broderick Cloete and trained by John Porter, who was based at Kingsclere in Hampshire and was very much involved in the establishment of the course at Newbury.

Porter had paid 700 guineas for Paradox as a yearling and at first owned him in partnership with a certain Captain Bowler until, on the strength of a very good gallop before his planned debut in the Middle Park Plate at

GOODWOOD RACECOURSE
1999
MEMBER

Newmarket, the colt was taken over by the first Duke of Westminster for the then considerable sum of £6,000. To put that amount of money in perspective, the winning owner's prize for the Derby at the time was £4,900.

Unfortunately for the Duke, Paradox was very disappointing in that first race and his new owner, advised by the 'expert friends' who are always around at such moments, decided that he would run no more in the Duke's yellow jacket and black cap. Paradox was passed on to Mr Cloete, who had only recently become one of John Porter's patrons, and the Duke felt he had done very much the right thing.

It did not take long, however, for the new owner to be rather happier than the vendor as Paradox romped home in the Dewhurst Plate of 1884 and the following year, starting at 3-1 on and ridden by Fred Archer, won the 2,000 Guineas. He was just pipped in the Derby by the Archer-ridden Melton, but after that, apart from the Sussex Stakes, he also won the Grand Prix de Paris, the Champion Stakes and the Free Handicap. In those days the senior Free Handicap was every bit as much a race as the junior version - run at the Craven meeting for the previous season's two-year-olds - is now.

Twenty-one years were to pass before another colt of comparable merit to Paradox won the Sussex Stakes. This was Troutbeck, who, rather ironically, belonged to the second Duke of Westminster, the grandson of the man who had temporarily owned Paradox.

Below: *Wool Winder won the Sussex Stakes of 1907, when his only defeat in nine races came when he was third in the Derby. He was later acquired by a syndicate from Austria and went on to a successful stud career in Czechoslovakia.*

Above: *Minoru - ridden by Herbert Jones - was the last of three Derby winners owned by King Edward VII, and the most recent to triumph at Epsom when racing for the reigning monarch, He won the Sussex Stakes in the year of his Epsom victory, 1909, but was later exported to Russia where he disappeared during the revolution of 1917.*

Troutbeck was one of the very best colts of his generation as he won seven other races in 1906, headed by the St Leger, and his only defeat in nine starts as a three-year-old was when he was third to Spearmint in the Derby.

The second Duke of Westminster did not enjoy racing and breeding in the same way as his grandfather had done, but he had some other notable victories including another Sussex Stakes with Hurry Off in 1923 and the 2,000 Guineas in 1941 with Lambert Simnel. Following the Duke's death, his fourth wife, Anne, Duchess of Westminster, owned the outstanding Arkle, the greatest steeplechaser of all time.

Wool Winder, who won the Sussex Stakes in 1907, had a very similar record to Troutbeck as he was beaten only in the Derby as a three-year-old. But whereas Troutbeck lost at Epsom simply because he was not good enough on the day, Wool Winder was involved in a collision with another runner on the hill down to Tattenham Corner. As a result he was last of all turning for home, and although he made up a lot of ground in the straight he was still two lengths behind the victorious Orby at the line.

He won the St Leger that same year, but in the next two seasons he was able to run only three times, and failed to win. Subsequently he enjoyed considerable success at stud when bought by a syndicate from Austria.

Wool Winder's owner was Brigadier-General 'Ned' Baird, who had been a member of the Jockey Club for 62 years by the time of his death in 1956.

Overleaf: *All to play for in the closing stages of the 1993 Sussex Stakes before Bigstone (with the noseband, Dominique Boeuf) gets the better of the 1,000 Guineas heroine Sayyedati (extreme right), who was to take the prize herself two years later. Odds-on Zafonic (pink cap) finishes only seventh.*

Wool Winder was the best horse he ever owned, but he had also won the 1888 Grand National with the half-bred black 40-1 chance Playfair.

The Sussex Stakes received the royal accolade in 1909 with victory for Minoru, who was the third and last Derby winner for King Edward VII (following Persimmon in 1896 and Diamond Jubilee in 1900) and the only one of the trio to triumph at Epsom when his owner was on the throne. Minoru later had a brief stud career in Ireland where his mating with the mare Gondolette began the line which resulted in due course in such top racehorse/sires as Hyperion, Mossborough and Sickle. Later Minoru was exported to Russia - and there is a mystery about what happened to him after that. He disappeared during the revolution of 1917 and there was a story that at one time he and the 1913 Derby winner Aboyeur were harnessed to a cart and driven several hundred miles to the Black Sea and thence to Serbia.

It is a general rule of thumb in racing that horses with inelegant names are not very good, although there are inevitably exceptions. One such was the 1910 Sussex Stakes winner Winkipop, who also won the 1,000 Guineas and the Coronation Stakes and was the ancestress of Oaks winner Pennycomequick, 2,000 Guineas winner Court Martial and the successful sire Wilwyn; her trainer William Waugh was also responsible for Troutbeck.

The 1911 winner Stedfast won 19 races apart from the Sussex Stakes, including the Jockey Club Stakes and the Coronation Cup, but his stud career was one of limited success, in contrast to that of Tracery, who was victorious in 1912 and later sired the Derby winner Papyrus, Black Panther (who won the 2,000 Guineas), and a number of other successful horses.

Tracery, who was bred in the United States, was running in England for the very first time when he was third to the filly Tagalie in the 1912 Derby. Later that year he won the St Leger and the St James's Palace Stakes, and as a four-year-old landed the Champion Stakes and the Eclipse Stakes.

In 1914 the winner was the talented but bad-tempered Black Jester, whose other good days included victories in the St Leger and the Coronation Cup. He had also won the Richmond Stakes the previous year, when he went to Goodwood as a two-year-old.

There was then a long spell, including the First World War (during which there was no racing at Goodwood from 1915 through to 1918), when the winners of the Sussex Stakes were of no great significance. The high-level thread was picked up once again by Dastur in 1932. He had the very frustrating experience - for his owner and trainer even if not for him! - of being second in all three colts' classics as well as in the Free Handicap and the Champion Stakes. It was not, however, all a case of 'so near and yet so far', as he won the Irish Derby, the King Edward VII Stakes, the Coronation Cup and the Champion Stakes. Dastur was the first of three winners in four years for the combination of the Aga Khan and Frank Butters, who also won in this spell with Badruddin and Hairan. There were, however, three different jockeys on the winners, with Michael Beary riding Dastur, Freddie Fox on Badruddin and Dick Perryrnan on Hairan.

***Left:** Landau was the last horse Sir Gordon Richards ever rode in a race. They were third in the 1954 Eclipse Stakes at Sandown and Sir Gordon's mount in the next race reared and fell on him as they were leaving the paddock, causing the injuries which forced him into retirement. In his absence Willie Snaith rode The Queen's horse to Sussex Stakes success.*

Gordon Richards then became the dominant factor of the next eleven years (racing at Goodwood was suspended from 1940 to 1945) as he won the Sussex Stakes on no fewer than seven occasions. No one apart from him and Charlie Smirke had a look-in for seven years after racing resumed at the end the Second World War.

The first of this sequence was Radiotherapy, who had been third in the Derby and, amazingly, was the longest-priced winner for the next nine years when he started at 7-4. The 1949 winner Krakatao had only one opponent and went off at 11-2 on, and My Babu, who was one of Charlie Smirke's two winners during that period, was a 3-1 on shot in 1948.

My Babu and the 1950 winner Palestine were both also successful in the 2,000 Guineas before their Goodwood triumphs - a feat later repeated by Brigadier Gerard in 1971 and the Italian-owned and ridden (Carlo d'Alessio and Gianfranco Dettori, father of Frankie, respectively) pair of Bolkonski and Wollow in 1975 and 1976, both horses trained by Henry Cecil.

Landau, who carried The Queen's colours to victory in 1954, would have been another Sussex winner for Sir (as he had by then become) Gordon Richards. He was in fact the last horse that Richards rode in a race when they were third in the Eclipse Stakes 18 days later. Sir Gordon was to have ridden a two-year-old filly called Abergeldie in the race after the Eclipse, but she threw and fell on him as they were leaving the paddock, fracturing his pelvis and causing the injuries which forced him into premature retirement. In his absence Willie Snaith rode Landau, a third Sussex winner in six years for Noel Murless.

"I RODE AGAINST GORDON RICHARDS FOR ABOUT FIVE OR SIX YEARS BEFORE HE RETIRED, AND HE WAS ALWAYS VERY COMPETITIVE. I REMEMBER ONE DAY WHEN I WAS RIDING A HORSE CALLED TINTINNABULUM AT BATH AND I WAS ABSOLUTELY RUNNING AWAY WITH THE RACE. I COULD HAVE WON BY FIVE OR SIX LENGTHS, BUT I THOUGHT I WOULD TRY TO BE CLEVER AND BEAT THE HORSE GORDON WAS RIDING BY ONLY A SHORT HEAD. I WON THE RACE, AND IT WAS VERY CLOSE, SIMPLY BECAUSE GORDON WAS SO DETERMINED HE ALMOST CARRIED HIS HORSE OVER THE LINE. HE WAS AN EXTREMELY NICE MAN, ALTHOUGH HE WAS ALSO QUITE HIGHLY STRUNG AWAY FROM THE COURSE. ONCE AT THE TRACK HE WAS VERY CALM, AND ALWAYS KIND AND HELPFUL TO YOUNGER JOCKEYS LIKE ME."

JIMMY LINDLEY

"The greatest jockey of the first half of the twentieth century, Gordon Richards owed his unprecedented success to his single-minded determination to ride as many winners as possible no matter how much work was involved, his unquestionable integrity and a natural intelligence which would have earned him rewards in most other professions."

THE BIOGRAPHICAL ENCYCLOPEDIA OF BRITISH FLAT RACING

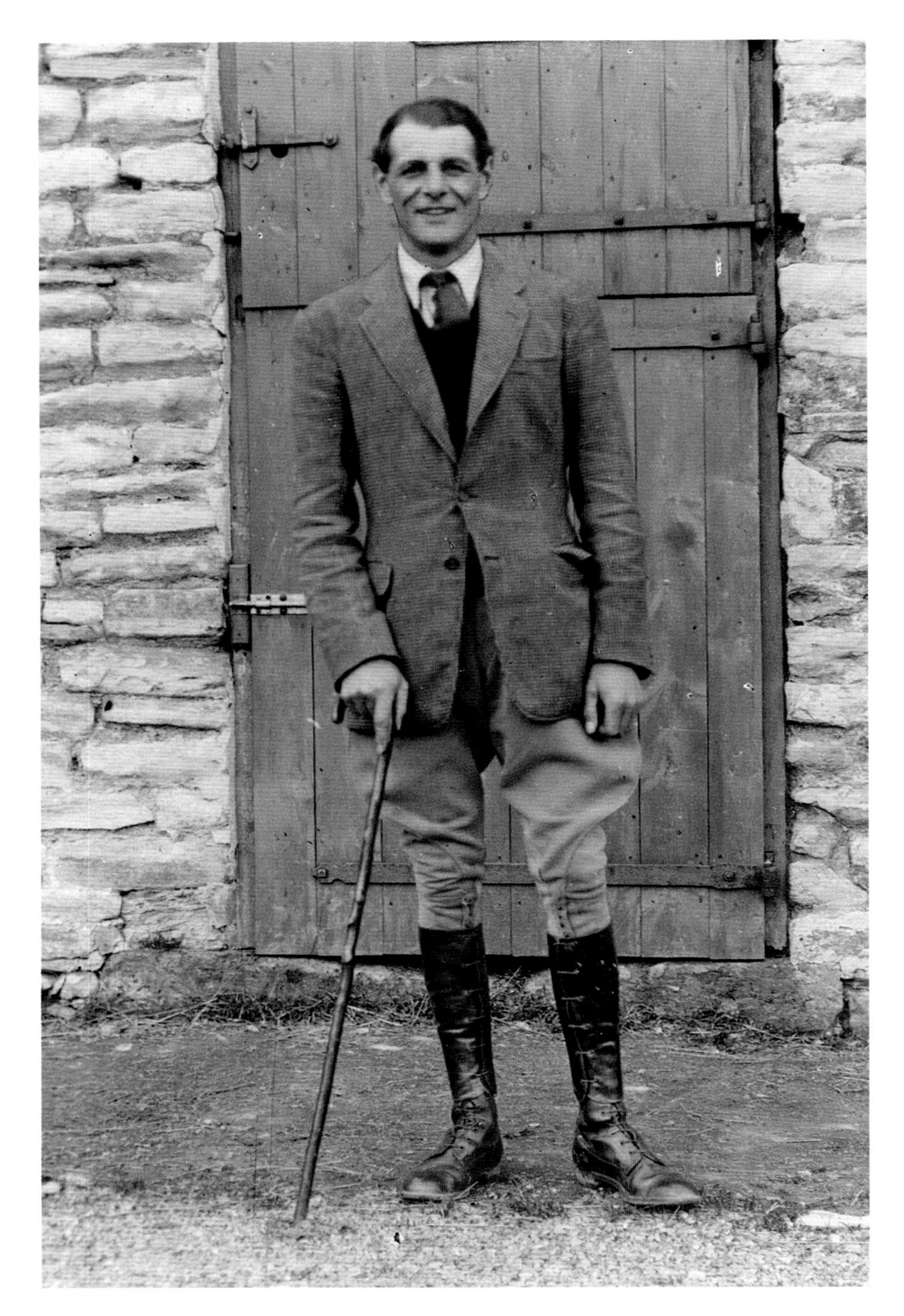

***Right:** Noel Murless was one of the outstanding trainers of his own or any era, and won just about every flat race worthy of the name. He began as a jump jockey and started training in North Yorkshire, gaining his first major success when Closeburn won the Stewards' Cup in 1947. During that year he was on a short list of three to take over from Fred Darling at Beckhampton; what clinched the decision for Darling was the fact that Murless, not his travelling head lad, carried the saddles from the weighing room to the saddling boxes.*

The 1957 winner Quorum was a rare big race success at Goodwood for his trainer Wilf Lyde and jockey Alec Russell. Although Russell is arguably best remembered for an afternoon earlier the same month when he rode the winners of all six races at the now defunct Scottish track of Bogside, near Ayr. Only Sir Gordon Richards before that, and Frankie Dettori afterwards, have been through the card at a flat race meeting in Britain.

Quorum also won the Free Handicap and the Jersey Stakes as well as being runner-up to Crepello in the 2,000 Guineas of 1957. He later sired some useful flat winners like Quartette and Beddard, but far and away the best known horse he produced was the triple Grand National hero Red Rum.

There was no shortage of quality among the winners of the Sussex Stakes around this time for after Quorum the next three were Major Portion, Petite Etoile and Venture VII. Major Portion and Venture VII were both runners-up in the 2,000 Guineas and gained wins respectively in the Queen Elizabeth II, St James's Palace and Middle Park Stakes on the one hand and the St James's Palace, Middle Park and Imperial Stakes on the other. Yet neither of them could equal the achievements of the outstanding Petite Etoile, the winner of 14 races including the 1,000 Guineas, the Oaks, the Yorkshire Oaks, the Champion Stakes and the Coronation Cup (twice). Sadly, like so many top-class racemares, she had a disastrous stud career.

While there was no lack of talent among the winners, there was a distinct shortage of runners. In no year from 1900 had there been a double-figure field; there were three consecutive years when only two horses took part, and one had to go back to 1925 to find a year in which full each-way betting was possible with a field of eight.

To avoid this problem it was decided in 1960 to open the race up to four-year-olds as well as the younger generation and two seniors, Sovereign Path and Ballylesson, ran behind Venture VII that year. Twelve months later the 100-7 chance Le Levanstell became the first four year-old to win the race when he beat Eagle and nine others.

Le Levanstell, one of three winners in six years who were trained in Ireland (he was trained by Seamus McGrath), went on to sire the Prix de l'Arc de Triomphe and Gold Cup-winner Levmoss, the top two-year-old My Swallow and the Prix de Diane heroine Sweet Mimosa.

The other Irish winners of this era were Carlemont and Paveh, trained by Paddy Prendergast and David Ainsworth respectively. Other winners of the early 1960s included Romulus, one of the many top horses for the US platinum tycoon Charles Engelhard (who also owned the Triple Crown winner Nijinsky), the race's longest-priced winner Queen's Hussar - whose 25-1 success was almost as big a shock as the fact that he managed to sire such a top-class horse as Brigadier Gerard - and the grey Roan Rocket, who cost only 1,800 guineas as a yearling and earned almost £35,000 in win money for his owner Tommy Frost.

On the whole, the welcome advent of larger fields did not prevent the Sussex Stakes from being an excellent race for favourites. Although there was a little rush of long-priced winners with Le Levanstall, Romulus and Queen's Hussar, there were only two occasions in the 14 years from 1967 through 1980 when the market leader was not successful.

Sir Gordon Richards, who had such a fine riding record in the race, gained his only success as a trainer with Reform in 1967, and Petingo, who won the following year, was the third win in the saddle for Lester Piggott. Earlier in the year Petingo had been second to Sir Ivor in the 2,000 Guineas with Jimmy Reppin in third place, but those placings were reversed later that season when Jimmy Reppin - in receipt of 6lb, admittedly - beat Petingo in the Wills Mile at Goodwood.

Jimmy Reppin, who won the Sussex Stakes in 1969, was later one of the victims of a ludicrous campaign for nominal correctness by *The Times*, whose executives decided that abbreviations and nicknames were to be taboo in their

"The Sussex Stakes is one of the most important all-aged mile events in Europe and certainly the highlight of the principal Goodwood meeting in terms of quality. The post-war roll call of success is impressive."

Jack Waterman,
The Punter's Friend

***Overleaf:** Kris (Joe Mercer), owned and bred by Lord Howard de Walden and trained by Henry Cecil, was one of the top milers of his time. He won 14 of 16 starts, including the 1979 Sussex Stakes, and later became a highly successful sire with classic winners Oh So Sharp, Unite and Rafha among his offspring.*

HC

Above: *Brigadier Gerard (Joe Mercer) was one of flat racing's fairytales. Unfashionably bred at the small stud of owners John and Jean Hislop, he established himself as one of the sport's true greats and was one of only two horses who beat the superb Mill Reef, which he did in the 2,000 Guineas of 1971. He won all but one of his 18 races, but sadly made no great impression at stud.*

hallowed pages. Names like Dick, Bob, Jim etc. were thus outlawed. Although Jimmy Reppin was officially registered with that name, as far as *The Times* was concerned he was James Reppin, which is how he appeared in their pages. Luckily it did not take long for the fatuity of such an idea to be exposed.

The first two winners of the 1970s were the very talented grey filly Humble Duty (the second of her sex and colour to win the race in 12 years, following Petite Etoile) and the outstanding Brigadier Gerard, who was beyond doubt one of the very best horses of the twentieth century, for all that his ability way outshone the potential of his pedigree and that the mating which produced him was a fluke.

His sire Queen's Hussar was a good horse, but one of the less distinguished winners of the Sussex Stakes - as is clear from his SP of 25-1 - and his dam La Paiva never won a race, though she had a good record as a broodmare. The story goes that the only reason that the mare went to the stallion was because their studs were close by and the mare's owners, John and Jean Hislop, were given a free nomination, rather discounting claims that the mating was the result of brilliant planning and analysis.

Whatever the finer points of that, the fact remains that Brigadier Gerard was an exceptional racehorse, beaten in only one of 18 starts with wins also taking in the 2,000 Guineas (in which he beat Mill Reef and My Swallow), the King George VI and Queen Elizabeth, the Eclipse and the Champion Stakes.

Ace Of Aces, whom TV commentator Jimmy Lindley rode to victory in the Sussex Stakes of 1974, was not one of the race's top winners, but his owner

Nelson Bunker Hunt is one of the more remarkable characters to have been involved in racing. At one time he had well over a hundred horses in training worldwide, most of them in his native United States, but also in England, Italy, Australia and New Zealand.

Bunker Hunt won top races with horses like the outstanding Dahlia and the Derby winners Empery and Youth, and at one time was the richest man in the entire United States. However, he and his brother tried to corner the world's silver market and, though they came very close to doing so, the whole venture came crashing down around them and Bunker Hunt went bankrupt. He has since returned to racing but at a much lower level.

After two surprises in the early 1980s from On The House (14-1) and Noalcoholic (16-1), who at six is to date the oldest winner of the race, things reverted to type with a series of short-priced winners, the first of which, in 1984, was the hugely charismatic Chief Singer, trained at Newmarket by the former jockey Ron Sheather.

Sheather never had a large string, but he knew a good horse when he saw one and he introduced Chief Singer in sensational fashion at Royal Ascot in 1983. Unfashionably bred and from a small stable, Chief Singer did not appear to be the sort of horse for a first-time-out gamble, but some knew better. He was backed at very fancy odds before winning the Coventry Stakes by four lengths at 20-1 and went on to bigger and better things.

Chief Singer was owned by Jeff Smith, whose company produced many parts for the interiors of aeroplanes. He has had horses in training for 25 years, owns the Littleton Stud in Hampshire and has also enjoyed much success with the splendid stayer Persian Punch, whose win in the 2001 Goodwood Cup was for many the highlight of that year's meeting.

Pat Eddery is the most successful current jockey in the race with five wins to his name, including one of the most exciting battles the Sussex Stakes has ever produced when the filly Marling just got the better of Selkirk in 1992. The previous year's winner Second Set was a close third, so that no horse has yet won the race more than once, although of course this could only have happened once the race had been opened up in 1960.

Only two horses above the age of four have won the race. The first was the six-year-old Noalcoholic, and in 1995 the prize fell to the five-year-old mare Sayyedati, who had won the 1,000 Guineas two years earlier. Sayyedati's trainer Clive Brittain began his racing life as an apprentice with (Sir) Noel Murless and worked for him as a lad for many years before setting up as a trainer in 1972. Brittain developed an oft-derided reputation for running horses in big races when they had no apparent chance, but his attacking policy has produced plenty of top dividends in races all over the world.

The win of Ali-Royal in 1997 was part of an excellent first season together for Henry Cecil and Kieren Fallon; few would have thought at the time that only two years to the day later the two men would have been standing in the Goodwood parade ring adjacent, but virtually speechless. On the day before the 1999 Sussex Stakes, in which Frankie Dettori gained his second win in the race

"I had been to Newbury a few times, but in all honesty I was not that interested in racing. Then Mum said to me, 'You must come to Goodwood and see this horse.' The horse was Kris, running in the Sussex Stakes. We went down to the one furlong marker. I could hear the jockeys shouting and the whips cracking, and the sound and the atmosphere really made an impression."

Clare Balding

Overleaf: *The battle of the nosebands, as the filly Marling (Pat Eddery) on the left just gets the better of the white-faced Selkirk (Ray Cochrane) in the brilliant finish to the Sussex Stakes of 1992.*

"It was an excellent race. I had Selkirk beaten, but he came back at me and went a head up. But Marling was so brave that she fought back in the last few strides and won by a head. She was very brave, a good little filly - certainly not over-big, but all guts. Goodwood is one of my favourite tracks; I have ridden well over 200 winners there. It is such a pretty place and a good track to ride on, although it can be tricky with all the ups and downs, and you have to be very careful to avoid getting trapped on the rail, especially in the big handicaps." PAT EDDERY, JOCKEY, MARLING

"They were two very high-class horses and it was a wonderful race, because they battled, not for as long as Bustino and Grundy in the King George, but all through the last two furlongs. First one was leading and then the other. Marling got her head in front and I think that we were coming back at her on the line. It was a great race and a shame that either of them had to lose. Selkirk was an absolutely top horse at the time so it was a bloody good performance on Marling's part. I think that really it was a fair result on the day. We were giving her 11lb as we were a four-year-old and she was a three-year-old filly, so even though it was weight for age and sex in a Group 1 race it was a lot of weight."

IAN BALDING, TRAINER, SELKIRK

Opposite: *Giant's Causeway was the 'iron horse' of 2000 when he battled to five Group 1 victories in a row, beginning with the St James's Palace Stakes at Royal Ascot and including the Sussex Stakes before he was beaten in the Queen Elizabeth II Stakes back at Ascot. All this came after he had been beaten in the 2,000 Guineas at Newmarket and the Curragh, prompting his trainer Aidan O'Brien to say he must have been too easy on him!*

Below: *Noverre (Frankie Dettori) had a rollercoaster of a season in 2001, of which his Sussex Stakes success was the highlight. The lows came when he failed a post-race test after 'winning' the Poule d'Essai des Poulains (the French 2,000 Guineas) and was disqualified, and when, following Sheikh Mohammed's description of him as "the best miler in Europe", he failed to win another race that year.*

when Godolphin's Aljabr made all the running and broke the track record, Cecil had sacked Fallon as his stable jockey among widespread rumours - constantly denied by the jockey - that he had had an affair with the trainer's then wife.

Aljabr tried his luck again in the 2000 running of the Sussex Stakes, but this time he could manage no better than fifth place as Giant's Causeway showed all his renowned battling qualities to get the better of Dansili. This was the third in a series of five consecutive Group 1 wins for Giant's Causeway, an achievement which no horse had managed since Mill Reef in 1971, and a series which came to a halt only when the colt was just beaten in the Queen Elizabeth II Stakes at Ascot that September.

The Godolphin team was back in pole position in 2001, though, when Noverre got the better of No Excuse Needed, taking revenge on Black Minnaloushe, who had just beaten him in the St James's Palace Stakes at Ascot but was only third this time. The result prompted Sheikh Mohammed to declare that Noverre was the best miler in Europe but, in the way that so often happens after such eulogies, Noverre did not win again and on his final appearance in England in 2001 was beaten by his 33-1 stablemate and presumed pacemaker Summoner in the Queen Elizabeth II Stakes.

The Sussex Stakes has come a very long way since its days of being a two-year-old race in which few were ever interested. Now it is on the agenda of any horse with pretensions to being regarded as the top miler in Europe, as its Group 1 status clearly indicates.

STEPPING FORWARD

As you walk towards the March Stand, which was opened by The Queen in 1980, it is impossible to miss the striking bronze statue of *The Horse*, which was created by Dame Elizabeth Frink and unveiled at the time the stand was opened. The statue is a brilliantly vivid reminder of why we all continue to assemble at Goodwood - to watch the cream of British racehorses competing at this beautiful Sussex venue.

The March Stand was one of the major features of the wholesale rebuilding programme which took place at Goodwood between 1976 and 1990, when all the facilities were vastly improved, so that racegoers could enjoy their visits in the comfortable conditions they deserve. In this era of ever fiercer competition for the leisure pound, it is imperative for racecourses to provide the very best facilities they can.

The new stand was the second major development in this period, following the re-siting of the weighing room and the parade ring four years earlier in 1976. Until then the parade ring had been situated at the extreme western end of the course so that racegoers in Tattersalls had a sabbath day's journey to reach it, and the weighing room was approximately where the Charlton Stand is now positioned.

Both were then moved to their current locations behind the main stand and thus became far more easily accessible. They have been there ever since, though both have been altered since that original switch. The most recent developments were the extra steppings around the parade ring and the building of the Kinrara Pavilion and the Double Trigger restaurant which were introduced in 2001. The much improved paddock viewing was very well received and the new pavilions also proved to be popular.

Above: *The maquettes which Dame Elizabeth Frink (right) used as she sculpted her masterful statue of* The Horse.

Incidentally, although Dame Elizabeth Frink was obviously best known for her expertise in the world of sculpture, she was no stranger to racing in its own right. She and her insurance broker husband Alex Csaky had a small stud with

"Goodwood is an inspirational place to call at. When you get up into the box and look across at the beautiful scenery of the Downs you feel it is a privilege to be doing the job. In the big sprints here the adrenalin really gets going when you see the horses coming over the brow of the hill. And there is an extra twist, because the commentary position is about 50 yards before the line you cannot really see from there what has won in a close finish. It is vital you swivel round to look at the monitor if the finish is tight. You have far more chance of calling it right if you do that."

Mike Cattermole

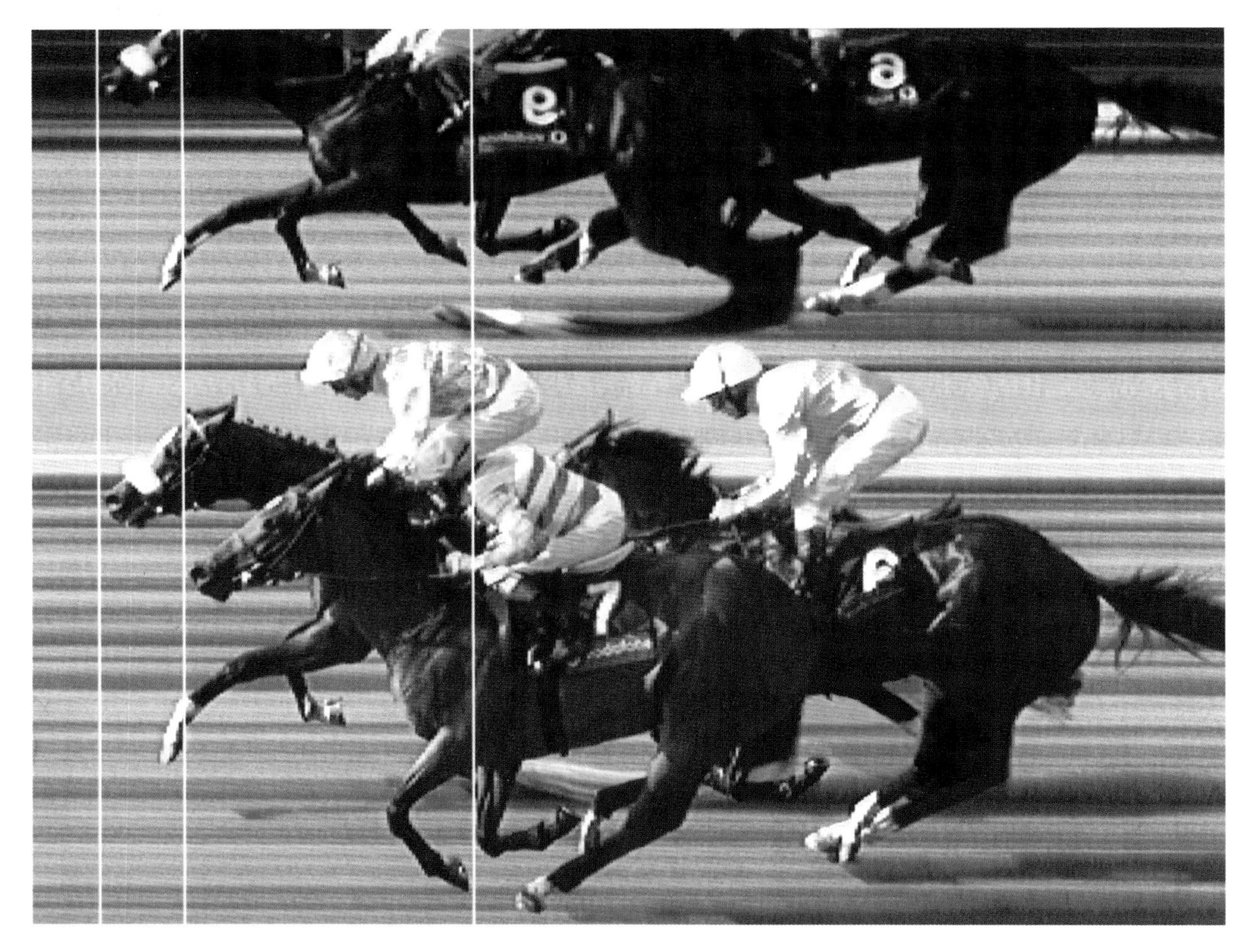

Above: *Why you need the photo finish camera, so that the judge can make sure which horse has beaten which, with a mirror image at top to show the action from both sides.*

Right: *Bob Haynes, the man who gave the first public commentary on a racecourse in Britain - at Goodwood in 1952. Haynes was ideal for the job: he was a superb race reader and had a wonderfully clear broadcasting voice.*

Overleaf: *Looking over the new pavilions to the parade ring and down towards the South Coast as the sun starts to set at the end of another Goodwood day.*

four mares near Blandford in Dorset, and he, as well as being a sometime racecourse commentator and Jockey Club judge, held a permit to train jumpers and won an all weather bumper at Lingfield in the 1989/90 season with Rawlsbury, ridden by the then up-and-coming Dean Gallagher.

It has been increasingly the trend in recent years for parade rings to be moved to more customer-friendly locations, but Goodwood was very much at the sharp end of that idea in 1976, and almost a quarter of a century before that they were the pioneers of one of the aspects of racing which we now all take for granted - the racecourse commentary.

It was back in 1952 that Goodwood provided the first such commentary. Until then spectators had to work out for themselves what was going on and how their fancy was running. If you did not have a pair of binoculars and a good vantage point and did not know your colours, that was just too bad: you had to wait until the result was called and the numbers hoisted into the frame to know if you had won. For many years, however, commentators were regarded as the poor relations of officialdom and the idea of listing their names on the racecards was clearly anathema. Clerks of the scales, by all means, judges certainly, but commentators - good heavens no.

That first commentary was given by Bob Haynes, who, with Michael Seth-Smith, Ken Grainger and Cloudesley Marsham, was to form the nucleus of the team which eventually expanded so that there were enough callers (even if of vastly varying accuracy) to cover every meeting every day.

GOODWOOD
GOODWOOD
GOODWOOD
super12.co.uk

Above: *Name the winner? Lester Piggott is about to drive Criterion (right, yellow and blue colours) to a dramatic victory in the 1982 Chesterfield Cup. The first five home were covered by less than half a length.*

Bob, whose son Nick maintains the family connection with racing and is a racecourse judge, was an outstanding commentator and race-reader as well as being an enthusiastic punter. For much of his time behind the microphone commentators were allowed to describe no more than the order in which the horses were racing, and Haynes was once sharply admonished for saying that a jockey was "sitting with a double handful"!

The racecourse commentary was introduced a few years after the photo-finish which came into use in 1947 and was first put into actual use at Epsom in April of that year. A couple of years later its interpretation at Goodwood by judge Malcolm Hancock caused a furore when he called High Stakes the short head winner of the Bentinck Stakes on the second day of the meeting. Further careful examination of the print indicated that the race should have been awarded to Hornet III, but in all fairness to the judge it is extremely easy to be confused by the photograph even when you are aware of what the result should have been.

These new and vastly improved facilities were part of the major general expansion at Goodwood which began in the mid-1960s. It is quite a thought that, in view of the fact that there have been 20 days' racing at Goodwood for the last three years, it was not until 1965 that there were more than four days - apart from 1947 and 1948, when there were six days, comprising the four-day July weekend and a two-day meeting in late August. At that time only Rothbury (which had only one day and closed in that same year) and Cartmel in Cumbria staged fewer days of racing.

In 1965 Goodwood introduced two new meetings in August and one in September and incorporated some important races into the new programmes. The first of these was the March Stakes, which has proved a useful testing ground for St Leger aspirants. Two of the March Stakes winners have gone on to success in the final classic - Commanche Run in 1984 and Michelozzo five years later, although in 1989 the St Leger was staged at Ayr because the track at Doncaster was unfit. Other horses like Ribofilio, Le Moss, Celestial Storm and Water Mill have gone on to put up very solid efforts at Doncaster.

Commanche Run, whose other major wins included the Phoenix Champion Stakes and the Benson and Hedges Gold Cup, and who also won Goodwood's Gordon Stakes, went on to be a successful sire under both codes with good winners like Commanche Court, She's Our Mare, Wavy Run and The Bajan Bandit. Le Moss became a top-class Cup horse in the two years after his March Stakes win and sired fine jumpers in Scotton Banks and Raymylette, while Zaffaran, successful in the March Stakes of 1988, has sired the Cheltenham Gold Cup winner Looks Like Trouble and other big chase winners in Beau and Frantic Tan.

Like the March Stakes, the Gordon Stakes, held on the first day of the July Meeting at Goodwood and marked its centenary in 2002, has given many indications as to what might happen at Doncaster six weeks later. In 2000 Millenary won the Gordon and then went on to St Leger triumph; the following year Alexius, who put up a remarkable display to win at Goodwood after losing about ten lengths at the start, would have gone off favourite at Doncaster had not injury forced his withdrawal on the eve of the race.

Nedawi, who dead-heated for the Gordon in 1998, Minster Son, who struck ten years earlier, and Athens Wood (1971) are others who have won both races. These horses were all well-fancied for the Gordon, but the race has also produced its share of surprises. Millenary went off at 9-1, Compton Ace in 1999 was a 12-1 chance, as was St Mawes in 1996. There have also been 25-1 winners in Electric in 1982 and Grey Thunder eight years before that. Big-priced winners for Grey Thunder's trainer Clive Brittain are not unexpected, but for a horse trained by (Sir) Michael Stoute, as was Electric, to start at such a price is very unusual.

One of the biggest surprises in the Gordon Stakes came in 1960 when the Derby winner St Paddy went off at 11-8 on but failed by half a length to give 5lb to Kipling, who was ridden by Geoff Lewis and trained by Peter Hastings-Bass, Ian Balding's late father-in-law.

Overleaf, inset: *Ian Balding and his daughter Clare are both highly accomplished riders.*

"When I was riding I was lucky enough to be champion amateur and top lady rider one year, and joint leading amateur in another, and I had some winners at Goodwood. I won the Royal Sussex Regiment Amateur Riders' Handicap two years running on Waterlow Park, once over a mile and the other over a mile and a half, but it was also at Goodwood that I was booed by a punter for the only time when I was riding. I was on an old horse called Mailman, who started favourite even though he was running over a trip too short for him. He could never really get into the race and finished sixth. As I was coming back one of the racegoers shouted, 'You ought to get going a bit earlier, darling'. I could not really try to explain to him that the horse was better over a longer trip. Dad has a great record at Goodwood - he has won the Chesterfield Cup six times and I particularly remember when he won the Goodwood Cup with Grey Shot. I was in Atlanta covering the Olympic Games and heard Dad being interviewed on Radio 5 by Cornelius (Lysaght). He loved that horse so much he was crying with the emotion of the result. It was very, very moving. I have presented the BBC TV racing coverage from Goodwood since 1998, after Julian Wilson retired, and worked with him and Willie Carson before that. We have always had a lovely, relaxed programme from Goodwood - you can still focus on the social and fashion side of things as well as the racing.

CLARE BALDING

Kipling was owned and bred by Lord Sefton, one of the most autocratic of men, who used to own Aintree racecourse until he sold it to the Topham family in 1949. He owned a number of good horses on the flat and over jumps and his Irish Lizard had a fine record over the big Liverpool fences. He won the Topham (now the John Hughes Memorial) Trophy in 1953 and was third in the Grand National two days later. He was third in the National again in 1954 and was also runner-up in the Grand Sefton of that season.

Lord Sefton, who vied with his contemporary Mr John Thursby (the owner of, among others, the Coronation Cup winner Sea Chimes) to have the best polished shoes in racing, did not give the impression of being a great believer in democracy.

There is one story of an encounter between Lord Sefton and a man whom he regarded as of inferior social stock (which would have taken in 99% of the population) when their paths crossed at an official gathering in the Liverpool area. The artisan, unaware of what he was letting himself in for, asked Lord Sefton what he did for a living. "Do?" expostulated Sefton. "What do I do?! You might as well ask a Hottentot who his tailor is."

Two years after the introduction of the August and September meetings and the March Stakes, the race now known as the Celebration Mile, was run for the first time. It has been won by some very smart horses in its 35-year history - the roll of honour includes Brigadier Gerard, Habitat, Humble Duty, Kris and Medicean.

The race has yet to achieve a double-figure field and, maybe in part for this reason, upsets have been few and far between. There have been a few, though, with the biggest of these coming in 1978 from the 25-1 shot Captain James. He raced for the McGrath family who were responsible for another big race Goodwood turn-up when Le Levanstell won the Sussex Stakes in 1961 at 100-7.

Further expansion in the Goodwood programme came in 1968 with the introduction of the May meeting; two years later the first running of the Derby trial, the Predominate Stakes, produced a royal winner with victory going to The Queen's colt Charlton, who was named after the England footballer Bobby Charlton.

Although only one Predominate winner, Troy in 1979, has gone on to Epsom triumph, there have been extremely good horses among the others. Three years ago the race was won by the outstanding Dubai Millennium, whose death in April 2001 was such a blow both to racing and breeding, and Pentire, Opera House and Minster Son are winners who have gone on to Group 1 victories.

Goodwood's racing programme was further augmented in 1970 with the addition of the Saturday to the festival meeting, so that there are 20 days each season running from May through September. The expansion to that total from just four days has inevitably led to a number of new races, one of the most successful of which has been the ten-furlong handicap on the Friday which was run in 2001 as the Mel Collier Handicap.

***Above:** Sheikh Hamdan al Maktoum's Ekraar (Richard Hills) strides on to victory in the Champagne Lanson Vintage Stakes in 1999.*

Since its first staging in 1962 this race has had a number of sponsors, most notably the *News Of The World* and the Exchange Telegraph and has been a real race for a gamble. There have been major touches like that with Indian Trail, who landed a big gamble for Robert Sangster, Barry Hills and Steve Cauthen in 1981, and has been much coveted by Luca Cumani, who won it three times in a row in the 1980s and got back again with Askham in 2001.

It was a major shock for racing generally when Schweppes pulled out of the big handicap hurdle which they used to sponsor at Newbury, for few races throughout the entire racing year used to attract more publicity, but Newbury's loss was Goodwood's gain with the introduction of the Schweppes Mile in 1987. When Schweppes abandoned that race the William Hill Organisation took it over and, fittingly for a race sponsored by bookmakers, every favourite has been beaten. To illustrate how competitive it is, only four times in 15 years has the winning margin been greater than a neck.

Sponsorship is now a vital, integral part of all racing and, with the exception of Royal Ascot, there is hardly a major race under either code at any course which does not have or has not had commercial support. The sums involved vary greatly and it is possible to sponsor a race at Goodwood for as little as £5,000. At the other end of the scale a sponsor of the Sussex Stakes has to contribute a six-figure sum towards the prize money. This is a reflection of

GOODWOOD
RACES
EVINGTON
557

"Sponsors are crucially important to the viability of the racecourse and the offering of high-level prize money. The ability to attract sponsorship is greatly assisted by the prospect of free to air television coverage, and the partnership with the BBC is always a great help. We have been lucky enough to have some very long-standing sponsors including the Lanson family, Racal - under their Vodafone banner - and William Hill, as well as many years of support from industry sponsors like the Tote and the EBF. It is all self-help, but that is what we are supposed to be doing."

Rod Fabricius, Clerk of the Course and General Manager, Goodwood Racecourse

the importance of the race and the British Horseracing Board's requirement that Group 1 races, like the Sussex and the Nassau at Goodwood, have to be supported at a suitably serious level.

It is inevitable with the way in which things fluctuate in the business world that sponsors should come and go, and there is quite an art not only in finding them in the first place but also in then keeping them involved and interested. Goodwood has done very well in this respect, so much so that nearly 30% of the total prize money in 2001 of £2,672,500 came from sponsors. Both these figures were records for the course.

In the last couple of decades the Sussex Stakes has been supported by Robert Sangster's Swettenham Stud and latterly by Champagne Lanson, who also enjoyed a long association with the Vintage Stakes, one of the two major two-year-old races at the July meeting. Although the house of Lanson ended their Goodwood sponsorship after the 2001 season and the house no longer belongs to the family, one member of the founding team has taken over the support of the two-year-old race. This is Victor Lanson, son of Pierre and Marie, who has his own brand of the sparkling liquid and decided to promote the event as the Champagne Victor Vintage Stakes.

Above: *Rod Fabricius, Goodwood's Clerk of the Course and General Manager, has been an integral part of all the many changes that have taken place at Goodwood since he came there for the 1983 season.*

The Nassau Stakes comes under the banner of Vodafone, whose visible presence in racing includes sponsorship of the Stewards' Cup, as well as the Derby, the Oaks and the Coronation Cup. Major sponsoring companies regard television exposure of "their" races as a vital part of the exercise, but many firms that support the smaller events do not feel that broadcasting of the races in which they are involved is in any way essential.

Goodwood's very successful Friday evening meetings in June - an idea which was pioneered by Clerk of the Course Rod Fabricius, have been aimed particularly at the local market, both as far as spectators and sponsors are concerned. Sponsorship is not only an opportunity to publicise a company and its operations, but also a chance for those companies to entertain clients with a day or an evening at the races.

The 49 boxes in the three Goodwood stands provide ideal facilities for guests. Entertainment for them can be pitched at a range varying from £50 to £450 per visitor per day, depending on how lavish a level of hospitality and how favoured a stand position the host may want. Boxes at Goodwood can be rented for such purposes on a daily or an annual basis.

The opening of the Sussex Stand in Tattersalls in 1990, a ceremony performed by Peter O'Sullevan, extended the number of boxes by 18 and provided vastly improved facilities for racegoers in Tattersalls.

Sir Peter had, of course, been professionally involved in racing at Goodwood for many years in his capacity as both commentator for BBC television and as correspondent for the *Daily Express*. In fact the television link-up goes back 45 years, as it was in July 1956 that the BBC television first covered racing at Goodwood.

Above: *The Duke of Richmond presents the winner's trophy to connections of Lively One after the Goodwood Handicap at Santa Anita in 1990. Trainer Charlie Whittingham (known as 'The Bald Eagle') and jockey Alex Solis join the celebrations. The Richmond family also has a twinning arrangement with the family of Le Duc de Brissac. In 1976 the present Duke of Richmond (then the Earl of March) and Le Duc (then Le Marquis de Brissac), chairman of the racecourse at Angers, discussed twinning the racecourses. As the courses were not particularly compatible for twinning, they created a race bringing the families together, with a race at each course. Goodwood's race is the Richmond-Brissac Trophy Stakes, one of only two races in Britain run as part of the programme of Fegentri (the Federation of Gentlemen Riders of Europe); the other is the Moet & Chandon Silver Magnum at Epsom.*

On that occasion they broadcast three races, headed by the Stewards' Cup, with Sir Peter providing the race description and Clive Graham, his colleague at both the BBC and the *Express*, contributing the paddock observations. In fact, Goodwood's involvement with the BBC goes back to 1937, five years after the 1932 Derby became the first race to be televised. Discussions then covered only the possibility of race commentaries being broadcast on the wireless, but the idea had to be abandoned due to technical difficulties. It was picked up again after the Second World War and in 1947 Goodwood charged 15 guineas a day for what were called 'full facilities'. On 30th July of that year Frank More O'Ferrall, who was also a leading player in the bloodstock agency world, commentated on the Goodwood Stakes - the first race to be transmitted from the course.

Over the years racing has become an increasingly international sport. Goodwood has had an American link for 20 years or more, highlighted by the Oak Tree Stakes for fillies on the third day of the July meeting. The naming of this race marks the close association between Goodwood and the Oak Tree Racing Association at Santa Anita racecourse, the outstandingly beautiful course with its backdrop of the San Gabriel Mountains just outside Los Angeles in California. In reciprocation Santa Anita stages a race each October named in honour of Goodwood.

There was an unusual link-up between the two courses at the July 2001 meeting when commentary on the Oak Tree Stakes was given by 16-year-old Jonathan Horowitz,who hails from Irvine in California and has called races in his native country. In spite of foul conditions, with the race being run in driving rain and a style of track with which he was totally unfamiliar, the young man gave a more than competent description of the all-the-way success by 20-1 Mauri Moon.

Opposite and previous pages: *The traditional raceweek ball at Goodwood was revived for the first time in 24 years in 1994, with the support of Tiffany, the Bond Street jewellers, and held again in 1995 (including the Goodwood Charity Stakes featuring pantomime horses). Balls were a feature of festival week since its inception, although the earliest took place in the Chichester Assembly Rooms, as the ballroom at Goodwood House had not yet been constructed; the ballroom had a spectacular opening in 1839. The raceweek ball was revived once more to celebrate the 200th anniversary of Goodwood Racecourse in 2002.*

Races have inevitably come and gone at Goodwood over the years, as has been the case across the country as the Pattern and Race Planning Committees have organised programmes on generally more sensible lines to avoid clashes, thus enabling owners and trainers of decent horses to map out a campaign for them.

One race which has disappeared from the festival meeting is the two-year-old seller, which was very popular in its day and was often the target for a big gamble. It was worth a good deal more than most races of its sort and invariably worth more than a number of events on the Goodwood card, and thus attracted runners who were some way above normal plating class.

In 1972 one of the runners was a certain Attivo, who finished fourth behind the favourite Angel Aboard. It is just as well for his owner (Sir) Peter O'Sullevan that he did not win the £1,476 first prize as he then might not have been able to carry the black jacket with its yellow crossbelts to those fine victories in the Chester Cup, the Northumberland Plate and the Triumph Hurdle. What excitement the 'voice of racing' would have missed.

Having secured its rightful place in the racing hierarchy Goodwood is determined to keep itself there and the huge improvements to the race programme and the stands that have taken place in the last 35 or so years will stand the course in very good stead.

Nor have Goodwood's owners and organisers forgotten why we all flock to the track in the first place. The next step in the round of improvements will include new boxes at the racecourse stables at Goodwood House and a new unloading ramp for horseboxes at the racecourse. The horse is the bottom line of the whole venture and will always be so - the Frink bronze is a fitting symbol of that. Long may it last.

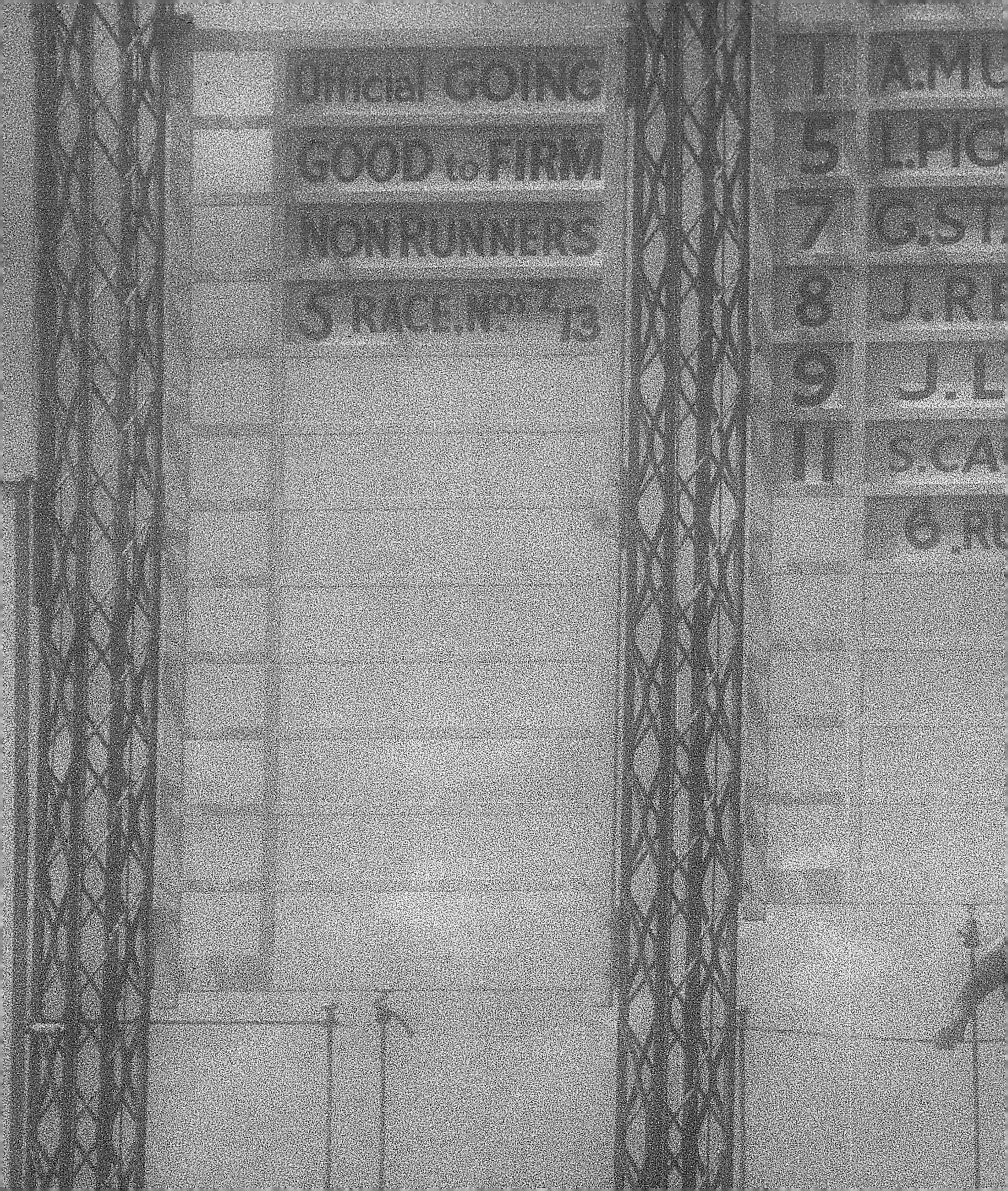

Official GOING
GOOD to FIRM
NON RUNNERS

GOODWOOD'S ROLL OF HONOUR

This section lists the winners of the principal races held at Goodwood since its inception to the present day, including the results in 2001 - and the results of the Goodwood Breeders' Cup at Santa Anita. For key races from the history of the racecourse - the Sussex Stakes, the Stewards' Cup, the Goodwood Cup, the Richmond Stakes, the Gordon Stakes, the Chesterfield Cup, and the Goodwood Stakes - early results are given. For all other races, results are from the resumption of racing at Goodwood after the Second World War or from the first running of the individual race. Alongside qualification criteria, length of the race and date of first running, the early results list information on the horse, age (where relevant), weight, and number of runners. In the post-war results additional data includes jockey, trainer, winning distance and starting price. Sponsors are as for the 2002 programme.

SUSSEX STAKES

Group One

Three-year-olds and up. One mile. First run 1841.

(1900-1941)

Year	Name	Age/Weight	Runners
1900	The Raft	3 8-04	5
1901	Energetic	3 8-03	9
1902	Royal Lancer	3 8-13	5
1903	Stephanas	3 8-03	5
1904	Mousqueton	3 8-10	5
1905	Thrush	3 8-13	2
1906	Troutbeck	3 9-01	3
1907	Wool Winder	3 9-01	3
1908	White Eagle	3 9-03	5
1909	Minoru	3 9-08	3
1910	Winkipop	3 9-01	5
1911	Stedfast	3 9-01	3
1912	Tracery	3 9-01	5
1913	Sun Yat	3 8-13	5
1914	Black Jester	3 9-01	5
1915-1918	No races		
1919	Glanmerin	3 8-13	4
1920	Braishfield	3 8-05	6
1921	Sunblaze	3 8-10	6
1922	Diligence	3 8-05	3
1923	Hurry Off	3 9-01	4
1924	Burslem	3 8-05	4
1925	The Monk	3 8-07	8
1926	Plimsol	3 8-05	4
1927	Rosalia	3 8-07	7
1928	Marconigram	3 8-13	6
1929	Le Phare	3 9-03	6
1930	Paradine	3 9-01	7
1931	Inglesant	3 8-05	6
1932	Dastur	3 9-03	2
1933	The Abbot	3 8-13	7
1934	Badruddin	3 9-03	3
1935	Hairan	3 8-12	7
1936	Corpach	3 8-02	5
1937	Pascal	3 9-03	6
1938	Faroe	3 9-01	6
1939	Olein	3 9-05	7
1940-1945	No races		

SUSSEX STAKES (1946-2000)

Year	Name	Age/Weight	Jockey	Trainer	Dist.	Runners	SP
1946	Radiotherapy	3 9-03	G Richards	F Templeman	½	6	7-4
1947	Combat	3 9-03	G Richards	F Darling	1½	2	13-8
1948	My Babu	3 9-08	C Smirke	F Armstrong	1	2	1-3F
1949	Kratatao	3 9-01	G Richards	N Murless	6	2	2-11F
1950	Palestine	3 9-08	C Smirke	M Marsh	1½	4	1-2F
1951	Le Sage	3 9-03	G Richards	T Carey	½	7	6-4F
1952	Agitator	3 9-01	G Richards	N Murless	4	5	8-15F
1953	King Of The Tudors	3 8-10	C Spares	W Stephenson	5	4	11-10F
1954	Landau	3 9-01	W Snaith	N Murless	5	4	6-4F
1955	My Kingdom	3 8-09	D Smith	W Nightingall	NK	5	13-2
1956	Lucero	3 9-01	E Mercer	H Wragg	1½	6	8-1
1957	Quorum	3 9-01	A Russell	W Lyde	½	4	10-11F
1958	Major Portion	3 9-07	E Smith	T Leader	1	5	8-11F
1959	Petite Etoile	3 9-04	L Piggott	N Mmurless	½	6	1-10F
1960	Venture VII	3 8-04	G Moore	A Head (Fr)	½	6	13-8F
1961	Le Levanstell	4 8-10	W Williamson	S McGrath (Ire)	NK	11	100-7
1962	Romulus	3 8-04	W Swinburn	R F J Houghton	4	8	9-1
1963	Queen's Hussar	3 8-03	R Hutchinson	T Corbett	Hd	10	25-1
1964	Roan Rocket	3 8-05	L Piggott	G Todd	½	8	4-6F
1965	Carlemont	3 8-03	R Hutchinson	P Prendergast (Ire)	3	11	7-2
1966	Paveh	3 8-03	R Hutchinson	T Ainsworth (Ire)	SHD	7	5-1
1967	Reform	3 8-3	A Breasley	Sir G Richards	1½	10	EVSF
1968	Petingo	3 8-04	L Piggott	F Armstrong	4	6	6-4F
1969	Jimmy Reppin	4 9-04	G Lewis	J Sutcliffe Jnr	3	5	7-4F
1970	Humble Duty	3 8-04	D Keith	P Walwyn	¾	5	11-8F
1971	Brigadier Gerard	3 8-07	J Mercer	W Hern	5	5	4-6f
1972	Sallust	3 8-10	J Mercer	W Hern	HD	3	9-2
1973	Thatch	3 8-10	L Piggott	M V O'Brien (Ire)	3	7	4-5F
1974	Ace Of Aces	4 9-07	J Lindley	M Zilber (Fr)	2	10	8-1
1975	Bolkonski	3 8-10	G Dettori	H Cecil	NK	9	1-2F
1976	Wollow	3 8-10	G Dettori	H Cecil	1	9	10-11F
1977	Artaius	3 8-10	L Piggott	M V Oíbrien (Ire)	1½	11	6-4F
1978	Jaazeiro	3 8-10	L Piggott	M V Oíbrien (Ire)	2	6	8-13F
1979	Kris	3 8-10	J Mercer	H Cecil	5	7	4-5F
1980	Posse	3 8-10	Pat Eddery	J Dunlop	HD	9	8-13F
1981	King's Lake	3 8-10	Pat Eddery	M V O'Brien (Ire)	HD	9	5-2
1982	On The House	3 8-07	J Reid	H Wragg	½	13	14-1
1983	Noalcoholic	6 9-07	G Duffield	G Pritchard-Gordon	2½	11	18-1
1984	Chief Singer	3 8-10	R Cochrane	R Sheather	½	5	4-7F
1985	Rousillon	4 9-07	G Starkey	G Harwood	2½	10	2-1JF
1986	Sonic Lady	3 8-07	W R Swinburn	M Stoute	1½	5	5-6F
1987	Soviet Star	3 8-10	G Starkey	A Fabre (Fr)	½	7	3-1
1988	Warning	3 8-10	Pat Eddery	G Harwood	1½	9	11-10F
1989	Zilzal	3 8-10	W R Swinburn	M Stoute	3	8	5-2
1990	Distant Relative	4 9-07	W Carson	B Hills	½	7	4-1
1991	Second Set	3 8-13	L Dettori	L Cumani	1½	8	5-1
1992	Marling	3 8-10	Pat Eddery	G Wragg	HD	8	11-10F
1993	Bigstone	3 8-13	D Boeuf	E Lellouche (Fr)	1½	10	14-1
1994	Distant View	3 8-13	Pat Eddery	H Cecil	½	9	4-1
1995	Sayyedati	5 9-04	B Doyle	C Brittain	NK	6	11-2
1996	First Island	4 9-07	M Hills	G Wragg	1	10	5-1
1997	Ali-Royal	4 9-07	K Fallon	H Cecil	¾	9	13-2
1998	Among Men	4 9-07	M Kinane	Sir M Stoute	1	10	4-1
1999	Aljabr	3 8-13	L Dettori	S Bin Suroor	1	8	11-10F

4th RACE
SAYAJIRAO
GLENDOWER
RICHARD III
ALLEGORY
CASTILIAN
PAT.

2000	Giant's Causeway	3 9-00	M Kinane	A O'Brien (Ire)	¾	10	3-1JF
2001	Noverre	3 9-00	L Dettori	S Bin Suroor	2	10	9-2

For three-year-olds only to 1959. For three- and four-year-olds only 1960-74.

NASSAU STAKES
(Sponsored by Vodafone)

Group One

Three-year-olds and up fillies and mares. One mile two furlongs. First run 1840.

(1946-2001)

Year	Name	Age/Weight	Jockey	Trainer	Dist.	Runners	SP
1946	Wayward Belle	3 9-01	E Smith	J Jarvis	¾	7	11-8F
1947	Wild Child	3 8-10	T Lowrey	R Perryman	HD	8	11-2
1948	Goblet	3 9-08	G Richards	N Murless	5	7	13-2
1949	Jet Plane	3 9-08	G Richards	J Lawson	¾	6	8-1
1950	Flying Slipper	3 9-01	W Carr	C Boyd-Rochfort	NK	7	8-1
1951	Sea Parrot	3 8-05	G Richards	N Murless	NK	7	7-4F
1952	Hortentia	3 8-10	D Smith	G Colling	SHD	7	11-2
1953	Happy Laughter	3 9-08	W Rickaby	J Jarvis	3	3	5-6F
1954	Key	3 9-05	W Snaith	N Murless	3	10	4-1
1955	Reel In	3 8-10	A Breasley	N Cannon	NK	6	13-8F
1956	Dilettante	3 8-10	D Smith	J F Watts	NK	9	6-1
1957	Swallowswift	3 8-10	E Mercer	G Colling	1	8	100-9
1958	Darlene	3 8-10	A Breasley	G Richards	3	6	100-3
1959	Crystal Palace	3 9-05	E Smith	T Leader	HD	6	3-1
1960	Desert Beauty	3 9-01	A Breasley	G Richards	½	5	2-1
1961	Rachel	3 8-05	J Lindley	J Gosden	1½	6	7-2
1962	Nortia	3 9-03	J Mercer	W Hern	½	7	100-30JF
1963	Spree	3 8-05	J Lindley	J Tree	HD	4	15-8F
1964	Cracker	3 8-10	J Mercer	W Wharton	1½	6	10-1
1965	Aunt Edith	3 8-05	L Piggott	N Murless	4	6	7-4F
1966	Haymaking	3 9-03	L Piggott	R F J Houghton	3	9	13-2
1967	Fair Winter	3 8-10	J Mercer	D Candy	6	5	7-2
1968	Hill Shade	3 8-00	A Barclay	N Murless	3	7	5-6F
1969	Lucyrowe	3 8-09	F Durr	P Walwyn	SHD	5	1-2F
1970	Pulchra	3 8-04	G Lewis	J Sirett	HD	5	20-1
1971	Catherine Wheel	3 8-04	G Lewis	B Hobbs	5	5	4-1
1972	Crespinall	3 8-08	R Hutchinson	R Hannon	2	4	25-1
1973	Cheveley Princess	3 8-08	L Piggott	H Wragg	2	9	15-2
1974	Mil's Bomb	3 8-08	G Lewis	N Murless	NK	4	10-11F
1975	Roussalka	3 8-08	L Piggott	H Cecil	1	6	9-4
1976	Roussalka	4 9-06	L Piggott	H Cecil	½	10	15-8F
1977	Triple First	3 8-05	G Starkey	M Stoute	NK	8	13-2
1978	Cistus	3 8-05	W Carson	W Hern	4	7	4-7F
1979	Connaught Bridge	3 8-05	J Mercer	H Cecil	1½	10	5-1
1980	Vielle	3 8-05	G Baxter	B Hobbs	2	7	8-15F
1981	Go Leasing	3 8-08	G Starkey	G Harwood	1	11	15-2
1982	Dancing Rocks	3 8-05	Pat Eddery	H Wragg	2	11	12-1
1983	Acclimatise	3 8-05	G Baxter	B Hobbs	3	6	4-1
1984	Optimistic Lass	3 8-08	W R Swinburn	M Stoute	2½	5	5-2F
1985	Free Guest	4 9-08	Pat Eddery	L Cumani	7	11	11-2
1986	Park Express	3 8-08	J Reid	J Bolger (Ire)	3	7	7-1
1987	Nom De Plume	3 8-07	S Cauthen	H Cecil	2½	5	11-4
1988	Ela Romara	3 8-06	Pat Eddery	G Wragg	3	7	10-1
1989	Mamaluna	3 8-06	G Starkey	G Harwood	1½	5	9-1
1990	Kartajana	3 8-06	W R Swinburn	M Stoute	2	6	11-2
1991	Ruby Tiger	4 9-04	T Quinn	P Cole	7	6	11-4
1992	Ruby Tiger	5 9-01	T Quinn	P Cole	NK	7	2-1
1993	Lyphard's Delta	3 8-06	W Ryan	H Cecil	1½	9	10-1
1994	Hawajiss	3 8-06	W R Swinburn	M Stoute	½	9	4-1JF
1995	Caramba	3 8-09	M Roberts	R Hannon	½	6	5-2F
1996	Last Second	3 8-06	G Duffield	Sir M Prescott	2	8	7-4F
1997	Ryafan	3 8-09	M Hills	J Gosden	2½	7	9-4F
1998	Alborada	3 8-09	G Duffield	Sir M Prescott	½	9	4-1
1999	Zahrat Dubai	3 8-06	G Stevens	S Bin Suroor	½	8	5-1
2000	Crimplene	3 8-06	P Robinson	C Brittain	1¾	7	7-4F
2001	Lailani	3 8-06	L Dettori	E Dunlop	1½	7	5-4F

For three-year-olds only to 1974.

STEWARDS' CUP
(Sponsored by Vodafone)

Handicap

Three-year-olds and up. Six furlongs. First run 1840.

(1840-1941)

Year	Name	Age/Weight	Runners
1840	Epirus	6 9-07	22
1841	Garry Owen	4 8-10	15
1842	Lady Adela	3 7-00	12
1843	Yorkshire Lady	4 6-04	17
1844	Sir Abstrupus	4 6-10	23
1845	Psalmsinger	3 5-04	21
1846	Lady Wildair	4 7-10	25
1847	The Cur	5 7-11	24
1848	The Admiral	4 7-03	28
1849	Cotton Lord	3 6-00	22
1850	Turnus	4 6-10	25
1851	Loadstone	6 7-07	24
1852	Kilmeny	4 6-13	35
1853	Longbow	4 9-04	24
1854	Pumicestone	3 6-00	37
1855	Clotilde	3 6-09	29
1856	New Brighton	6 8-03	32
1857	Tournament	3 7-00	34
1858	Glenmasson	4 7-05	28
1859	Maid of Kent	4 6-07	34
1860	Sweetsauce	3 7-01	37
1861	Croagh Patrick	3 5-09	45
1862	Lady Clifden	4 8-09	34
1863	Birdhill	4 7-05	29
1864	Marigold	4 7-06	40
1865	Out And Outer	3 6-06	36
1866	Sultan	4 8-03	24
1867	Tibthorpe	3 5-10	35
1868	Vex	3 6-00	22
1869	Fichu	3 6-00	29
1870	Typhoeus	5 8-10	28
1871	Anton	3 7-00	39
1872	Oxonian	6 8-12	28
1873	Sister Helen	5 7-08	N/A
1874	Modwena	5 7-01	25
1875	Trappist	3 7-10	22
1876	Monaco	4 6-07	27
1877	Herald	5 7-00	23
1878	Midlothian	4 7-02	20
1879	Peter	3 8-00	30
1880	Elf King	4 7-09	28
1881	Mazurka	3 6-10	28
1882	Lowland Chief	4 8-06	19
1883	Hornpipe	6 8-09	18
1884	Sweetbread	5 9-03	23
1885	Dalmeny	5 6-13	18
1886	Crafton	4 7-11	25
1887	Upset	4 6-03	23
1888	Tib	5 6-07	21
1889	Dog Rose	6 7-12	18
1890	Marvel	3 7-06	22
1891	Unicorn	3 6-02	24
1892	Marvel	5 8-08	30
1893	Medora	3 6-12	19
1894	Gangway	4 8-07	21
1895	Wise Virgin	3 6-06	22
1896	Chasseur	4 8-05	24
1897	Amphora	4 8-08	23
1898	Altesse	4 8-04	15
1899	Northern Farmer	5 7-06	19
1900	Royal Flush	N/A 7-13	19
1901	O'Donovan Rossa	4 7-00	28
1902	Mauvezin	6 8-02	23
1903	Dumbarton Castle	3 7-04	21
1904	Melayr	3 6-09	19
1905	Xeny	4 7-09	17
1906	Rocketter	3 7-06	13
1907	Romney	3 6-03	15
1908	Elmstead	3 7-00	18
1909	Mediant	3 7-13	21
1910	Golden Rod	4 8-01	21
1911	Braxted	3 7-05	19
1912	Golden Rod	6 8-13	21
1913	Lord Annandale	3 6-10	20
1914	*Golden Sun	4 8-12	23
	*Lord Annandale	4 7-09	
1915-1918	No races		
1919	KIng Sol	5 7-00	14
1920	Western Wave	4 8-07	21
1921	Service Kit	4 6-12	20
1922	Tetrameter	5 7-07	30
1923	Epinard	3 8-06	14
1924	Compiler	4 7-09	24
1925	Defiance	4 7-08	24
1926	Perhaps So	5 8-01	29
1927	Priory Park	5 9-00	24
1928	Navigator	3 7-05	16
1929	Fleeting Memory	4 8-01	19
1930	Le Phare	4 8-01	28
1931	Poor Lad	4 7-11	15
1932	Solenold	3 7-10	21
1933	Pharacre	4 7-05	26
1934	Figaro	4 8-05	22
1935	Greenore	6 8-08	17
1936	Solerina	4 8-11	20
1937	Firozepore	3 8-03	30
1938	Harmachis	5 7-06	25
1939	Knight's Caprice	4 8-06	23
1940	No Race		
1941	#Valthema	4 7-02	N/A
1942-1945	No races		

STEWARDS' CUP (1946-2001)

Year	Name	Age/Weight	Jockey	Trainer	Dist.	Runners	SP
1946	Commissar	6 7-12	A Richardson	E Stedall	HD	15	10-1
1947	Closeburn	3 8-10	G Richards	N Murless	NK	19	100-7

1948	Dramatic	3 7-07	E Smith	G Todd	1½	16	9-1
1949	The Bite	4 7-07	H Packham	J Wood	SHD	21	33-1
1950	First Consul	4 8-13	E Britt	F Armstrong	1	21	100-9
1951	Sugar Bowl	4 7-12	W Snaith	F Armstrong	HD	21	100-6
1952	Smokey Eyes	5 8-10	C Smirke	R Jarvis	1	18	100-7
1953	Palpitate	4 7-13	W Snaith	F Armstrong	HD	22	5-1F
1954	Ashurst Wonder	4 6-11	A Shrive	L Hall	½	28	50-1
1955	King Bruce	4 8-11	W Rickaby	P Hastings-Bass	HD	26	100-6
1956	Matador	3 9-02	E Smith	J Waugh	NK	24	100-8
1957	Arcandy	4 8-09	T Gosling	G Beeby	2	16	100-7
1958	Epaulette	7 9-00	F Durr	W O'Gorman	1	20	33-1
1959	Tudor Monarch	4 7-13	G Lewis	W Nightingall	NK	21	25-1
1960	Monet	3 8-05	J Lindley	J Tree	SHD	18	20-1
1961	Skymaster	3 8-12	A Breasley	G Smyth	SHD	22	100-7
1962	Victorina	3 8-09	W Williamson	P Nelson	NK	26	10-1F
1963	Creole	4 9-01	S Smith	J Jarvis	SHD	25	20-1
1964	Dunme	5 7-12	P Cook	R Read	½	20	9-1JF
1965	Potier	3 8-05	R Hutchinson	J Jarvis	¾	20	100-7
1966	Patient Constable	3 7-07	R Reader	R Smyth	1½	25	33-1
1967	Sky Diver	4 7-05	D Cullen	P Payne-Gallwey	1½	31	20-1
1968	Sky Diver	5 7-06	T Sturrock	P Payne-Gallwey	SHD	18	100-6
1969	Royal Smoke	3 7-09	M L Thomas	W O'Gorman	½	15	100-7
1970	Jukebox	4 8-11	L Piggott	H Wallington	NK	24	100-6
1971	Apollo Nine	4 9-05	J Lindley	P Nelson	1½	26	14-1
1972	Touch Paper	3 8-02	P Cook	B Hobbs	HD	22	25-1
1973	Alphadamus	3 7-11	P Cook	M Stoute	HD	27	16-1
1974	Red Alert	3 9-02	J Roe	D Weld (Ire)	1½	25	16-1
1975	Import	4 8-00	M L Thomas	W Wightman	½	21	14-1
1976	Jimmy The Singer	3 7-08	E Johnson	B Lunness	1	17	15-1
1977	Calibina	5 8-05	G Baxter	P Cole	¾	24	8-1F
1978	Ahonoora	3 8-00	P Waldron	B Swift	½	23	50-1
1979	Standaan	3 7-10	P Bradwell	C Brittain	2	16	5-1F
1980	Repetitious	3 7-02	A Clark	G Harwood	SHD	28	15-1
1981	Crews Hill	5 9-09	G Starkey	F Durr	¾	30	11-1
1982	Soba	3 8-04	D Nicholls	D Chapman	2½	30	18-1
1983	Autumn Sunset	3 8-02	W Carson	M Stoute	HD	23	6-1F
1984	Petong	4 9-10	B Raymond	M Jarvis	¾	26	8-1JF
1985	Al Trui	5 8-01	M Wigham	S Mellor	SHD	28	9-1F
1986	Green Ruby	5 8-12	J Williams	G Balding	NK	24	20-1
1987	Madraco	4 7-02	P Hill	P Calver	4	30	50-1
1988	Rotherfield Greys	6 8-08	N Day	C Wall	2	28	14-1
1989	Very Adjacent	4 7-04	D Gibson	G Lewis	SHD	22	12-1
1990	Knight Of Mercy	4 9-00	B Raymond	R Hannon	NK	30	14-1
1991	Notley	4 8-07	R Perham	R Hannon	2½	29	14-1
1992	Lochsong	4 8-00	W Carson	I Balding	½	30	10-1
1993	King's Signet	4 9-10	W Carson	J Gosden	1½	29	16-1
1994	For The Present	4 8-03	J Fortune	T Barron	SHD	26	16-1
1995	Shikari's Son	8 8-13	R Hughes	J White	¾	27	40-1
1996	Coastal Bluff	4 8-05	J Fortune	T Barron	3	30	10-1JF
1997	Danetime	3 8-10	Pat Eddery	N Callaghan	NK	30	5-1F
1998	Superior Premium	4 8-12	R Winston	R Fahey	1½	29	14-1
1999	Harmonic Way	4 8-06	R Hughes	R Charlton	1½	30	12-1
2000	Tayseer	6 8-11	R Hughes	D Nicholls	1½	30	13-2
2001	Guinea Hunter	5 9-00	J Spencer	T Easterby	NK	30	33-1

** Dead heat # Run at Newmarket as Stewards Handicap*

GOODWOOD CUP
(Sponsored by JP Morgan Private Bank)

Group Two

Three-year-olds and up. Two miles. First run 1812.

(1812-1939)

Year	Name	Age/Weight	Runners
1812	Shoestrings	4 7-12	5
1813	Camerton	5 8-12	4
1814	Banquo	4 7-12	4
1815	No race		
1816	Scarecrow	6 9-05	5
1817 - 1824	No races		
1825	Cricketer	3 7-00	3
1826	Stumps	4 8-11	WO
1827	Link Boy	4 8-04	4
1828	Miss Craven	4 8-01	2
1829	Fleur de Lis	N/A 9-03	6
1830	Fleur de Lis	N/A 9-09	9
1831	Priam	4 9-05	3
1832	Priam	5 9-13	8
1833	Rubini	5 9-09	9
1834	Glencoe	3 7-04	10
1835	Rockingham	5 9-04	10
1836	Hornsea	4 8-10	10
1837	Carew	4 8-01	10
1838	Harkaway	4 8-08	8
1839	Harkaway	5 9-04	9
1840	Beggarman	5 8-05	9
1841	Charles XII	5 8-13	10
1842	Charles XII	6 9-09	9
1843	Hyllus	N/A 9-07	13
1844	Alice Hawthorn	6 9-05	9
1845	Miss Elis	3 7-00	12
1846	Grimston	3 7-04	9
1847	The Hero	4 9-06	9
1848	Van Tromp	4 9-03	9
1849	Canezou	4 8-11	8
1850	Canezou	5 9-07	8
1851	Nancy	3 7-00	10
1852	Kingston	3 7-06	11
1853	Jouvence	3 5-08	15
1854	Virago	3 7-03	3
1855	Baroncino	3 5-13	6
1856	Rogerthorpe	3 7-02	10
1857	Monarque	5 8-09	14
1858	Saunterer	4 9-00	8
1859	Promised Land	3 7-07	12
1860	Sweetsauce	3 7-07	8
1861	Starke	6 6-10	9
1862	Tim Whiffler	3 7-07	7
1863	Isoline	3 7-03	7
1864	Dollar	4 9-00	10
1865	Ely	4 9-07	9
1866	The Duke	4 9-00	5
1867	Vauban	3 7-07	5
1868	Speculum	3 7-07	5
1869	Restitution	4 9-00	5
1870	Siderolite	4 9-00	6
1871	Shannon	3 7-04	5
1872	Favonius	4 9-03	5
1873	Flageolet	3 7-07	3
1874	Doncaster	4 9-03	6
1875	Adventuriere	4 8-07	7
1876	New Holland	4 8-10	6
1877	Hampton	5 9-00	5
1878	Kincsem	4 8-07	3
1879	Isonomy	4 9-03	6
1880	Dresden China	4 8-07	2
1881	Madame du Barry	6 8-11	4
1882	Friday	5 7-11	4
1883	Border Minstrel	3 7-05	5
1884	St Slmon	3 8-00	3
1885	Althorp	3 7-07	5
1886	The Bard	3 7-07	WO
1887	Savile	3 7-07	5
1888	Rada	3 7-04	4
1889	Trayles	4 9-10	2
1890	Philomel	5 8-13	5
1891	Gonsalvo	4 9-06	5
1892	Martagon	5 9-10	3
1893	Barmecide	N/A 8-06	5
1894	Kilsallaghan	4 8-02	6
1895	Florizel II	4 9-06	2
1896	Count Schomberg	4 8-02	WO
1897	Count Schomberg	5 10-02	4
1898	King's Messenger	3 7-07	5
1899	Merman	N/A 9-05	3
1900	Mazagan	4 9-03	8
1901	Fortunatus	3 8-00	5
1902	Perseus	3 7-01	6
1903	Rabelais	3 7-02	8
1904	Saltpetre	4 7-10	5
1905	Red Robe	4 7-10	5
1906	Plum Tree	3 7-12	8
1907	The White Knight	4 9-10	6
1908	Radium	5 9-02	6
1909	Carrousel	3 7-08	5
1910	Magic	3 7-02	3
1911	Kilbroney	4 9-03	5
1912	Tullibardine	4 8-12	3
1913	Catmint	4 9-03	6
1914	Son-in-Law	3 7-08	5
1915 - 1918	No races		
1919	Queen's Square	4 9-00	5
1920	Mount Royal	3 7-07	4
1921	Bucks	3 7-08	5
1922	Flamboyant	4 9-03	5
1923	Triumph	4 9-03	3
1924	Teresina	4 9-00	6
1925	Cloudbank	4 9-03	6
1926	Glommen	4 9-03	9
1927	Dark Japan	4 9-03	3
1928	Kinchinjunga	4 9-03	7
1929	Old Orkney	5 9-07	6
1930	Brown Jack	6 9-07	5
1931	Salmon Leap	4 9-03	6
1932	Brulette	4 9-04	5
1933	Sans Peine	3 7-11	5
1934	Loosestrife	5 9-06	4
1935	Tiberius	4 9-07	3
1936	Cecil	5 9-06	9
1937	Fearless Fox	4 9-02	6
1938	Epigram	5 9-06	11
1939	Dubonnet	4 8-01	5

1940 - 1945	No races		
1946	Marsyas II	6 9-11	4
1947	Monsieur l'Amiral	6 9-12	4
1948	Tenerani	4 8-12	4
1949	Alycidon	4 8-12	4
1950	Val Drake	4 8-12	4
1951	Pan II	4 8-12	4

GOODWOOD CUP (1952-2001)

Year	Name	Age/Weight	Jockey	Trainer	Dist.	Runners	SP
1952	Medway	4 8-12	D Smith	F N Winter	1	4	5-1
1953	Souepi	5 9-00	C Elliott	G Digby	SHD	8	2-1F
1954	Blarney Stone	5 9-00	W Rickaby	V Smyth	15	5	13-2
1955	Double Bore	4 9-00	T Gosling	J Tree	1½	8	9-1
1956	Zarathustra	5 9-00	W Carr	C Boyd-Rochfort	½	4	10-11F
1957	Tenterhooks	3 7-10	E Britt	C Elsey	½	7	2-1F
1958	Gladness	5 8-11	L Piggott	M V O'Brien (Ire)	1½	4	1-2F
1959	Dickens	3 7-10	D Smith	C Boyd-Rochfort	¾	4	9-4
1960	Exar	4 9-00	L Piggott	N Murless	2	4	4-9F
1961	Predominate	9 9-00	E Smith	T Leader	SHD	4	11-4
1962	Sagacity	4 9-00	W Carr	C Boyd-Rochfort	2	4	5-1
1963	Trelawny	7 9-00	A Breasley	G Todd	6	4	8-13F
1964	Raise You Ten	4 9-00	S Clayton	C Boyd-Rochfort	¾	5	EVSF
1965	Apprentice	5 9-00	S Clayton	C Boyd-Rochfort	2½	5	8-1
1966	Gaulois	3 7-10	R Hutchinson	C Boyd-Rochfort	3	7	15-2
1967	Wrekin Rambler	4 9-00	A Breasley	G Richards	1½	5	2-1F
1968	Ovaltine	4 9-00	B Taylor	J F Watts	2½	7	5-2F
1969	Richmond Fair	5 9-00	J Gorton	B Hobbs	2	3	5-4
1970	Parthenon	4 9-00	G Starkey	H Cecil	2	5	3-1
1971	Rock Roi	4 9-00	D Keith	P Walwyn	4	5	4-6F
1972	Erimo Hawk	4 9-00	Pat Eddery	G Barling	½	4	10-11F
1973	Proverb	3 7-10	E Johnson	B Hills	½	4	6-4JF
1974	Proverb	4 9-00	L Piggott	B Hills	3	4	4-5F
1975	Girandole	4 9-00	L Piggott	M Stoute	2	8	7-2
1976	Mr Bigmore	4 9-00	G Starkey	P Robinson	1	6	3-1
1977	Grey Baron	4 9-03	G Lewis	B Hobbs	1½	8	11-4
1978	Tug Of War	5 9-00	B Rouse	D Whelan	¾	5	20-1
1979	Le Moss	4 9-07	J Mercer	H Cecil	7	5	1-2F
1980	Le Moss	5 9-07	J Mercer	H Cecil	NK	5	4-7F
1981	Ardross	5 9-07	L Piggott	H Cecil	1	6	2-9F
1982	Heighlin	6 9-00	S Cauthen	D Elsworth	½	8	8-1
1983	Little Wolf	5 9-07	W Carson	W Hern	½	7	4-9F
1984	Gildoran	4 9-07	S Cauthen	B Hills	8	4	9-4
1985	Valuable Witness	5 9-00	Pat Eddery	J Tree	5	7	11-10F
1986	Longboat	5 9-07	W Carson	W Hern	10	5	1-3F
1987	Sergeyevich	3 7-10	W Carson	J Dunlop	¾	5	EVSF
1988	Sadeem	5 9-07	G Starkey	G Harwood	1	6	4-6F
1989	Mazzacano	4 9-00	Pat Eddery	G Harwood	NK	5	15-2
1990	Lucky Moon	3 7-10	W Carson	J Dunlop	2½	6	11-8F
1991	Further Flight	5 9-00	M Hills	B Hills	1	10	9-2
1992	Further Flight	6 9-05	M Hills	B Hills	SHD	11	7-1
1993	Sonus	4 9-03	Pat Eddery	J Gosden	1	9	4-1
1994	Tioman Island	4 9-05	T Quinn	P Cole	¾	15	10-1
1995	Double Trigger	4 9-05	J Weaver	M Johnston	NK	9	2-1F
1996	Grey Shot	4 9-00	Pat Eddery	I Balding	HD	7	3-1
1997	Double Trigger	6 9-00	M Roberts	M Johnston	1½	10	16-1
1998	Double Trigger	7 9-05	D Holland	M Johnston	¾	9	11-2
1999	Kayf Tara	5 9-07	L Dettori	S Bin Suroor	4	7	9-4JF
2000	Royal Rebel	4 9-02	M Kinane	M Johnston	½	8	10-1
2001	Persian Punch	8 9-05	T Quinn	D Elsworth	1½	12	6-1

Established as a three-mile race in 1812, the distance soon dropped back to 2m 5f, to 2m 4f in 1990, then to two miles.

RICHMOND STAKES
(Sponsored by Gerrard Investment Management)

Group Two

Two-year-old colts and geldings. Six furlongs. First run 1877.

(1877-1939)

Year	Name	Runners	Year	Name	Runners
1877	Jannette	15	1899	Winifreda	4
1878	Wheel Of Fortune	13	1900	Handicapper	5
1879	Bend Or	8	1901	Duke Of Westminster	6
1880	Bal Gal	11	1902	Mead	7
1881	Dutch Oven	8	1903	Queen's Holiday	6
1882	Sigmophone	11	1904	Polymeius	7
1883	Duke Of Richmond	12	1905	Lally	4
1884	Rosy Morn	6	1906	Weathercock	8
1885	Sunrise	7	1907	Bolted	9
1886	Panzerschiff	5	1908	Bayardo	4
1887	Friar's Balsam	3	1909	Charles O'Malley	5
1888	Gulliver	6	1910	Pietri	9
1889	Golden Gate	6	1911	Sweeper II	6
1890	Siphonia	2	1912	Seremond	9
1891	Orme	8	1913	Black Jester	7
1892	Inverdon	9	1914	Pommern	10
1893	Galloping Dick	8	1915-1918	No races	
1894	The Nipper	10	1919	Golden Guinea	4
1895	Persimmon	5	1920	Sunblaze	4
1896	Chillingham	5	1921	Fodder	5
1897	Paladore	4	1922	Bombay Duck	2
1898	St Gris	5	1923	Halcyon	5

Year	Name	Runners	Year	Name	Runners
1924	Manna	9	1933	Colombo	8
1925	Pantera	6	1934	Bobsleigh	11
1926	The Satrap	4	1935	Mahmoud	11
1927	Gang Warily	13	1936	Perlfox	12
1928	Rattlin The Reefer	7	1937	Unbreakable	8
1929	Challenger	9	1938	Chancery	13
1930	Four Course	11	1939	Moradabad	8
1931	Spenser	7	1940-1945	No races	
1932	Solar Boy	1			

RICHMOND STAKES (1946-2001)

Year	Name	Weight	Jockey	Trainer	Dist.	Runners	SP
1946	Petition	9-00	H Wragg	F Butters	3	4	1-5F
1947	Birthday Greetings	8-07	J Simpson	H Jelliss	2	10	11-10F
1948	Star King	9-00	S Wragg	J Waugh	1	10	8-11F
1949	Palestine	9-00	G Richards	F Butters	4	3	6-100F
1950	Grey Sovereign	9-00	W Carr	G Beeby	NK	7	5-2
1951	Gay Time	8-07	A Breasley	N Cannon	½	4	100-7
1952	Artane	8-07	G Richards	P Prendergast (Ire)	½	5	13-8
1953	The Pie King	9-00	G Richards	P Prendergast (Ire)	2	6	8-13F
1954	Eubulides	9-00	E Britt	C Elsey	SHD	7	6-5F
1955	Ratification	9-00	W Rickaby	V Smyth	2	4	11-8F
1956	Red God	9-00	W Carr	C Boyd-Rochfort	½	5	7-2
1957	Promulgation	9-00	E Smith	T Leader	2	7	11-8F
1958	Hieroglyph	9-00	W Carr	C Boyd-Rochfort	½	7	9-4
1959	Dollar Piece	9-00	J Mercer	H Cottrill	½	4	100-6
1960	Typhoon	9-00	R Hutchinson	P Prendergast (Ire)	1½	5	4-11F
1961	Sovereign Lord	9-00	G Lewis	G Smyth	HD	7	8-1
1962	Romantic	9-00	L Piggott	N Murless	1	5	8-11F
1963	Gentle Art	9-00	R Hutchinson	J Jarvis	½	5	8-11F
1964	Ragtime	9-00	R Hutchinson	G Smyth	½	3	13-8
1965	Sky Gipsy	9-00	R Hutchinson	G Smyth	SHD	3	3-1
1966	Hambledon	9-00	A Breasley	T Corbett	2½	7	2-1F
1967	Berber	9-00	A Breasley	G Richards	1½	3	8-11F
1968	Tudor Music	9-00	F Durr	M Jarvis	2½	3	5-1
1969	Village Boy	9-00	W Williamson	G Todd	NK	5	9-2
1970	Swing Easy	9-00	L Piggott	J Tree	½	5	4-5F
1971	Sallust	8-11	J Mercer	W Hern	½	10	2-1F
1972	Master Sing	9-00	J Mercer	D Candy	1½	7	13-8F
1973	Dragonara Palace	8-11	L Piggott	B Hills	½	7	4-9F
1974	Legal Eagle	8-11	G Baxter	W Marshall	NK	6	4-1
1975	Stand To Reason	8-11	W Carson	B Hills	1½	9	12-1
1976	J.O. Tobin	8-11	L Piggott	N Murless	1½	5	8-11F
1977	Persian Bold	8-11	L Piggott	A Ingham	1½	5	4-6F
1978	Young Generation	8-11	G Starkey	G Harwood	3	5	12-1
1979	Castle Green	8-11	P Cook	M Stoute	NK	5	20-1
1980	Another Realm	8-11	J Mercer	F Durr	HD	10	16-1
1981	Tender King	8-11	P Waldron	J Sutcliffe Jnr	NK	7	11-4
1982	Gallant Special	8-11	L Piggott	R Armstrong	2	4	4-6F
*1983	Godstone	8-11	G Sexton	P Haslam	*	9	14-1
1984	Primo Dominie	8-11	J Reid	B Swift	NK	6	10-11F
1985	Nomination	8-11	T Quinn	P Cole	2½	10	8-1
1986	Rich Charlie	8-11	J Reid	C Nelson	HD	8	11-4JF
1987	Warning	8-11	Pat Eddery	G Harwood	1½	7	4-11F
1988	Heart Of Arabia	9-00	R Cochrane	C Brittain	1½	6	11-1
1989	Contract Law	8-11	B Raymond	W Jarvis	2½	5	9-2
1990	Mac's Imp	8-11	A Munro	W O'Gorman	1	7	2-1F
1991	Dilum	8-11	A Munro	P Cole	3½	4	2-7F
1992	Son Pardo	8-11	J Reid	R Hannon	1	6	7-1
1993	First Trump	8-11	M Hills	G Wragg	½	5	100-3
1994	Sri Pekan	8-11	T Quinn	P Cole	¾	6	9-4
1995	Polaris Flight	8-11	J Reid	P Chapple-Hyam	NK	6	9-4
1996	Easycall	8-11	B Doyle	B Meehan	3	7	7-2
1997	Dagggers Drawn	8-11	K Fallon	H Cecil	1½	6	8-13F
1998	Muqtarib	8-11	R Hills	J Dunlop	2	4	9-2
1999	Bachir	8-11	L Dettori	J Gosden	1½	7	11-8F
2000	Endless Summer	8-11	J Fortune	J Gosden	1	8	2-1F
2001	Mister Cosmi	8-11	K Darley	M Johnstone	1	8	7-1

**Godstone finished a 1¾ third to Vacarme, but the latter was disqualified and placed last after a stewards' enquiry, while an objection by Godstone's jockey to runner-up Creag-an-Sgor was sustained.*

CELEBRATION MILE

Group Two

Three-year-olds and up. One mile. First run 1967.

(1967-2001)

Year	Name	Age/Weight	Jockey	Trainer	Dist.	Runners	SP
1967	St Chad	3 8-03	G Moore	N Murless	1	7	9-4
1968	Jimmy Reppin	3 7-13	G Lewis	J Sutcliffe Jnr	2	6	5-1
1969	Habitat	3 8-06	L Piggott	R F J Houghton	½	6	9-2
1970	Humble Duty	3 8-04	D Keith	P Walwyn	1	5	4-6F
1971	Brigadier Gerard	3 8-06	J Mercer	W Hern	10	3	1-6F
1972	Sallust	3 8-13	J Mercer	W Hern	¾	3	8-13F
1973	Jacinth	3 8-10	J Gorton	B Hobbs	2	5	2-5F
1974	Pitcairn	3 8-08	R Hutchinson	J Dunlop	1½	3	4-9F
1975	Gay Fandango	3 8-08	Pat Eddery	M V O'Brien (Ire)	3	8	5-1
1976	Free State	3 8-03	Pat Eddery	P Walwyn	SHD	6	13-8F
1977	Be My Guest	3 8-07	L Piggott	M V O'Brien (Ire)	HD	6	6-4F
1978	Captain James	4 8-13	J Mercer	S McGrath (Ire)	NK	6	25-1
*1979	Kris	3 8-12	J Mercer	H Cecil	¾	8	30-100F

1980	Known Fact	3 8-12	W Carson	J Tree	NK	6	5-2
1981	To-Agori-Mou	3 8-12	G Starkey	G Harwood	½	6	5-4F
1982	Sandhurst Prince	3 8-05	G Starkey	G Harwood	1½	8	7-4
1983	Montekin	4 8-13	B Rouse	J Dunlop	½	6	8-1
1984	Rousillon	3 8-06	G Starkey	G Harwood	½	5	8-13F
1985	Abandoned - Course Waterlogged						
1986	Then Again	3 8-07	G Starkey	L Cumani	½	8	8-1
1987	Milligram	3 8-07	W R Swinburn	M Stoute	½	4	5-2
1988	Prince Rupert	4 9-03	M Hills	B Hills	1½	6	16-1
1989	Distant Relative	3 8-09	M Hills	B Hills	2½	5	2-1
1990	Shavian	3 9-00	S Cauthen	H Cecil	2½	5	5-2F
1991	Bold Russian	4 9-00	W Carson	B Hills	NK	5	100-3
1992	Selkirk	4 9-03	R Cochrane	I Balding	2½	7	1-2F
1993	Swing Low	4 9-03	J Reid	R Hannon	½	6	10-1
1994	Mehthaaf	3 8-11	W Carson	J Dunlop	2½	6	5-2
1995	Harayir	3 8-12	W Carson	W Hern	½	6	5-4F
1996	Mark Of Esteem	3 9-01	L Dettori	S Bin Suroor	3½	7	11-4F
**1997	Among Men	3 8-09	M Kinane	M Stoute	**	4	8-11F
1998	Muhtathir	3 8-09	R Hills	J Gosden	1¾	9	11-4F
1999	Cape Cross	5 9-07	J Reid	S Bin Suroor	1½	5	5-2
2000	Medicean	3 8-09	Pat Eddery	Sir M Stoute	1	6	5-2
2001	No Excuse Needed	3 8-09	K Fallon	Sir M Stoute	1½	6	8-11F

**Run at Ascot*

***Among Men was originally second, but was awarded the race on disqualification of 2½l winner Cape Cross for causing interference.*

PRESTIGE STAKES
(Sponsored by Touchdown In Malaysia)
Group Three
Two-year-old fillies only. Seven furlongs. First run 1974.
(1974-2001)

Year	Name	Weight	Jockey	Trainer	Dist.	Runners	SP
1974	One Over Parr	8-11	Pat Eddery	P Walwyn	¾	7	15-8F
1975	Cappuccilli	8-08	L Piggott	H Cecil	2	9	15-2
1976	Triple First	8-08	G Starkey	M Stoute	4	7	7-1
1977	Cistus	8-08	W Carson	W Hern	NK	8	7-2
1978	Formulate	8-08	M Roberts	H Cecil	1	12	20-1
*1979	Schweppes Forever	8-11	B Tayor	R Price	2	9	15-2
1980	Fairy Footsteps	8-03	Pat Eddery	H Cecil	4	10	4-1
1981	Stratospheric	8-06	Pat Eddery	J Dunlop	2½	6	16-1
1982	Flamenco	8-09	J Matthias	I Balding	4	9	5-1
1983	Shoot Clear	8-09	W R Swinburn	M Stoute	1	8	3-1
1984	Bella Colora	8-06	W R Swinburn	M Stoute	¾	6	4-1
1985	Asteroid Field	8-06	B Thomson	B Hills	4	6	11-1
1986	Invited Guest	8-07	S Cauthen	R Armstrong	2½	6	4-1
1987	Obeah	8-09	C Asmussen	B Hills	2½	6	16-1
1988	Life At The Top	8-12	M Roberts	A Stewart	½	7	5-1
1989	Moon Cactus	8-12	S Cauthen	H Cecil	1½	7	4-7F
1990	Jaffa Line	8-09	S Cauthen	D Elsworth	NK	5	5-2
1991	Musicale	9-00	Pat Eddery	H Cecil	1	5	15-8F
1992	Love Of Silver	8-09	M Roberts	C Brittain	NK	7	9-1
1993	Glatisant	8-09	M Hills	G Wragg	HD	6	1-2F
1994	Pure Grain	8-09	J Reid	M Stoute	1¼	9	2-1
1995	Bint Shadayid	8-09	W Carson	J Dunlop	HD	6	EVSF
1996	Red Camellia	8-12	G Duffield	Sir M Prescott	6	5	10-11F
1997	Midnight Line	8-09	W Ryan	H Cecil	SHD	6	11-2
1998	Circle Of Gold	8-09	J Reid	P Chapple-Hyam	1	9	8-13F
1999	Icicle	8-09	R Cochrane	J Fanshawe	SHD	9	10-1
2000	Freefourracing	8-09	T Quinn	B Meehan	NK	6	8-1
2001	Gossamer	8-09	J Spencer	L Cumani	7	6	5-4F

**Run at Ascot*

GORDON STAKES
(Sponsored by Peugeot)
Group Three
Three-year-olds only. One mile four furlongs. First run 1902.
(1902-1939)

Year	Name	Weight	Runners
1902	Osbech	9-04	3
1903	Zindafel	8-10	3
1904	Delaunay	9-07	3
1905	Dinneford	8-07	6
1906	Victorious	9-04	3
1907	Galvani	9-07	7
1908	Putchamin	8-07	7
1909	Moscato	9-07	5
1910	Cardinal Beaufort	9-00	5
1911	Prince Palatine	9-07	4
1912	Fantasio	8-07	4
1913	Augur	8-04	8
1914	My Prince	9-07	6
1915 - 1918	No races		
1919	Sir Douglas	10-00	2
1920	The Alder	8-00	2
1921	Stanislaus	8-00	4
1922	Tamar	9-00	3
1923	Bold And Bad	9-10	3
1924	Black Sheep	8-00	3
1925	Kentish Knock	9-10	4
1926	Thistledown	8-03	4
1927	Tiger Hill	8-03	6
1928	Cyclonic	9-10	10
1929	Defoe	8-03	7
1930	*Press Gang	9-10	4
	*Ut Majeur	9-00	
1931	Rose en Soleil	9-00	6
1932	Firdaussi	9-03	5
1933	Tavern	8-00	4
1934	Bright Bird	9-10	4
1935	Bideford Bay	8-11	5
1936	Magnet	9-00	9
1937	Perifox	9-04	5
1938	Valedictory	8-03	7
1939	Wheatland	9-04	4
1940 - 1945	No races		

GORDON STAKES (1946-2001)

Year	Name	Weight	Jockey	Trainer	Dist.	Runners	SP
1946	Fast And Fair	9-02	C Richards	J Lawson	NK	5	5-1
1947	Merry Quip	9-02	T Weston	N Cannon	2	4	4-11F
1948	Nathoo	9-07	G Richards	F Butters	3	6	7-2
1949	Royal Forest	9-02	G Richards	N Murless	10	3	1-6F
1950	Foxboro	8-07	W Rickaby	V Smyth	SHD	8	100-9
1951	Prince d'Ouilly	8-07	G Richards	R Warden	½	3	4-7F
1952	Gay Time	8-07	G Richards	W Nightingall	1½	3	2-15F
1953	Prince Canarina	8-07	D Smith	H Leader	4	4	1-3F
1954	Brilliant Green	7-13	E Smith	D Watson	4	9	5-2F
1955	Manati	8-07	W Carr	C Boyd-Rochfort	4	6	100-8
1956	Dacian	8-07	W Snaith	H Cottrill	1½	6	10-1
1957	Pipe Of Peace	8-12	A Breasley	G Richards	½	6	4-6F
1958	Guersillus	8-12	E Hide	C Elsey	5	5	13-8
1959	Above Suspicion	8-12	D Smith	C Boyd-Rochfort	NK	4	EVSF
1960	Kipling	8-12	G Lewis	P Hastings-Bass	½	8	6-1
1961	Pardao	8-12	W Carr	C Boyd-Rochfort	1½	5	10-11F
1962	Gay Challenger	8-07	R Hutchinson	J Oxx (Ire)	2	9	5-1
1963	Tiger	8-12	A Breasley	G Richards	2	9	100-3
1964	Sweet Moss	8-12	L Piggott	N Murless	1½	7	11-2
1965	King Log	8-02	R Hutchinson	G Todd	3	6	4-1
1966	Khalekan	8-02	D Lake	P Prendergast (Ire)	2½	6	2-1F
1967	Sun Rock	8-12	G Moore	N Murless	HD	7	11-4JF
1968	Mount Athos	8-12	R Hutchinson	J Dunlop	1	3	4-7F
1969	Harmony Hall	8-12	W Williamson	G Smyth	3	3	5-1
1970	Rock Roi	8-07	G Lewis	P Walwyn	2	4	3-1
1971	Athens Wood	8-07	G Starkey	H Thomson Jones	½	5	7-4F
1972	Scottish Rifle	8-10	R Hutchinson	J Dunlop	½	3	4-6F
1973	Duke Of Ragusa	8-10	J Gorton	B Hobbs	6	4	11-8
1974	Grey Thunder	8-10	W Carson	C Brittain	½	8	25-1
1975	Guillaume Tell	8-10	L Piggott	M V O'Brien (Ire)	2	9	11-8F
1976	Smuggler	8-13	J Mercer	W Hern	SHD	6	7-2
1977	Pollerton	8-10	C Roche	P Prendergast (Ire)	7	4	11-2
1978	Sexton Blake	8-10	E Hide	B Hills	SHD	5	100-3
1979	More Light	8-10	W Carson	W Hern	¼	6	5-2
1980	Prince Bee	8-10	W Carson	W Hern	2½	6	5-4F
1981	Burtomi	8-02	W Carson	W Hern	1½	5	3-1
1982	Electric	8-13	G Starkey	M Stoute	3	6	25-1
1983	John French	8-10	L Piggott	H Cecil	2½	6	4-1
1984	Commanche Run	8-10	L Piggott	L Cumani	5	8	7-2JF
1985	Kazaroun	8-10	W R Swinburn	M Stoute	8	5	10-1
1986	Allez Milord	8-10	G Starkey	G Harwood	½	5	11-10F
1987	Love The Groom	9-02	W Carson	J Dunlop	3	6	6-4F
1988	Minster Son	8-10	W Carson	W Hern	2	5	2-1F
1989	Warrshan	8-10	W R Swinburn	M Stoute	HD	4	3-1
1990	Karinga Bay	8-10	B Rouse	Denys Smith	½	6	13-2
1991	Stylish Senor	8-10	G Duffield	J Fanshawe	½	3	11-4
1992	Bonny Scot	8-10	L Dettori	L Cumani	2	6	6-1
1993	Right Win	8-10	J Reid	R Hannon	2½	8	3-1F
1994	Broadway Flyer	8-13	M Hills	J Hills	NK	9	11-2
1995	Presenting	8-10	L Dettori	J Gosden	1½	7	7-4F
1996	St Mawes	8-10	K Darley	J Dunlop	HD	12	12-1
1997	Stowaway	8-10	K Darley	S Bin Suroor	3	10	100-30F
1998	*Rabah	8-10	R Hills	J Dunlop	*	6	5-2
	*Nedawi	8-10	L Dettori	S Bin Surror	*		5-1
1999	Compton Ace	8-10	K Fallon	G Butler	1½	6	12-1
2000	Millenary	8-13	T Quinn	J Dunlop	SHD	10	9-1
2001	Alexius	8-10	K Fallon	Sir M Stoute	NK	11	7-1

Open to three-year-olds and up in 1902, restricted to three-year-olds thereafter.

**Dead heat*

KING GEORGE STAKES
Group Three
Three-year-olds and up. Five furlongs. First run 1911.
(1946-2001)

Year	Name	Age/Weight	Jockey	Trainer	Dist.	Runners	SP
1946	Honeyway	5 9-11	E Smith	J Jarvis	½	2	7-100F
1947	Daily Mail	4 9-02	G Richards	W Nightingall	2	2	1-8F
1948	Royal Barge	4 9-00	G Richards	P Allden	½	4	7-4
1949	Abernant	3 9-00	G Richards	N Murless	2	8	30-100F
1950	Abernant	4 9-11	G Richards	N Murless	5	3	4-9F
1951	Bakshishi	3 8-01	G Richards	H Wragg	SHD	5	100-3
1952	Royal Serenade	4 9-11	G Richards	H Wragg	NK	6	7-2

1953	Fairy Flax	4 9-06	A Breasley	J Lawson	HD	5	6-1
1954	Four Of Spades	3 8-03	W Johnstone	G Beeby	4	5	100-3
1955	Democratic	3 8-03	A Breasley	P Prendergast (Ire)	¾	5	11-10F
1956	Palariva	3 9-00	R Poincelet	A Head (Fr)	1	4	6-1
1957	Refined	3 8-00	D Smith	P Prendergast (Ire)	½	4	5-2
1958	Right Boy	4 9-09	L Piggott	W Dutton	1½	5	8-13F
1959	Right Boy	5 9-09	L Piggott	P Rohan	2	5	8-13F
1960	Bleep-Bleep	4 9-02	W Carr	H Cottrill	HD	3	100-8
1961	Floribunda	3 8-03	R Hutchinson	P Prendergast (Ire)	3	4	4-6F
1962	La Tendresse	3 8-00	G Bougoure	P Prendergast (Ire)	½	3	11-1
1963	Secret Step	4 9-06	A Breasley	P Hastings-Bass	1	5	11-10F
1964	Matatina	4 9-06	L Piggott	F Armstrong	HD	5	EVSF
1965	Pugnacity	3 8-07	L Piggott	W Wharton	1	4	9-4
1966	Polyfoto	4 9-09	B Taylor	E Reavey	1	9	8-1
1967	Right Strath	6 8-09	J Mercer	W Nightingall	½	5	100-6
1968	So Blessed	3 9-03	F Durr	M Jarvis	1	5	4-5F
1969	Laser Light	3 8-03	R Hutchinson	J Dunlop	2½	3	2-1
1970	Raffingora	5 9-09	L Piggott	W Marshall	1	4	4-1
1971	Constans	6 8-13	L Piggott	J Tree	1½	6	9-4
1972	Stilvi	3 8-05	J Gorton	B Hobbs	SHD	5	100-3
1973	Sandford Lad	3 8-04	A Murray	R Price	½	5	6-5F
1974	Singing Bede	5 9-00	G Baxter	D Marks	HD	9	12-1
1975	Auction Ring	3 8-04	J Mercer	W Hern	½	8	85-4
1976	Music Boy	3 8-05	G Starkey	B Lunness	NK	8	16-1
1977	Scarcely Blessed	3 8-02	R Hutchnson	R F J Houghton	NK	9	6-1
1978	Music Maestro	3 9-01	G Starkey	M Stoute	NK	7	6-1
1979	Ahonoora	4 9-03	G Starkey	F Durr	2	7	EVSF
1980	Valeriga	4 9-06	L Piggott	L Cumani	2	9	9-2
1981	King Of Spain	5 9-08	P Cook	P Cundell	NK	8	4-1
1982	Tina's Pet	4 9-00	L Piggott	G Huffer	2	12	6-1
1983	Soba	4 9-00	D Nicholls	D Chapman	2½	14	9-4F
1984	Anita's Prince	3 8-08	L Piggott	R Lister (Ire)	4	13	2-1F
1985	Primo Dominie	3 8-13	W R Swinburn	M Stoute	½	11	5-4F
1986	Double Schwartz	5 9-05	Pat Eddery	C Nelson	SHD	14	6-4F
1987	Singing Steven	3 8-13	B Rouse	R Hannon	HD	9	14-1
1988	Silver Fling	3 8-05	Pat Eddery	I Balding	1	13	2-1F
1989	Statoblest	3 8-08	R Cochrane	L Cumani	¾	13	11-1
1990	Argentum	3 9-00	J Reid	J Holt	1½	14	4-1F
1991	Title Roll	3 8-07	W Carson	T Stack (Ire)	¾	15	8-1
1992	Freddie Lloyd	3 9-00	J Reid	N Callaghan	NK	11	5-1
1993	Lochsong	5 8-11	L Dettori	I Balding	HD	11	13-8F
1994	Lochsong	6 9-07	L Dettori	I Balding	1¼	15	10-11F
1995	Hever Golf Rose	4 9-05	J Weaver	J Naughton	½	11	10-1
1996	Rambling Bear	3 8-10	R Cochrane	M Blanshard	1	14	10-1
1997	Averti	6 9-00	K Fallon	W Muir	½	15	11-1
1998	Land Of Dreams	3 8-07	D Holland	M Johnston	¾	15	5-1
1999	Rudi's Pet	5 9-00	S Sanders	D Nicholls	1¼	15	6-1F
2000	Cassandra Go	4 8-10	M Roberts	G Wragg	SHD	13	11-2
2001	Deitrich	3 8-12	M Kinane	A O'Brien (Ire)	¾	15	11-2

VINTAGE STAKES

Champagne Victor

Group Three

Two-year-olds only. Seven furlongs. First run 1975.

(1975-2001)

Year	**Name**	**Weight**	**Jockey**	**Trainer**	**Dist.**	**Runners**	**SP**
1975	Riboboy	8-11	J Merer	W Hern	1	10	8-11F
1976	Sky Ship	9-03	J Mercer	W Hern	HD	8	10-11F
1977	Conte Santi	8-06	B Taylor	R Price	2	10	7-2JF
1978	Troy	9-00	W Carson	W Hern	2½	5	2-1F
1979	Marathon Gold	9-00	J Mercer	H Cecil	2½	7	9-4
1980	Church Parade	8-11	W Carson	W Hern	HD	6	8-13F
1981	Treboro	9-00	G Starkey	G Harwood	1	5	5-4F
1982	All Systems Go	8-11	G Duffield	G Pritchard-Gordon	HD	7	5-1
1983	Trojan Fen	9-00	L Piggott	H Cecil	1½	5	4-11F
1984	Petoski	9-00	J Mercer	W Hern	¾	8	2-1F
1985	Faustus	9-00	S Cauthen	H Cecil	NK	10	9-4F
1986	Don't Forget Me	8-11	Pat Eddery	R Hannon	½	5	7-1
1987	Undercut	9-00	Pat Eddery	G Harwood	1½	6	EVSF
1988	High Estate	9-02	S Cauthen	H Cecil	½	6	6-5F
1989	Be My Chief	9-00	S Cauthen	H Cecil	½	5	8-15F
1990	Mukaddamah	8-11	W Carson	P Walwyn	1½	6	6-4F
1991	Dr Devious	9-00	W Carson	P Chapple-Hyam	1½	7	9-4
1992	Maroof	8-11	W Carson	R Armstrong	1½	10	8-1
1993	Mister Baileys	8-11	D McKeown	M Johnston	2½	6	13-8F
1994	Eltish	8-11	Pat Eddery	H Cecil	2½	8	8-11F
1995	Alhaarth	8-11	W Carson	W Hern	1	6	5-6F
1996	Putra	8-11	T Quinn	P Cole	2	8	100-30
1997	Central Park	9-00	Pat Eddery	P Cole	3	6	5-4F
1998	Aljabr	8-11	L Dettori	S Bin Suroor	3	7	4-6F
1999	Ekraar	8-11	R Hills	M Tregoning	2	5	7-4
2000	No Excuse Needed	8-11	J Murtagh	Sir M Stoute	1¾	10	12-1
2001	Naheef	8-11	L Dettori	D Loder	2	10	8-1

MOLECOMB STAKES

Group Three

Two-year-olds only. Five furlongs. First run 1833.

(1946-2001)

Year	**Name**	**Weight**	**Jockey**	**Trainer**	**Dist.**	**Runners**	**SP**
1946	Rule Britannia	8-07	H Wragg	W Earl	1	4	8-11F
1947	Phaetonia	8-07	G Richards	F Darling	2	6	5-4F
1948	Integrity	9-02	C Smirke	J Leach	1	7	7-2
1949	Diableretta	9-07	G Richards	F Butters	¾	2	1-8F
1950	Crawley Beauty	8-12	G Richards	N Murless	2	12	4-6F
1951	Tayeh	8-07	G Richards	M Marsh	3	10	9-4F
1952	Tessa Gillian	8-07	W Rickaby	J Jarvis	1½	7	5-4F
1953	Urshalim	8-11	C Smirke	M Marsh	¾	8	11-2
1954	Brave Venture	8-11	W Rickaby	J Jarvis	1½	11	100-6
*1955	Palariva	8-11	R Poincelet	A Head (Fr)	*	6	4-9F
1956	Pharsalia	8-11	W Snaith	H Cottrill	2	6	11-8F
1957	Abelia	8-11	L Piggott	N Murless	3	4	1-5F
1958	Krakenwake	8-11	A Breasley	N Bertie	2	8	11-4
1959	Queensbury	8-11	E Smith	J Waugh	6	5	5-4F
1960	Cynara	8-11	J Mercer	H Wragg	3	4	2-9F
1961	La Tendresse	8-11	R Hutchinson	P Prendergast (Ire)	6	7	EVSF
1962	Royal Indiscretion	8-11	G Bougoure	P Prendergast (Ire)	HD	7	11-8F
1963	Crimea II	8-11	W Carr	C Boyd-Rochfort	¾	8	11-2
1964	Regal Pink	8-11	G Bougoure	P Prendergast (Ire)	3	7	5-2F
1965	Reet Lass	8-11	B Connorton	W Gray	1½	6	100-9
1966	Smooth	8-11	L Piggott	R F J Houghton	1½	5	9-2
1967	Lowna	8-11	G Moore	N Murless	4	7	7-4
1968	Flying Legs	8-11	L Piggott	M Jarvis	½	5	4-1
1969	Mange Tout	8-11	B Foy	K Cundell	4	4	8-11F
1970	Cawston's Pride	8-11	B Taylor	F Maxwell	4	4	1-5F
1971	Pert Lassie	8-08	G Starkey	H Cecil	1	4	4-7F
1972	Miss Slip	8-11	J Lindley	W Marshall	HD	3	6-4
1973	Bitty Girl	9-01	B Raymond	M Jarvis	½	6	7-4
1974	Lady Rowley	8-13	L Piggott	N Callaghan	1	4	4-5F
1975	Hayloft	8-10	L Piggott	R F J Houghton	NK	8	3-1
1976	Be Easy	8-10	R Hutchinson	J Dunlop	½	7	9-1
1977	Hatta	8-10	R Hutchinson	J Dunlop	2½	7	7-1
1978	Greenland Park	9-04	H White	Lord Huntingdon	2½	6	5-6F
1979	Keep Off	8-10	W Carson	J Dunlop	HD	6	7-1
1980	Marwell	8-10	L Piggott	M Stoute	2½	7	4-6F
1981	Prowess Prince	8-10	L Piggott	E Eldin	1½	6	4-5F
1982	Kafu	8-10	G Starkey	G Harwood	3	4	6-5
1983	Precocious	9-00	L Piggott	H Cecil	2½	7	30-100F
1984	Absent Chimes	8-10	P Robinson	D Thom	1½	8	11-4F
1985	Hotbee	8-07	T Williams	J Bridger	NK	9	100-1
1986	Gemini Fire	8-12	S Cauthen	P Felgate	SHD	6	33-1
1987	Classic Ruler	8-12	J Reid	C Nelson	1½	7	5-2
1988	Almost Blue	8-12	J Carroll	J Berry	¾	13	10-1
1989	Haunting Beauty	8-07	Pat Eddery	J Etherington	¾	10	3-1
**1990	Poets Cove	8-12	J Reid	W Carter	*	4	11-2
1991	Sahara Star	8-07	J Reid	M Stoute	1½	7	2-1F
1992	Millyant	8-07	M Roberts	R Guest	1	11	9-2
1993	Risky	8-12	W R Swinburn	R Hannon	3½	5	4-9F
1994	Hoh Magic	8-10	M Hills	M Bell	2½	7	EVSF
1995	Almaty	9-03	K Darley	C Collins (Ire)	1½	7	9-2
1996	Carmine Lake	8-07	J Reid	P Chapple-Hyam	NK	7	6-1
1997	Lady Alexander	8-11	P Shanahan	C Collins (Ire)	½	13	100-30F
1998	Inya Lake	8-07	T Quinn	M Channon	1	9	20-1
1999	Misty Miss	8-07	J Egan	P Evans	1	10	33-1
2000	Misty Eyed	8-10	L Newman	N Dutfield	1¼	9	3-1
2001	Whitbarrow	9-01	B Marcus	R Millman	½	14	10-1

For two-year-old fillies only 1932-80.

**Palariva was beaten a head by La Fresnes, but the latter was disqualified and placed last after a stewards' enquiry.*

***Poets Cove was beaten ½l by Jimmy Barnie, but the latter was disqualified and placed last after a stewards' enquiry.*

SELECT STAKES

Group Three

Three-year-olds and up. One mile two furlongs. First run 1965.

(1965-2001)

Year	**Name**	**Age/Weight**	**Jockey**	**Trainer**	**Dist.**	**Runners**	**SP**
1965	Derring Do	4 9-04	A Breasley	A Budgett	6	3	4-11F
1966	Antiquarian	5 8-13	R Hutchinson	H Blagrave	2	5	9-4
1967	Haymaking	4 8-13	L Piggott	R F J Houghton	NK	4	13-8
1968	Abandoned - Local Flooding						
1969	Jimmy Reppin	4 9-07	G Lewis	J Sutcliffe Jnr	4	4	EvsF
1970	Northern Wizard	4 8-11	G Lewis	W Marshall	½	4	10-1
1971	Ortis	4 9-07	D Keith	P Walwyn	4	4	1-10F
1972	Wenceslas	4 8-12	L Piggott	M V O'Brien (Ire)	1	1	10-11F
1973	So Royal	3 7-09	D Cullen	D Candy	HD	7	EvsF
1974	Abandoned - Waterlogged						
1975	Escapologist	3 7-08	E Johnson	A Budgett	HD	7	13-8F
1976	Obstacle	3 7-12	P Waldron	H Candy	1	8	11-1
1977	Balmerino	5 9-09	R Hutchinson	J Dunlop	5	9	6-1
1978	Gunner B	5 9-09	J Mercer	H Cecil	½	3	4-9F
*1979	Bolide	3 7-13	W Carson	W Hern	7	6	13-8F
1980	Welsh Chanter	4 9-03	J Mercer	H Cecil	1½	6	4-1
1981	Prince Bee	4 9-09	J Mercer	W Hern	3	4	7-4F
1982	Peacetime	3 8-10	Pat Eddery	J Tree	¾	6	3-1
1983	Morcon	3 8-07	W Carson	W Hern	SHD	6	9-4
1984	Bob Back	3 8-05	B Raymond	M Jarvis	5	5	8-1
1985	Iroko	3 8-04	B Rouse	M Stoute	2	8	7-2
1986	Dancing Brave	3 8-13	G Starkey	G Harwood	10	6	No SP
1987	Most Welcome	3 8-06	Paul Eddery	G Wragg	2	6	6-4F
1988	Mtoto	5 9-09	M Robets	A Stewart	2½	5	1-4F
1989	Legal Case	3 8-06	L Dettori	L Cumani	4	5	7-4F
1990	Missionary Ridge	3 8-12	R Cochrane	B Hills	½	5	9-2

Year	Name	Age/Weight	Jockey	Trainer	Dist.	Runners	SP
1991	Filia Ardross	5 8-11	M Roberts	A Stewart	½	6	11-2
1992	Knifebox	4 9-00	D Holland	J Gosden	½	10	25-1
1993	Knifebox	5 9-03	M Roberts	J Gosden	¾	6	6-4F
1994	Alderbrook	5 9-00	Paul Eddery	Mrs J Cecil	HD	7	7-2
1995	Triarius	5 9-00	G Carter	S Bin Suroor	1½	6	7-4F
1996	Singspiel	4 9-03	C Asmussen	M Stoute	1	4	11-10F
1997	Fahris	3 8-07	R Cochrane	B Hanbury	6	5	100-30
1998	Mutamam	3 8-10	M Roberts	A Stewart	4	4	11-8F
1999	Lear Spear	4 9-05	T Quinn	D Elsworth	½	7	9-2
2000	Ekraar	3 8-10	R Hills	M Tregoning	5	5	10-11F
2001	Nayef	3 8-10	R Hills	M Tregoning	6	3	8-13F

For four-year-olds and up 1965-72; handicap 1966 only; three and four-year-olds 1973-75.
**Run at Sandown*

CHARLTON HUNT SUPREME STAKES

Group Three
Three-year-olds and up. Seven furlongs. First run 1981.
(1981-2001)

Year	Name	Age/Weight	Jockey	Trainer	Dist.	Runners	SP
1981	Belmont Bay	4 9-04	L Piggott	H Cecil	2	5	10-11F
1982	Hays	3 8-10	G Starkey	G Harwood	½	7	11-8F
1983	Larionov	3 8-07	B Taylor	J Winter	¾	9	14-1
1984	Sarab	3 8-07	T Quinn	P Cole	3	8	15-8F
1985	Efisio	5 8-04	W Carson	J Dunlop	¾	10	9-4F
1986	Sarab	5 9-01	T Quinn	P Cole	HD	10	7-4F
1987	Asteroid Field	4 8-06	M Hills	B Hills	HD	10	7-1
1988	Fair Judgement	4 8-12	J Reid	M V O'Brien (Ire)	1½	8	7-4F
1989	Kerita	3 8-05	Pat Eddery	R F J Houghton	HD	8	7-1
1990	Anshan	3 8-09	Pat Eddery	J Gosden	2	6	2-1F
1991	Osario	4 8-12	M Roberts	R Hannon	NK	13	20-1
1992	Hazaam	3 8-09	W R Swinburn	M Stoute	HD	7	7-1
1993	Abandoned - Waterlogged						
1994	Soviet Line	4 9-02	W R Swinburn	M Stoute	¾	9	2-1F
1995	Inzar	3 8-08	T Quinn	P Cole	Shd	10	3-1
1996	Tagula	3 8-09	K Darley	I Balding	Hd	9	4-1
1997	Decorated Hero	5 9-02	O Peslier	J Gosden	1½	6	6-4F
1998	Decorated Hero	5 9-05	L Dettori	J Gosden	½	8	2-1JF
1999	Abandoned - Waterlogged						
2000	Mount Abu	3 8-09	J Fortune	J Gosden	Hd	8	2-1JF
2001	Late Night Out	6 8-12	M Tebbutt	W Jarvis	2	4	EVSF

LUPE STAKES
(Sponsored by Victor Chandler)

Listed Race
Three-year-old fillies only. One mile two furlongs. First run 1972.
(1972-2001)

Year	Name	Weight	Jockey	Trainer	Dist.	Runners	SP
1972	Star Ship	8-08	A Murray	R Price	1	7	9-1
1973	Rosolini	8-08	R Hutchinson	P Nelson	3	8	4-1JF
1974	Northern Princess	8-08	A Kimberley	J Hindley	¾	5	11-4
1975	Misoptimist	8-08	A Kimberley	J Hindley	1	7	15-2
1976	Laughing Girl	8-03	Pat Eddery	H Wragg	¾	9	6-1
1977	Western Star	8-08	Pat Edery	P Walwyn	2	5	6-1
1978	Cistus	8-08	W Carson	W Hern	4	8	6-4F
1979	Britannia's Rule	8-03	P Waldron	H Candy	½	5	7-1
*1980	Vielle	8-08	G Baxter	B Hobbs	½	8	7-4F
1981	Golden Bowl	8-08	J Matthias	I Balding	3	4	11-10F
1982	Height Of Fashion	8-11	W Carson	W Hern	2	4	1-5F
1983	Current Raiser	8-03	T Ives	C Brittain	6	8	33-1
1984	Miss Beaulieu	8-08	L Piggott	G Wragg	¾	15	4-1
1985	Bella Colora	8-11	W R Swinburn	M Stoute	2½	6	8-11F
1986	Tralthee	8-11	Pat Eddery	L Cumani	2½	6	9-4
1987	Scimitarra	8-11	S Cauthen	H Cecil	2	16	8-1
1988	Miss Boniface	8-11	M Roberts	P Kelleway	HD	4	5-1
1989	Lady Shipley	8-11	G Starkey	M Stoute	4	7	8-1
1990	Moon Cactus	9-03	S Cauthen	H Cecil	1½	7	5-4F
1991	Fragrant Hill	8-11	R Cochrane	I Balding	1½	7	33-1
1992	Oumaldaaya	8-11	W Carson	J Dunlop	3	6	3-1
1993	Gisarne	8-11	W Carson	J Dunlop	NK	9	3-1
1994	Bulaxie	9-00	W Carson	J Dunlop	4	6	4-9F
1995	Subya	8-11	W Carson	J Dunlop	1¼	9	11-2
1996	Whitewater Affair	8-11	R Cochrane	M Stoute	1¾	9	4-1F
1997	Maid Of Camelot	8-08	T Sprake	R Charlton	1¼	7	10-1
1998	Napoleon's Sister	8-08	K Fallon	D Elsworth	2½	8	20-1
1999	Claxon	8-11	P Eddery	J Dunlop	2¼	8	7-4F
2000	Love Divine	8-08	T Quinn	H Cecil	4	6	3-1
2001	Foodbroker Fancy	8-08	D O'Neill	D Elsworth	HD	9	14-1

Race distance 1m 4f 1981-83.
**Run at Kempton*

PREDOMINATE STAKES
(Sponsored by Letheby & Christopher)

Listed Race
Three-year-olds only. One mile three furlongs. First run 1970.
(1970-2001)

Year	Name	Weight	Jockey	Trainer	Dist.	Runners	SP
1970	Charlton	8-11	J Mercer	W Hern	2½	4	5-4
1971	Levanter	9-00	L Piggott	H R Price	½	5	10-11F
1972	Scottish Rifle	8-11	R Hutchinson	J Dunlop	½	8	6-1
1973	Buoy	8-11	J Mercer	W Hern	4	9	3-1
1974	English Prince	9-00	Pat Eddery	P Walwyn	6	11	9-2
1975	No Alimony	9-00	Pat Eddery	P Walwyn	SHD	6	4-7F
1976	General Ironside	8-11	L Piggott	H Cecil	4	6	11-2
1977	Royal Blend	8-11	J Mercer	H Cecil	3	6	11-4F
1978	English Harbour	8-11	W Carson	I Balding	1½	9	9-1
1979	Troy	9-00	W Carson	W Hern	7	4	4-11F
*1980	Prince Bee	8-06	W Carson	W Hern	¾	8	6-1
1981	Abandoned Due To Waterlogging						
1982	Peacetime	9-00	J Mercer	J Tree	½	9	11-4F
1983	Morcon	8-06	W Carson	W Hern	6	6	11-4JF
1984	Ilium	8-06	A Murray	H Thomson Jones	½	12	4-1JF
1985	Lanfranco	9-00	S Cauthen	H Cecil	3	8	11-10F
1986	Allez Milord	8-12	G Starkey	G Harwood	5	8	5-6F
1987	Ibn Bey	8-12	T Quinn	P Cole	2	9	20-1
1988	Minster Son	9-01	W Carson	W Hern	1½	7	3-1
1989	Warrshan	8-12	W R Swinburn	M Stoute	2	8	7-2
1990	Razeen	8-12	S Cauthen	H Cecil	4	6	7-2
1991	Man From Eldorado	8-12	R Cochrane	G Harwood	NK	8	10-1
1992	Jeune	8-12	M Hills	G Wragg	5	9	7-1
1993	Geisway	8-12	L Piggott	R Hannon	SHD	6	9-2
1994	Opera Score	8-08	Pat Eddery	H Cecil	½	5	4-1
1995	Pentire	9-00	M Hills	G Wragg	SHD	6	11-8F
1996	Don Micheletto	8-08	M Kinane	S Bin Suroor	½	9	5-1
1997	Grapeshot	8-11	J Reid	L Cumani	2½	6	2-1F
1998	Rabah	8-08	Pat Eddery	J Dunlop	½	6	15-2
1999	Dubai Millennium	8-08	L Dettori	S Bin Suroor	3½	6	4-11F
2000	Roscius	8-08	L Dettori	S Bin Suroor	SHD	8	9-2
2001	Asian Heights	8-08	Keiren Fallon	G Wragg	1¾	11	3-1F

Race distance 1m 4f up to 1987, then 1m 2f up to 2000.
**Run at Kempton*

FESTIVAL STAKES

Listed Race
Four-year-olds and up. One mile two furlongs. First run 1975.
(1975-2001)

Year	Name	Age/Weight	Jockey	Trainer	Dist	Runners	SP
1975	Taros	4 8-12	J Mercer	P Walwyn	SHD	5	5-6F
1976	Rose Bowl	4 9-04	W Carson	R F J Houghton	4	6	4-6F
1977	Lucky Wednesday	4 9-07	J Mercer	H Cecil	½	7	4-5F
1978	Balmerino	6 9-07	G Starkey	J Dunlop	¾	6	8-11F
1979	Ile De Bourbon	4 9-07	J Reid	R F J Houghton	4	6	EVSF
*1980	Sea Chimes	4 9-00	W Carson	J Dunlop	4	6	13-8
1981	Triomphe	4 8-11	Pat Eddery	M V O'Brien (Ire)	1	8	9-4
1982	Castle Keep	5 9-00	W Carson	J Dunlop	2	6	2-1F
1983	Fine Sun	6 9-00	Pat Eddery	M Lambert	HD	8	8-1
1984	Morcon	4 9-03	W Carson	W Hern	½	6	7-4
1985	Rainbow Quest	4 9-06	Pat Eddery	J Tree	2	6	1-3F
1986	Dihistan	4 8-11	W R Swinburn	M Stoute	12	7	11-4F
1987	Rakaposhi King	5 9-00	S Cauthen	H Cecil	2	3	8-15F
1988	Race Void (Won By Mtoto)**						
1989	Sweet Chesne	4 8-11	S Cauthen	H Cecil	1	6	2-1
1990	Relief Pitcher	4 9-01	Pat Edery	P Walwyn	½	7	12-1
1991	Spritsail	5 9-01	Pat Edery	H Cecil	2½	6	9-4
1992	Flashfoot	4 8-12	R Cochrane	I Balding	HD	9	7-4F
1993	Red Bishop	5 9-01	M Roberts	J Gosden	NK	6	5-1
1994	Alderbrook	5 8-12	Paul Eddery	Mrs J Cecil	½	12	4-1
1995	Baron Ferdinand	5 8-12	Pat Eddery	R Charlton	2	4	11-10F
1996	Captain Horatius	7 9-01	T Quinn	J Dunlop	2½	6	4-1
1997	Germano	4 8-12	M Hills	G Wragg	HD	10	4-1
1998	Faithful Son	4 8-12	J Reid	S Bin Suroor	3	5	4-6F
1999	Great Dane	4 9-04	K Fallon	H Cecil	1¼	8	9-4F
2000	Island House	4 8-12	M Roberts	G Wragg	NK	5	6-4F
2001	Mubtaker	4 8-12	R Hills	M Tregoning	HD	5	7-2

For four-year-olds only 1975-77.
**Run at Kempton. ** 'Won' by Mtoto, but the horses had been sent on to the wrong course and the race was declared void.*

LADY O MEMORIAL GLORIOUS RATED STAKES

Listed Handicap
Four-year-olds and up. One mile four furlongs. First run 1979.
(1979-2001)

Year	Name	Age/Weight	Jockey	Trainer	Dist.	Runners	SP
1979	Bohemian Grove	3 8-03	A Murray	A Maxwell (Ire)	4	5	4-6F
1980	Water Mill	3 8-02	W Carson	W Hern	4	7	11-10F
1981	Capstan	3 7-11	W Carson	W Hern	¾	5	5-4
1982	Capstan	4 9-01	W Carson	W Hern	12	4	4-7F
1983	Seymour Hicks	3 8-05	W Carson	J Dunlop	1½	7	7-4F
1984	Longboat	3 8-02	B Rouse	W Hern	2½	6	10-1
1985	Shernazar	4 9-01	W R Swinburn	M Stoute	1½	9	10-1
1986	Nisnas	3 8-02	T Quinn	P Cole	1½	8	EVSF
1987	Knockando	3 8-05	R Cochrane	L Cumani	3	9	4-1
1988	Maksud	3 8-02	M Roberts	R Armstrong	1½	4	6-1
1989	Knoosh	3 8-05	Pat Eddery	M Stoute	2½	3	6-4F
1990	Hajade	3 8-06	L Dettori	L Cumani	2½	4	6-4
1991	Fly Away Soon	3 8-03	T Quinn	P Cole	¾	5	8-1
1992	Spinning	5 9-02	R Cochrane	I Balding	1½	6	7-2
1993	Usaidit	4 8-07	J Reid	T Mills	1	12	7-1
1994	Duke Of Eurolink	5 8-08	Pat Eddery	J Dunlop	¾	8	7-2
1995	Midnight Legend	4 9-07	L Dettori	L Cumani	1½	7	7-2
1996	Salmon Ladder	4 9-05	T Quinn	P Cole	1¼	9	7-2F
1997	Bahamian Sunshine	6 8-07	J Weaver	B Akehurst	3½	7	20-1

1998	Sabadilla	4 9-07	L Dettori	J Gosden	½	9	7-2
1999	Danish Rhapsody	6 9-07	G Stevens	Lady Herries	1½	8	9-1
2000	Murghem	5 9-07	D Holland	M Johnston	½	7	5-2F
2001	Compton Bolter	4 9-07	K Darley	G Butler	NK	12	12-1

Run as Alycidon Stakes up to 1986; as Alycidon Glorious Stakes 1987-88.

OAK TREE STAKES

Listed Race

Three-year-olds and upwards fillies and mares. Seven furlongs. First run 1980.

(1980-2001)

Year	Name	Age/Weight	Jockey	Trainer	Dist.	Runners	SP
1980	Trevita	3 8-05	P Cook	H Thomson Jones	¾	10	11-2
1981	Star Pastures	3 8-11	B Taylor	J Hindley	1	6	11-10F
1982	Chalon	3 9-00	L Piggott	H Cecil	¾	5	2-11F
1983	Fenny Rough	3 8-07	S Cauthen	B Hills	1	6	14-1
1984	Brocade	3 8-08	G Starkey	G Harwood	1½	10	9-2JF
1985	Ever Genial	3 8-05	S Cauthen	H Cecil	3	6	2-1JF
1986	Roya Loft	3 8-07	R Cochrane	W Jarvis	SHD	12	14-1
1987	Gayane	3 8-10	S Cauthen	H Cecil	1½	6	1-3F
1988	Ohsomellow	3 8-10	R Cochrane	L Cumani	3	7	4-1
1989	Kerita	3 8-07	Pat Eddery	R F J Houghton	¾	6	2-1
1990	Alidiva	3 8-09	S Cauthen	H Cecil	2½	9	11-2
1991	Himiko	3 8-07	M Hills	B Hills	1½	8	10-1
1992	Storm Dove	3 8-07	Paul Eddery	R Charlton	7	9	5-2F
1993	Moon Over Miami	3 8-07	J Reid	C James	HD	11	33-1
1994	Blue Siren	3 8-10	M Hills	I Balding	1½	10	6-1
1995	Brief Glimpse	3 8-07	M Hills	D Chappell	2	10	14-1
1996	Thrilling Day	3 8-13	D Harrison	N Graham	1¾	14	12-1
1997	Dazzle	3 8-07	J Reid	M Stoute	½	8	11-4
1998	Beraysim	3 8-07	L Dettori	M Jarvis	3½	9	15-8F
1999	Selfish	5 9-00	K Fallon	H Cecil	HD	6	13-2
2000	Danceabout	3 8-07	K Darley	G Wragg	HD	11	15-8F
2001	Mauri Moon	3 8-07	D Holland	G Wragg	NK	13	20-1

MARCH STAKES

(Sponsored by San Miguel)

Listed Race

Three-year-olds and up. One mile six furlongs. First run 1965.

(1965-2001)

Year	Name	Age/Weight	Jockey	Trainer	Dist.	Runners	SP
1965	Vivat Rex	3 8-11	J Roe	W Wharton	5	5	6-1
1966	Wrekin Rambler	3 9-02	T Stringer	G Richards	1	7	5-1
1967	Dart Board	3 9-07	A Breasley	G Richards	HD	6	15-8
1968	Deep Sapphire	3 9-02	S Smith	C Boyd-Rochfort	2½	3	6-4
1969	Ribofilio	3 8-11	L Piggott	R F Johnson Houghton	5	2	1-7F
1970	Hazy Idea	3 8-08	L Piggott	W Hern	1½	4	9-4
1971	Alderney	3 8-01	G Baxter	A Budgett	SHD	6	8-1
1972	Scottish Rifle	3 9-07	R Hutchinson	J Dunlop	2	4	4-9F
1973	Honey Crepe	3 8-11	P Cook	J F Watts	7	4	8-11F
1974	Crash Course	3 8-11	A Kimberley	J Hindley	NK	5	15-2
1975	Whip It Quick	3 8-11	A Murray	H R Price	½	5	7-1
1976	Marquis De Sade	3 9-05	B Taylor	H R Price	1½	5	11-8F
1977	Sporting Yankee	3 8-11	Pat Eddery	P Walwyn	3	3	8-13F
1978	Le Moss	3 9-05	J Mercer	H Cecil	2	5	5-2
*1979	Torus	3 8-11	J Reid	R F Johnson Houghton	¾	5	11-2
1980	Water Mill	3 8-11	W Carson	W Hern	7	3	1-7F
1981	Capstan	3 9-01	J Mercer	W Hern	8	3	4-7F
1982	Santella Man	3 8-11	G Starkey	G Harwood	SHD	6	7-2
1983	Band	3 9-01	W Carson	W Hern	3	5	4-11F
1984	Commanche Run	3 9-05	D McHargue	L Cumani	15	4	2-5F
1985	Abandoned - Waterlogged						
1986	Celestial Storm	3 8-11	W R Swinburn	L Cumani	3	7	3-1
1987	Ala Hounak	3 8-11	W Newnes	F Durr	¾	5	11-2
1988	Zaffaran	3 8-11	W R Swinburn	M Stoute	¾	5	9-4
1989	Michelozzo	3 8-11	S Cauthen	H Cecil	5	4	11-8F
1990	River God	3 9-01	S Cauthen	H Cecil	1½	4	4-7F
1991	Jahafil	3 8-11	W Carson	W Hern	1½	5	9-2
1992	Rain Rider	3 9-01	W Carson	J Dunlop	HD	4	11-10F
1993	Shaiba	3 8-11	M Roberts	M Stoute	¾	4	11-2
1994	Midnight Legend	3 8-11	L Dettori	L Cumani	2½	5	5-4F
1995	Jellaby Askhir	3 8-11	R Cochrane	R Akehurst	2	2	4-6F
1996	Sharaf Kabeer	3 8-11	L Dettori	S Bin Suroor	2½	7	11-4F
1997	Pentad	3 8-11	L Dettori	R Charlton	½	5	9-4
1998	Ta-Lim	3 8-11	R Hills	Sir M Stoute	2½	3	EVSF
1999	Yavana's Pace	7 9-10	R Hughes	M Johnston	½	5	7-1
2000	Alva Glen	3 8-07	P Eddery	Sir M Stoute	3	5	5-2
2001	Shamaiel	4 9-02	J Spencer	G Butler	¾	8	3-1

Three-year-olds only to 1998, opened to older horses in 1999

**Run at Ascot*

CONQUEROR STAKES

(Sponsored by E.B.F.)

Listed Race

Three-year-olds and up. One mile. First run 1997.

(1997-2001)

Year	Name	Age/Weight	Jockey	Trainer	Dist.	Runners	SP
1997	Out West	3 8-02	A McGlone	H Cecil	¾	9	6-1
1998	Digitalize	3 8-02	J Quinn	H Cecil	1½	6	EVSF
1999	Hawriyah	3 8-02	R Hills	J Dunlop	2	7	9-4
2000	Corinium	3 8-05	T Quinn	H Cecil	1¾	6	10-11F
2001	Sheppard's Watch	3 8-02	M Dwyer	M Tregoning	½	8	10-1

STARDOM STAKES

Listed Race

Two-year-olds only. One mile. First run 1978.

(1978-2001)

Year	Name	Weight	Jockey	Trainer	Dist.	Runners	SP
1978	Bonnie Isle	8-13	W Carson	J Dunlop	NK	5	7-1
*1979	Morayshire	9-02	J Lynch	B Hobbs	N/A	2	2-11F
1980	Clear Verdict	9-02	J Mercer	H Cecil	NK	6	9-4
1981	Jalmood	9-02	Pat Eddery	J Dunlop	4	6	4-1
1982	Lofty	9-05	P Cook	H Thomson Jones	½	4	5-4
1983	Gambler's Cup	8-11	A Clark	G Harwood	HD	9	6-1
1984	Royal Coach	9-03	Paul Eddery	H Cecil	2	8	1-2F
1985	Mashkour	8-11	Paul Eddery	H Cecil	2½	7	8-11F
1986	Beeshi	8-11	P Waldron	P Cole	2	7	7-1
1987	Church Lyric	8-11	G Starkey	G Harwood	1½	6	11-10F
1988	Zalazl	9-01	M Roberts	H Cecil	NK	3	5-4
1989	Champagne Gold	8-11	B Raymond	D Smith	NK	4	10-1
1990	Selkirk	8-11	J Reid	I Balding	4	5	20-1
1991	Seattle Rhyme	8-11	Pat Eddery	D Elsworth	3	5	EVSF
1992	Blush Rambler	8-11	C Asmussen	M Stoute	4	6	3-1
1993	Innishowen	8-11	T Quinn	R Hannon	2½	6	6-L
1994	Fahal	8-11	R Cochrane	D Morley	2½	6	3-1
1995	Bonarelli	8-11	W R Swinburn	M Stoute	HD	5	9-4JF
1996	Falkenham	8-11	T Quinn	P Cole	1	5	8-11F
1997	Alboostan	8-11	G Carter	D Morley	1	5	11-2
1998	Mutaahab	8-11	G Carter	E Dunlop	½	3	100-30
1999	Sarafan	8-11	G Duffield	Sir M Prescott	1¾	5	6-4F
2000	Atlantis Prince	8-11	O Peslier	S Woods	NK	8	6-1
2001	Henri Lebasque	8-11	J Fortune	P Cole	¾	6	3-1

**Run at Sandown*

FOUNDATION STAKES

Listed Race

Three-year-olds and up. One mile two furlongs. First run 1986.

(1986-2001)

Year	Name	Age/Weight	Jockey	Trainer	Dist.	Runners	SP
1986	Chinoiserie	3 8-08	R Cochrane	L Cumani	1	7	9-2
1987	Street Line	3 8-09	B Raymond	M Jarvis	2	5	6-1
1988	Alwuhush	3 8-06	R Cochrane	J Dunlop	6	4	2-1F
1989	Monastery	3 8-06	R Cochrane	Mrs L Piggott	1	3	6-4
1990	Noble Patriarch	3 8-08	J Reid	J Dunlop	½	8	5-1
1991	Perpendicular	3 8-08	W Ryan	H Cecil	NK	4	5-2
1992	King's Loch	3 8-08	W Ryan	H Cecil	2½	8	12-1
1993	Abandoned - Waterlogged						
1994	Luhuk	3 8-11	R Hughes	J Dunlop	2½	6	4-1
1995	Revere	5 9-03	T Quinn	P Cole	1½	9	2-1F
1996	Hagwah	4 8-09	M Roberts	B Hanbury	2½	5	5-2
1997	Danish Rhapsody	4 9-00	Paul Eddery	Lady Herries	½	5	3-1
1998	Danish Rhapsody	5 9-00	Paul Eddery	Lady Herries	½	4	5-1
1999	Diamond White	4 8-09	T Sprake	M Ryan	4	8	5-1
2000	Albarahin	5 9-00	R Hills	M Tregoning	1½	6	5-6F
2001	Mont Rocher	6 9-00	K Fallon	M Hammond (Fr)	NK	5	7-4

THOROUGHBRED STAKES

(Sponsored by Vodafone)

Listed Race

Three-year-olds only. One mile. First run in 1998.

(1998-2001)

Year	Name	Weight	Jockey	Trainer	Dist.	Runners	SP
1998	Great Dane	8-12	K Fallon	H Cecil	2½	7	100-30
1999	Slip Stream	8-12	L Dettori	S Bin Suroor	3	4	4-5F
2000	Adilabad	8-12	P Eddery	Sir M Stoute	NK	5	100-30
2001	Goggles	8-12	C Rutter	H Candy	½	7	7-1

CHESTERFIELD CUP

Handicap

Four-year-olds and up. One mile two furlongs. First run 1840.

(1840-1939)

Year	Name	Age/Weight	Runners
1840	Potentate	N/A 8-05	20
1841	Dr Caius	4 8-11	11
1842	Retriever	6 7-09	14
1843	Scaltheen	4 7-10	22
1844	Knight Of The Whistle	6 9-00	14
1845	Aegis	3 6-00	21
1846	Mongrel	4 7-00	13
1847	Collingwood	4 6-11	15
1848	Marquis Of Conyngham	5 7-03	14
1849	Woolwich	3 6-00	13
1850	Turnus	4 6-12	14
1851	Miss Ann	5 7-07	12
1852	Harbinger	3 7-00	19
1853	Nabob	4 7-03	12
1854	Catspaw	4 7-04	23
1855	Pumicestone	4 7-12	17
1856	Termagant	3 5-07	17
1857	Comquot	3 6-10	19
1858	Sunbeam	3 7-04	18
1859	Zuyder Zee	5 8-12	23
1860	Orlanda	4 6-07	26
1861	Croagh Patrick	3 6-00	26

1862	Prince Plausible	4 7-08	26
1863	Ace Of Clubs	4 7-09	21
1864	King Of Utopia	4 7-07	25
1865	Redmire	3 6-00	30
1866	Broomielaw	4 9-00	21
1867	Ostreger	5 9-00	25
1868	Charnwood	3 7-06	23
1869	Vespasian	6 10-04	19
1870	Soucar	3 6-09	16
1871	Botheration	3 6-07	27
1872	Napolitain	3 6-10	20
1873	Drummond	4 8-04	19
1874	Dalham	3 5-12	17
1875	Coomassie	3 6-07	17
1876	Coomassie	4 8-08	23
1877	Mousquetaire	4 7-05	16
1878	Midlothian	4 7-10	9
1879	Villager	3 6-08	14
1880	Victor Emanuel	3 6-07	15
1881	Victor Emanuel	4 8-05	19
1882	Vibration	3 5-12	9
1883	Vibration	4 8-01	11
1884	Prism	4 8-11	11
1885	Hermitage	4 8-12	10
1886	Saraband	3 8-05	17
1887	Spot	3 6-00	9
1888	Candlemas	5 7-06	8
1889	Veracity	5 9-03	10
1890	Father Confessor	5 9-06	7
1891	Shrine	4 6-06	9
1892	Lottery	4 6-06	12
1893	Pensioner	4 7-09	6
1894	Worcester	4 7-04	6
1895	Pitcher	5 8-11	9
1896	Phoebus Apollo	3 6-12	11
1897	Birchrod	4 7-07	15
1898	Chaleureux	4 7-04	6
1899	Calveley	4 8-06	14
1900	Spectrum	4 6-11	9
1901	Glenapp	3 6-01	14
1902	Ypsilanti	4 7-12	6
1903	Lady Help	3 6-05	10
1904	Union Jack	4 8-13	9
1905	Song Thrush	3 6-13	9
1906	Gold Riach	3 7-12	8
1907	Velocity	5 9-10	11
1908	King's Courtship	4 6-13	12
1909	Succour	6 8-08	12
1910	Land League	N/A 8-03	12
1911	Dean Swift	N/A 8-03	8
1912	Southannan	N/A 8-06	10
1913	Junior	4 8-07	9
1914	Kiltoi	4 7-11	14
1915 - 1918	No races		
1919	Tangiers	3 7-09	7
1920	Alasnam	4 7-09	4
1921	Illuminator	4 8-11	10
1922	Statuary	5 8-01	13
1923	Evander	5 8-11	12
1924	Frater	3 8-00	9
1925	Warden of the Marches	3 8-00	14
1926	Warden of the Marches	4 9-08	11
1921	Volta's Pride	4 8-04	9
192B	Silver Hussar	3 7-10	14
1929	Double Life	3 7-05	13
1930	The MacNab	4 8-11	18
1931	Lord Bill	4 8-11	10
1932	Seraph Boy	3 7-01	14
1933	Colorado Kid	4 9-06	15
1934	Alcazar	3 7-09	12
1935	Irongrey	4 8-01	10
1936	William Of Valence	4 8-08	20
1937	Finalist	5 9-07	14
193B	Pylon II	5 8-01	15
1939	Bacardi	5 7-12	11
1940 - 1945	No races		

CHESTERFIELD CUP
(Now Bet Direct Summer Stakes)
(1946-2001)

Year	Name	Age/Weight	Jockey	Trainer	Dist.	Runners	SP
1946	Signalman	3 8-04	H Wragg	H Leader	2	9	7-4F
1947	Avignon	4 7-13	K Gethin	G Hardy	1	6	20-1
1948	Royal Tara	5 8-13	K Gethin	J Beary	SHD	10	6-1JF
1949	Impeccable	5 9-12	G Richards	J Powell	4	7	2-1F
1950	Krakatao	4 9-07	G Richards	N Murless	4	10	7-4F
1951	Grani	5 7-11	L Piggott	J Waugh	HD	12	8-1
1952	Sunny Brae	4 8-05	E Fordyce	D Watson	1½	9	6-1
1953	Hilltop	4 8-12	W Carr	C Boyd-Rochfort	SHD	16	11-2F
1954	Prefect	4 8-03	A Breasley	N Cannon	1½	15	100-8
1955	Royal Maid	4 7-13	P Robinson	H Wragg	HD	7	5-1
1956	Athenien II	3 8-05	W Carr	C Pratt	1	15	10-1
1957	Rowland Ward	5 9-00	E Mercer	J Jarvis	¾	13	100-8
1958	London Cry	4 8-12	A Breasley	G Richards	1½	8	5-1
1959	Aggressor	4 8-13	J Lindley	J Gosden	1	8	100-3
1960	Rocky Royale	4 9-01	W Carr	D Whelan	2	15	100-8
1961	Stupor Mundi	4 8-09	W Carr	C Boyd-Rochfort	NK	13	7-1
1962	Robson's Choice	6 8-04	A Breasley	E Goddard	SHD	11	8-1
1963	St Gulliver	4 9-02	L Piggott	F Armstrong	3	15	4-1F
1964	Early To Rise	4 8-07	G Lewis	I Balding	1½	11	10-1
1965	Tarqogan	5 9-01	W Williamson	G McGrath (Ire)	3	13	8-1
1966	Polymint	6 6-09	R Dicey	J Sutcliffe Jnr	2	10	20-1
1967	Midnight Marauder	5 8-03	J Mercer	J Tree	1½	11	8-1
1968	Scottish Sinbad	4 8-13	R Hutchinson	J Dunlop	HD	11	100-6
1969	Cheval	4 9-10	R Hutchinson	J Dunlop	1½	10	7-1
1970	Harken	4 8-11	J Mercer	W Hern	2	10	100-8
1971	Tandy	5 9-04	J Mercer	B Swift	NK	9	10-1
1972	King Midas	4 9-10	J Mercer	D Candy	1	5	2-1F
1973	Prominent	6 9-01	G Baxter	A Budgett	4	5	7-4F
1974	Hail The Pirates	4 10-00	L Piggott	M V O'Brien (Ire)	1½	9	7-4F
1975	Edwards Hill	4 8-03	R Street	B Hills	½	7	33-1
1976	Blaskette	5 8-06	P Cook	N Vigors	2	3	2-1
1977	Fluellen	4 10-00	Pat Eddery	H Wragg	HD	6	4-1
1978	Town And Country	4 9-13	W Carson	W Hern	2	5	13-8F
1979	Philodantes	4 9-01	S Cauthen	B Hills	4	5	4-1
1980	Borderline	4 7-05	S Payne	I Balding	½	9	17-2
1981	Commodore Blake	4 7-04	B Crossley	M Stoute	5	14	13-2
1982	Criterion	3 9-10	L Piggott	G Harwood	HD	7	7-1
1983	Morcon	3 9-00	W Carson	W Hern	4	15	9-2F
1984	Mailman	5 8-10	T Quinn	I Balding	3	7	11-2
1985	Iroko	3 8-13	S Cauthen	M Stoute	HD	9	9-2JF
1986	Mailman	7 8-06	Pat Eddery	I Balding	2	11	11-1
1987	Loud Appeal	3 8-11	R Cochrane	M Stoute	HD	10	4-1
1988	Apache	3 8-06	J Bleasdale	C Thornton	SHD	7	9-4F
1989	Pelorus	4 10-00	B Rouse	W Jarvis	½	10	12-1
1990	Song Of Sixpence	6 9-05	S Cauthen	I Balding	2½	7	9-2
1991	Ijtihaad	4 9-05	W Carson	W Hern	1½	10	11-2
1992	Knock Knock	7 9-00	R Cochrane	I Balding	SHD	10	9-2F
*1993	Rose Alto	5 8-13	G Duffield	J Fanshawe	*	13	25-1
1994	Desert Shot	4 8-13	J Tate	M Stoute	¾	13	12-1
1995	Silver Groom	5 7-06	M Henry	R Akehurst	2½	14	6-1
1996	Grand Selection	4 8-03	M Fenton	M Bell	NK	13	12-1
1997	Danish Rhapsody	4 8-06	J Reid	Lady Herries	½	18	14-1
1998	Supply & Demand	4 9-00	K Fallon	G L Moore	1½	17	3-1F
1999	Ormelie	4 9-00	J Fortune	P Chapple-Hyam	NK	8	6-1
2000	Sharp Play	5 9-09	D Holland	M Johnston	SHD	11	11-2
2001	Kuster	5 8-06	J Spencer	L Cumani	1¼	12	6-1

Called the Bet Direct Summer Stakes Handicap since 2000.

**Rose Alto was beaten ¾l by Knowth, but the placings were reversed after a stewards' enquiry*

THE GOODWOOD STAKES
(Sponsored by Marriott Hotels)
Handicap

Three-year-olds and up. Two miles five furlongs. First run 1823.

(1823-1939)

Year	Name	Age/Weight	Runners
1823	Dandizette	3 6-06	2
1824	Vitellina	3 5-08	3
1825	Stumps	3 6-13	4
1826	Stumps	4 9-00	4
1827	Miss Craven	3 7-02	4
1828	Souvenir	5 8-06	WO
1829	The Alderman	N/A 8 9-00	2
1830	Aaron	4 7-13	11
1831	Conciliation	3 6-12	15
1832	Lucetta	6 9-05	13
1833	Little Red Rover	6 8-06	14
1834	Rob Roughead	4 7-07	16
1835	Glaucus	5 9-08	14
1836	Felix	4 7-08	18
1837	Lucifer	5 7-10	18
1838	Loutherbourg	4 7-01	11
1839	Barnacles	6 8-01	16
1840	Orelia	4 6-09	15
1841	Orelia	5 8-08	19
1842	Retriever	6 7-11	20
1843	Lucy Banks	4 7-07	12
1844	Franchise	5 6-00	18
1845	Miss Elis	3 5-07	23
1846	Jonathan Wild	3 4-07	21
1847	Hydrangea	4 6-10	14
1848	Chanticleer	5 9-02	16
1849	Maid Of Lyme	6 6-13	21
1850	Windischgratz	3 5-10	17
1851	Backbiter	6 7-09	13
1852	Weathergage	3 5-06	12
1853	Adine	4 7-08	17
1854	Bribery	3 5-11	16
1855	Quince	4 6-10	10
1856	Pretty Boy	3 7-08	25

1857	Leamington	4 8-06	19
1858	The Roman Candle	4 7-00	16
1859	Starke	4 7-07	17
1860	Wallace	3 7-04	17
1861	Elcho	3 5-13	11
1862	Boaddily	4 6-06	16
1863	Blackdown	3 6-02	13
1864	Blondin	4 7-06	7
1865	Suspicion	4 6-13	11
1866	Rama	3 5-12	10
1867	Gomera	5 9-00	12
1868	Tabouret	3 6-00	17
1869	Starter	3 5-10	10
1870	Paganini	5 8-10	11
1871	Taraban	N/A 8-05	14
1872	Spennithorne	4 7-07	16
1873	Uhlan	4 8-08	19
1874	Scamp	3 6-08	14
1875	Freeman	6 8-05	13
1876	Hampton	4 7-09	9
1877	Prince George	4 7-00	12
1878	Norwich	4 7-03	14
1879	Bay Archer	3 6-08	10
1880	Reveller	4 7-04	9
1881	Brown Bess	5 6-08	7
1882	Fortissimo	4 8-03	11
1883	Corrie Roy	5 9-00	9
1884	Stockholm	4 6-08	11
1885	Void		
1886	Winter Cherry	3 5-07	N/A
1887	Carlton	4 9-00	5
1888	Stourhead	N/A 7-11	12
1889	Ingram	4 7-01	6
1890	Papyrus	4 7-12	14
1891	White Feather	3 6-10	6
1892	Ralph Neville	5 7-12	9
1893	Red Eyes	4 8-01	8
1894	Spindle Leg	4 6-13	8
1895	Campanajo	3 7-00	7
1896	Carlton Grange	4 7-00	6
1897	Gluten	4 7-01	7
1898	Marius II	5 7-12	7
1899	Merman	N/A 9-00	10
1900	Jiffy II	5 7-09	10
1901	Avidity	5 7-06	14
1902	Templemore	4 7-08	10
1903	Genius	5 7-13	10
1904	Sandboy	4 7-06	9
1905	His Majesty	4 8-03	8
1906	Winwick	4 6-13	12
1907	Royal Dream	4 8-01	11
1908	Asticot	5 6-12	14
1909	Lagos	4 8-06	7
1910	Queen's Journal	4 7-04	11
1911	Ignition	3 6-04	6
1912	Irish Marine	4 8-01	9
1913	Washing Day	4 7-05	10
1914	Collodion	3 6-07	14
1915-1918	No races		
1919	Haki	N/A 9-00	11
1920	Rowland	4 6-13	11
1921	Arravale	6 6-13	7
1922	Flint Jack	5 8-03	6
1923	Trossach Girl	3 7-00	9
1924	London Cry	5 8-08	13
1925	Diapason	4 8-10	9
1926	Broken Faith	N/A 7-02	8
1927	Try Try Again	5 7-10	13
1928	Arctic Star	4 8-05	19
1929	Clear Cash	4 7-09	14
1930	Joyous Greeting	6 7-02	18
1931	Noble Star	4 8-11	14
1932	Forum II	5 6-08	13
1933	Prince Oxendon	5 7-13	19
1934	Claran	5 7-13	12
1935	Hoplite	4 8-11	14
1936	Avondale	8 7-04	16
1937	Epigram	4 7-08	19
1938	*Naval Display	4 7-12	11
	*Snake Lightning	4 7-09	
1939	Valedictory	4 7-13	18
1940 - 1945	No races		

GOODWOOD STAKES (1946-2001)

Year	Name	Age/Weight	Jockey	Trainer	Dist.	Runners	SP
1946	Reynard Volant	4 8-10	E Smith	J Jarvis	¾	6	7-4F
1947	Strathmore	4 6-10	T Sidebotham	E Bennett	4	11	100-8
1948	Auralia	5 9-06	D Smith	R Day	HD	15	100-8
1949	Harlech	4 8-08	C Elliott	E Williams	1½	10	9-2
1950	Strathspey	5 9-00	A Breasley	N Cannon	2	16	3-1F
1951	Veuillin	4 7-13	E Mercer	J Bisgood	1½	11	8-1
1952	French Design	5 6-12	R Arnold	G Todd	1	8	100-8
1953	Papillio	4 8-06	W Carr	C Boyd-Rochfort	3	12	11-2
1954	Osborne	7 9-07	W Carr	C Boyd Rochfort	2	13	100-7
1955	French Design	8 8-07	V Gardner	G Todd	1	17	9-1
1956	Terrington	5 6-10	N Pearson	W Marshall	½	13	100-6
1957	Persian Flag	4 8-07	W Carr	W Nightingall	½	15	13-2F
1958	Predominate	6 8-08	E Smith	T Leader	6	14	100-9
1959	Predominate	7 9-05	E Smith	T Leader	1	7	3-1
1960	Predominate	8 9-05	E Smith	T Leader	4	10	15-8F
1961	Alcove	4 8-03	D Smith	J F Watts	8	8	11-2
1962	Golden Fire	4 7-10	D Yates	D Marks	¾	11	13-2
1963	Golden Fire	5 8-06	D Yates	D Marks	¾	18	10-1
1964	Tree Leopard	4 8-08	J Mercer	W Hern	½	11	100-8
1965	Gold Aura	5 7-12	S Clayton	C Boyd-Rochfort	1½	10	5-1
1966	All Found	4 7-06	D Maitland	H Blagrave	NK	14	10-1
1967	Tubalcain	6 8-13	G Lewis	E Goddard	¾	12	8-1
1968	Acharacle	4 8-07	B Taylor	T Leader	½	14	100-8
1969	Amberwood	4 8-00	A Errington	J Benstead	1½	10	7-1
1970	Pride Of Alcide	4 8-07	G Starkey	H Cecil	1½	11	5-1
1971	Cossall	4 7-10	Pat Eddery	R Jarvis	½	6	5-1
1972	Biskrah	5 9-03	J Mercer	A Breasley	1	12	6-1
1973	Pamroy	4 8-04	G Lewis	A Breasley	SHD	8	4-1
1974	Reine Beau	4 7-07	A Bond	M Masson	10	14	10-1
1975	Dubrovnik	4 8-08	P Waldron	H Candy	2	8	5-1
1976	Sea Anchor	4 10-00	J Mercer	W Hern	1½	8	5-2F
1977	Sea Kestrel	7 7-07	D McKay	Mrs R Lomax	¾	10	10-1
1978	Caporello	4 9-02	E Eldin	G Pritchard-Gordon	3	7	6-1
1979	The Solent	3 8-07	J Mercer	H Cecil	2½	5	5-2F
1980	Heighlin	4 9-12	Pat Eddery	D Elsworth	½	4	5-4F
1981	Castelnau	5 8-05	Pat Eddery	P Cole	5	11	3-1
1982	Atlantic Traveller	5 8-07	E Hide	J Watts	2	8	17-2
1983	Morgan's Choice	6 8-06	W Carson	C Hill	5	11	5-2F
1984	Ack Ack Regiment	4 7-13	R Fox	P Cole	NK	12	6-1
1985	Obertura	3 8-11	G Starkey	G Harwood	½	10	9-4F
1986	Sarfraz	3 9-07	G Starkey	G Harwood	2	9	4-1
1987	Actinium	4 9-03	Pat Eddery	J Jenkins	1½	7	5-1
1988	Dam Busters	3 9-09	Pat Eddery	Mrs L Piggott	NK	9	7-1
1989	Late Cut	4 8-04	M Rimmer	H Collingridge	2	9	20-1
1990	Make Contact	4 9-02	Pat Eddery	R Akehurst	4	7	9-4F
1991	Haitham	4 9-05	Pat Eddery	R Akehurst	1½	10	5-1
1992	Bardolph	5 8-10	T Quinn	P Cole	SHD	13	13-2
1993	Aahsaylad	7 9-08	J Williams	J White	1½	9	4-1JF
1994	Harlestone Brook	4 9-04	W Carson	J Dunlop	2½	13	15-2
1995	Imad	5 7-12	D Gibson	J White	½	8	16-1
1996	Southern Power	5 10-00	T Quinn	R Akehurst	NK	9	7-2
1997	Cloud Inspector	6 9-04	J Weaver	M Johnston	¾	12	8-1
1998	Puteri Wentworth	4 8-06	J Fortune	Miss G Kelleway	½	11	10-1
1999	High And Mighty	4 10-00	L Dettori	J Gosden	1	9	2-1F
2000	Laffah	5 8-05	R Hughes	G Moore	1½	8	6-1
2001	Hugs Dancer	4 8-04	D McKeown	J Given	2½	14	11-1

WILLIAM HILL MILE

Handicap

Three-year-olds and up. One mile. First run 1987.

(1987-2001)

Year	Name	Age/Weight	Jockey	Trainer	Dist.	Runners	SP
1987	Waajib	4 9-10	M Roberts	A Stewart	NK	20	8-1
1988	Strike Force	3 8-06	M Hills	B Hills	NK	21	8-1
1989	Safawan	3 8-00	W Carson	M Stoute	HD	14	11-2
1990	March Bird	5 7-08	N Adams	J Sutcliffe	1½	16	15-1
1991	Sky Cloud	5 8-07	T Quinn	R Akehurst	NK	15	20-1
1992	Little Bean	3 8-02	M Hills	G Wragg	2	21	9-1
1993	Philidor	4 8-04	N Kennedy	J Eustace	SHD	19	13-2
1994	Fraam	5 9-09	W R Swinburn	A Scott	NK	19	10-1
1995	Khayrapour	5 7-13	B Doyle	B Meehan	SHD	21	15-2
1996	Moscow Mist	5 7-10	Declan O'Shea	Lady Herries	SHD	18	66-1
1997	Fly To The Stars	3 9-06	O Peslier	M Johnston	1¼	20	14-1
1998	For Your Eyes Only	4 9-06	J Weaver	T Easterby	NK	22	14-1
1999	Lonesome Dude	4 9-07	G Stevens	Sir M Stoute	NK	20	7-1
2000	Persiano	5 8-12	D Harrison	J Fanshawe	SHD	22	10-1
2001	Riberac	5 8-12	K Darley	M Johnstone	3½	21	12-1

SEABEACH STAKES

Handicap

Three-year-olds only. One mile two furlongs. First run 1962.

(1965-2001)

Year	Name	Weight	Jockey	Trainer	Dist.	Runners	SP
1962	Tamerlo	9-00	A Breasley	G Richards	1½	26	100-7
1963	Fraximus	7-07	D Yates	W Wightman	NK	21	25-1
1964	French Possession	7-09	D Smith	G Brooke	3	19	20-1
1965	Super Sam	7-09	P Robinson	J F Watts	7	16	5-1
1966	Le Cordonnier	9-02	G Lewis	S Ingham	½	19	100-7
1967	Sucaryl	8-08	G Moore	N Murless	1½	12	5-6F
1968	Principal Boy	8-01	E Eldin	J Clayton	SHD	12	4-1F
1969	Irish Maill II	8-00	E Eldin	J Waugh	½	8	7-1
1970	Sol' Argent	7-07	D Cullen	T Gosling	½	13	20-1
1971	Spoiled Lad	9-03	B Taylor	B Van Cutsem	NK	8	7-2F
1972	Warpath	8-04	A Russell	S Hall	½	15	11-1
1973	Cupid	7-07	D Cullen	W Hern	½	12	10-1

1974	Take A Reef	9-11	J Gorton	B Hobbs	½	19	13-1
1975	Duboff	8-00	W Carson	B Hills	2½	12	7-1
1976	Il Padrone	8-01	R Fox	J Sutcliffe Jnr	HD	13	14-1
1977	Ad Lib Ra	9-00	L Piggott	R F J Houghton	1½	14	4-1F
1978	Crimson Beau	8-02	G Baxter	P Cole	HD	7	4-1
*1979	Lindoro	9-00	W Carson	W Hern	*	9	6-4F
1980	Karamita	7-07	P Robinson	M Stoute	6	10	6-4F
1981	Indian Trail	8-03	S Cauthen	B Hills	HD	9	3-1F
1982	Busaco	9-01	W Carson	W Hern	NK	10	7-1
1983	Millfontaine	8-13	G Starkey	G Harwood	1½	12	6-1
1984	Free Guest	8-06	D McHargue	L Cumani	5	15	4-1F
1985	Fish 'n' Chips	8-03	Pat Eddery	L Cumani	2	13	9-4F
1986	Chinoiserie	8-11	T Ives	L Cumani	½	13	14-1
1987	Broken Hearted	9-03	T Quinn	P Cole	7	13	7-2
1988	Kazaviyna	7-10	G Carter	M Stoute	¾	14	16-1
1989	Biennial	9-02	Pat Eddery	G Harwood	1	8	2-1F
1990	Kawtuban	9-02	W Carson	R Charlton	HD	8	7-1
1991	Green Danube	8-02	A Munro	Lord Huntingdon	3½	16	25-1
1992	Party Cited	9-04	J Williams	D Elsworth	HD	18	12-1
1993	Western Cape	8-12	Pat Eddery	R Charlton	NK	18	14-1
1994	Frustration	8-06	D Harrison	Lady Herries	1½	10	5-1
1995	Jalfrezi	7-10	S Sanders	J Toller	½	14	6-1
1996	Fahim	8-13	R Hills	A Stewart	¾	14	5-2F
1997	Future Perfect	8-09	C Rutter	P Cole	1½	18	25-1
1998	Gypsy Passion	8-10	O Peslier	M Johnston	NK	10	6-1
1999	Azouz Pasha	8-09	K Fallon	H Cecil	1¼	17	9-1
2000	Happy Diamond	9-06	J Reid	M Johnston	1¼	11	15-2
2001	Askham	8-10	J Spencer	L Cumani	3	11	11-4F

**Lindoro was beaten ¾l by Red Rufus but the latter was disqualified and placed last after a stewards' enquiry.*

LENNOX STAKES
(Sponsored by Theo Fennell)

Group Three
Three-year-olds only. Seven furlongs. Goodwood acquired this Group race in 2000.
(2000–2001)

Year	Name	Age/Weight	Jockey	Trainer	Dist.	Runners	SP
2000	Observatory	3 8-12	K Darley	J Gosden	1½	8	11-4
2001	Fath	4 9-00	M Dwyer	M Tregoning	¾	9	14-1

RICHMOND-BRISSAC TROPHY STAKES

Handicap
Three-year-olds and up. One mile one furlong. First run 1977. A Fegentri race.
(1977–2001)

Year	Name	Age/Weight	Jockey	Trainer	Dist.	Runners	SP
1977	Roaming Cloud	3 10-00	R Hutchinson	G Hunter	SHD	8	6-1
1978	Mandalus	4 12-00	A Esler	Sir M Prescott	SHD	8	9-4F
*1979	Can Run	6 10-00	R Hutchinson	D Gandolfo	¾	5	15-8F
1980	Princes Gate	3 11-07	J Hills	H Thomson Jones	4	5	2-1
1981	Liberated	5 11-07	J Busutil	R Baker	NK	8	33-1
1982	Fiesta Fun	4 11-04	R Hutchinson	P Cole	2	8	6-4F
1983	Cornish Gem	4 11-03	R Hutchinson	G Lewis	1½	10	9-1
1984	Sunoak	4 11-07	A J Wilson	G Harwood	4	4	4-11F
1985	Abandoned Due To Waterlogging						
1986	Blenders Choice	4 10-11	T Thomson Jones	J King	8	9	5-2F
1987	Tarleton's Oak	4 10-07	H Van De Veuer	G Harwood	1½	9	7-1
1988	Sabatina	3 11-02	H Van De Veuer	G Harwood	2	7	13-8F
1989	Amber Loch	4 11-07	P Fenton	P Cole	4	4	15-8F
1990	Gilderdale	8 11-03	C Segner	J Hills	1½	6	15-8F
1991	Jurz	3 10-07	F Grasso-Caprioli	H Thomson Jones	¾	7	5-1
1992	Surrey Dancer	4 10-13	F Grasso-Caprioli	B Hanbury	1½	10	9-2
1993	Talent	5 11-09	L Urbano	Lord Huntingdon	5	9	6-1
1994	Second Chance	4 10-13	R Teal	P Mitchell	NK	7	5-1
1995	Adolescence	5 11-06	L Urbano	K McAuliffe	NK	6	100-3
1996	Night Wink	4 11-10	K Goble	G Moore	¾	11	11-1
1997	Show Faith	7 10-03	C Vigors	R Hannon	3½	9	7-1
1998	Vola Via	5 11-05	A Balding	I Balding	3	10	8-1
1999	Thatchmaster	8 10-6	A Evans	C Horgan	1¾	13	9-1
2000	Bound For Pleasure	4 11-10	T Scudamore	J Gosden	8	14	11-8F
2001	Noble Calling	4 11-04	K O'Brien	R Hodges	NK	12	16-1

Race distance 1m up to 2984, 1m 2f 1986-89.
**Run at Sandown*

ON THE HOUSE STAKES

Listed Race
Three-year-olds and up. One mile. First run 1999.
(1999–2001)

Year	Name	Age/Weight	Jockey	Trainer	Dist.	Runners	SP
1999	Ramooz	6 9-08	R Hills	B Hanbury	½	7	6-1
2000	Swallow Flight	4 9-05	R Hughes	G Wragg	4	2	1-3F
2001	Late Night Out	6 9-05	M Tebbutt	W Jarvis	1¼	4	7-4

TOTE GOLD TROPHY STAKES

Handicap
Three-year-olds only. One mile four furlongs. First run 1990.
(1990–2001)

Year	Name	Age/Weight	Jockey	Trainer	Dist.	Runners	SP
1990	Black Monday	4 8-07	L Dettori	L Cumani	1½	12	4-1F
1991	Tidemark	4 8-08	L Dettori	L Cumani	1	11	100-30F
1992	Spinning	5 9-10	R Cochrane	I Balding	½	16	14-1
1993	Dana Springs	3 8-11	L Dettori	R Hannon	NK	16	10-1
1994	Midnight Legend	3 9-07	J Weaver	L Cumani	3	17	9-2F
1995	Pilsudski	3 8-12	W R Swinburn	M Stoute	NK	15	11-2
1996	Freequent	3 8-09	Pat Eddery	L Cumani	¾	12	9-1
1997	Maylane	3 9-04	M Roberts	A Stewart	½	15	13-2
1998	Muhib	3 9-01	R Hills	Sir M Stoute	¾	15	10-1
1999	Mary Stuart	3 8-09	G Stevens	Sir M Stoute	HD	11	9-4F
2000	Blue Gold	3 9-01	J Reid	R Hannon	HD	10	14-1
2001	Ovambo	3 8-11	S Sanders	P Makin	1	12	9-1

For three-year-olds and up 1990-92

GOODWOOD BREEDERS' CUP HANDICAP, SANTA ANITA

Grade Two
Three-year-olds and up. One mile one furlong. First run 1982.
(1982–2001)

Year	Name	Age/Weight	Jockey	Trainer
1982	Cajun Prince	5 8-03	W Guerra	L Barrera
1983	Peltrax	5 8-05	K Black	W Charlton
1984	Lord At War	4 8-05	W Shoemaker	C Whittingham
1985	Lord At War	5 8-13	W Shoemaker	C Whittingham
1986	Super Diamond	6 8-10	L Pincay	E Gregson
1987	Ferdinand	4 8-11	W Shoemaker	C Whittingham
1988	Cutlass Really	6 8-09	G Stevens	C Lewis
1989	Present Value	5 8-07	E Delahoussaye	J Fanning
1990	Lively One	5 8-08	A Solis	C Whittingham
1991	The Prime Minister	4 8-03	C McCarron	C Whittingham
1992	Reign Road	4 8-04	K Desormeaux	J Robbins
1993	Lottery Winner	4 8-02	K Desormeaux	J Robbins
1994	Bertrando	5 8-08	G Stevens	J Shirreffs
1995	Soul Of The Matter	4 8-09	K Desormeaux	R Mandella
*1996	Savinio	6 8-05	C Nakatini	W Greenman
1997	Benchmark	6 8-04	E Delahoussaye	R W Wells
1998	Silver Charm	4 8-12	G Stevens	B Baffert
1999	Budroyale	6 8-07	G K Gomez	Ted West
2000	Tiznow	4 8-04	C McCarron	J Robbins
2001	Freedom Crest	5 8-04	K Desormeaux	R Baltas

**Savinio finished a length behind Alphabet Soup but the latter was disqualified for causing interference and placed third.*

TIME AND DISTANCE (records since 1990)

STANDARD AND RECORD TIMES

Distance	Time	Age	Weight	Going	Horse	Date
5f	56.01	5	9-00	Fast	Rudi's Pet	July 27 1999
5f (2 yo)	57.53	2	8-12	Fast	Poets Cove	Aug 3 1990
6f	1.09.58	4	8-03	Firm	For The Present	July 30 1994
6f (2 yo)	1.09.81	2	8-11	Firm	Bachir	July 28 1999
7f	1.23.88	3	8-07	Fast	Brief Glimpse,	July 25 1995
7f (2 yo)	1.24.99	2	8-11	Firm	Ekraar	July 29 1999
8f	1.35.66	3	8-13	Firm	Aljabr	July 28 1999
8f (2 yo)	1.38.94	2	9-00	Good	Mutawwaj	Sept 24 1997
9f	1.52.81	3	9-06	Firm	Vena	July 27 1995 *
1m 1f 192y	2. 04.96	3	8-06	Firm	Kartajana	Aug 4 1990
12f	2.31.57	3	8-10	Firm	Presenting	July 25 1995
14f	2.58.57	4	9-02	Gd-Firm	Mowbray	July 27 1999
16f	3.23.57	4	9-05	Firm	Tioman Island	July 28 1994
20f	4.11.75	3	7-10	Firm	Lucky Moon	Aug 2 1990

** Flag Start*

Previous Records (up to 1989)

Distance	Time	Age	Weight	Going	Horse	Date
5f	56.92	4	9-00	Firm	Tina's Pet	July 29 1982
5f (2 yo)	58.07	2	8-10	Firm	Kafu	July 27 1982
6f	1.09.58	3	8-04	Firm	Soba	July 27 1982
6f (2 yo)	1.11.05	2	8-11	Fast	Vacarme (disq.)	July 27 1983
7f	1.24.70	3	7-13	Ylding	Alcindoro	Sept 14 1970
7f (2 yo)	1.26.61	2	9-00	Firm	Be My Chief	July 27 1989
8f	1.36.77	3	8-10	Firm	Zilzal	July 26 1989
8f (2 yo)	1.40.66	2	8-13	Firm	Bonnie Isle	Sept 18 1978
1m 2f	2.04.72	5	9-00	Good	Rakaposhi King	May 20 1987
12f	2.32.73	4	9-01	Firm	Capstan	July 30 1982
14f	2.58.83	4	9-13	Firm	Capstan	Aug 19 1981
19f (2m 3f)	4.08.30	4	9-13	Firm	El Conquistador	May 21 1987
21f (2m 5f)	4.30.42	3	7-10	Firm	Sergeyevich	July 30 1987

Standard Times (since 1990)

Distance	Time	Distance	Time
5f	56.7.00	1m 1f 192y	2.04.8
6f	1.09.80	12f	2.33.7
7f	1.24.80	14f	2.59.00
8f	1.36.5	16f	3.21.5
9f	1.52.00	20f	4.11.00

Previous Standard Times (up to 1989)

Distance	Time	Distance	Time
5f	58.4	1m 4f	2.33.7
6f	1.11	1m 6f	2.58
7f	1.26	2m 3f (est)	4.50
Old Mile	1.38.5	2m 5f	4.31
1m 2f	2.05.3		

ACKNOWLEDGEMENTS

Camilla Cecil would like to thank Seamus Buckley, Kate Fox, the Edward James Foundation at West Dean Park, David Legg-Willis, Richard Pailthorpe, the Royal Archive at Windsor, and everyone at Goodwood.

George Ennor would like to give grateful thanks for their time and help to Clare Balding, Ian Balding, Willie Carson, Mike Cattermole, Tony Clark, Pat Eddery, John Gosden, the late Major Dick Hern, Darryll Holland and his agent Matt Chapman, Richard Hughes, Mark Johnston, Jimmy Lindley, Jim A. McGrath, Simon Morant, Peter Willett and Julian Wilson.

Richard Onslow would like to thank Peter Willett and Philip Dodd.

The publishers would like to thank all those who helped make this book possible, including David Ashforth, Sir Peter O'Sullevan, Dawn Sharpe and Jacqui Thomas. Special thanks to The Duke of Richmond and The Earl of March; to Peter Willett and Rosemary Baird for their sage advice and expert knowledge; to Rod Fabricius, Seamus Buckley, Patricia Cooke, Emma Doran, Brenda Hamilton and John Thompson at Goodwood Racecourse; and to Jane Bartholomew, Marion Calver-Smith, Rebecca Evans, Alison Sweeney and Ellen Westbrook at Goodwood House.

A selective bibliography includes *Goodwood* by David Hunn; *The Biographical Encyclopedia Of British Flat Racing* by Roger Mortimer, Richard Onslow and Peter Willett; *The Derby Stakes* by Roger Mortimer, *The Encyclopedia Of Flat Racing* by Howard Wright; *The Punter's Friend* by Jack Waterman; *Racecourses On The Flat* by John Tyrrel; *British Racecourses* by B.W.R. Curling; *The Racing Life Of Lord George Bentinck* by John Kent, *The Dukes Of Richmond* by John Kent, *Why Did They Call Me Archibald?* by Richard Pailthorpe and Janet Holt; *Goodwood Country* by Richard Pailthorpe and Ian Serraillier.

Picture credits: Goodwood archive; page 6 top and bottom, 21, 22, 23, 24, 25, 26, 38,44, 45, 46, 47, 54, 56, 70, 73, 80, 109, 110, 111, 112, 113, 116, 117, 119, 120/1, 122, 123, 125, 127, 134, 139, 146, 147, 148/9, 150, 151, 158, 160, 161, 182, 183, 207 · Goodwood archive (Mark Aspland); page 28, 30/31, 48/49, 107, 202 · Goodwood archive (George Selwyn); page 1, 2/3, 132/3, 181 · Goodwood archive (Jon Franklin); pages 4/5, 16, 18/19, 32, 37, 72, 90/1, 194/5, 222/3 · Goodwood archive (Trevor Jones); page 40 middle and last, 64, 87, 98/9, 170, 180 · Goodwood archive (Mike Caldwell); page 15, 34/5, 78/9, 186/7, 197 · Goodwood archive (Nigel Millard); page 27, 33, 39, 66, 68, 75, 76, 81 · Goodwood archive (Elizabeth Furth); page 52, 163, 212/3, 216/7 · Goodwood archive (Graham Piggott); page 8, 102 · Goodwood archive (Stephen Hayward); pages 82/3, 192 · Goodwood archive (John Blythe); page 17· Goodwood archive (Paul Lund); pages 42/3 · Goodwood archive (John Crofts); page 188 · Goodwood archive (Gerry Cranham); page 191 · Goodwood archive (Four Foot Fotos); page 196 · Goodwood archive (Dan Stevens); page 200/1 background, and twenty scattered images, 202 · Goodwood archive (Racetech); page 184 · Goodwood archive (Chris Joyce); pages 136/137 · 204/5· George Selwyn; page 11, 12, 29, 62, 63, 105, 129, 140, 141, 166/7 174/5, 178, 181 198, 199 · Trevor Jones; page 40 top, 60, 85 · Antoinette Eugster; pages 200/1, twenty scattered images · Chris Joyce; 136/137 · 204/5 · Mary Evans Picture Library; page 89, 92, 153 · By courtesy of The National Portrait Gallery; page 108, 144 · Hulton Archive; page 69 · 'PA' Photos; page 106 · By courtesy of Nick Haynes; page 185 · By courtesy of Lady Penn; page 125

Goodwood's Roll of Honour based on the *Goodwood Media Guide 2002*, compiled in conjunction with Goodwood Racecourse by Racenews Ltd. Extracts from King George V's Diary (RA King George V's Diary [GVD]) by kind permission of the Royal Archive at Windsor.